Transformations of *La Familia* on the U.S.-Mexico Border

LATINO PERSPECTIVES

Gilberto Cárdenas, series editor

INSTITUTE *for*

Latino Studies

UNIVERSITY OF NOTRE DAME

*The Institute for Latino Studies, in keeping with the distinctive
mission, values, and traditions of the University of Notre Dame,
promotes understanding and appreciation of the social, cultural,
and religious life of U.S. Latinos through advancing research,
expanding knowledge, and strengthening community.*

Transformations of *La Familia* on the U.S.-Mexico Border

Edited by
Raquel R. Márquez
and
Harriett D. Romo

University of Notre Dame Press
Notre Dame, Indiana

Library of Congress Cataloging-in-Publication Data

Transformations of la familia on the U.S.-Mexico border /
edited by Raquel R. Márquez and Harriett D. Romo.
    p.   cm. — (Latino perspectives)
Includes bibliographical references and index.
ISBN-13: 978-0-268-03509-9 (pbk. : alk. paper)
ISBN-10: 0-268-03509-1 (pbk. : alk. paper)
1. Family—Mexican-American Border Region. 2. Mexican American
women—Mexican-American Border Region—Social conditions.
3. Women immigrants—Mexican-American Border Region—
Social conditions. I. Márquez, Raquel R. II. Romo, Harriett.
HQ549.T73   2008
306.850972'1—dc22
                                                                2008010456

To the women who lovingly and skillfully shape the lives of their families along the U.S.-Mexico border, as well as to our own mothers and daughters

CONTENTS

Tables

Figures

ACKNOWLEDGMENTS

We wish to thank Ana Marie Argilagos, senior consultant, Planning, Research, and Development Unit, Southwest Border/Indian Country, and the Annie E. Casey Foundation for funding the Working Group on Families on the Border. We also wish to thank Gilberto Cárdenas, director of the Institute for Latino Studies at the University of Notre Dame and the Inter-University Program for Latino Research (IUPLR), for his support of the Working Group and this project. The opportunity to bring together women scholars with common research interests to share ideas and offer criticism in border family studies was invaluable in making this collection a reality. Ana Marie Argilagos and Gilberto Cárdenas helped to identify Mexican scholars and provided funds for Working Group meetings throughout the collaboration.

As editors, we are grateful for the privilege of directing the Working Group, which allowed us to confer with talented women scholars concerned about Latino families in the borderlands. The border has a special meaning for each of us, but we hope that together this body of work draws attention to the extensive needs of families in the region.

We are also indebted to the Sociology Department graduate students who worked on this project, particularly Tamara Casso, Crissy Rivas, and Todd Garrard, at the University of Texas, San Antonio. Their efforts in organizing the meetings, coding data, tracking the multiple versions of the chapters, and preparing the final manuscript ultimately contributed to the success of this volume. Lastly, we offer our most sincere thanks to Caroline Domingo of the IUPLR, who served as our liaison to the University of Notre Dame Press and who guided us throughout the entire manuscript process.

Introduction

Raquel R. Márquez and Harriett D. Romo

The U.S.-Mexico border is in many ways a unique space where family ties, Mexican and U.S. policies, and the Spanish and English languages are central components of everyday life. The borderlands is a place where families negotiate identities while interacting within changing social, political, and economic dynamics. For example, one resident, Mercedes, describes this complexity: "There are three worlds. You have the Mexican, the American, and the one here at the border, because here you have a combination of both cultures and it's different from the Mexican and the American." Her relatives from Nuevo Laredo, Mexico, treat her American home as their base on the U.S. side. They visit often, shop in the United States, participate in community activities on both sides of the border, and feel comfortable in Spanish and English. This is a "transborder" family.

Twenty-seven-year-old Nancy is a resident of an extended border urban area. She has a four-year-old son and a seven-month-old daughter who were born in the United States and are U.S. citizens. Her Mexican-born husband is presently serving in the U.S. military in Iraq. Nancy's mother came to *el norte* as an undocumented immigrant when she was eight months pregnant with Nancy, thus making Nancy, who was herself born in the United States, an American citizen. Her mother returned to Mexico with Nancy while her father continued to work in construction in Texas. Her father returned annually to see his family. Nancy continued her schooling in Mexico until seventh grade, when her mother rejoined her father, who was by then a U.S. citizen living in San Antonio. She earned her high-school diploma in San Antonio. Thus, Nancy has lived a transnational life as a U.S. citizen growing up in Mexico, attending school on both sides of the border, and celebrating traditional milestones in both countries. Nancy and her husband were raised in the same rural village in Mexico, and relatives living in the United States and Mexico maintain close contacts.

Mercedes and Nancy are representative of the families whom we write about in this book—families who live as if there are no borders. The complexity of their lives illustrates why we have chosen to include the terms "transborder," "transnational," and "binational" in this volume even though each of these terms reflects a different conceptual approach. Some families are "transborder"—they go back and forth on a daily basis to work, attend school, or tend to family needs. Other families live in the United States and have less frequent contact with their community of origin, but they have relatives who reside in Mexico and the United States, own homes in both countries, run businesses that have clients or markets on both sides of the border, and are economically, socially, and emotionally "transnational." Still other families have qualified for dual nationality and are legal citizens of both countries. Their relationships with the border are shaped by the legal status that allows many forms of incorporation that noncitizenship denies. Many of the families whom we write about in these chapters include members who are undocumented, naturalized citizens, residents with various types of visas, U.S.-born citizens, or citizens with dual nationality. While using the terms transborder, transnational, and binational may seem analytically murky, all three indeed reflect the reality of border families.

Introducing Our Objectives

We enter this discussion fully recognizing that the wide expanse of the international border presents a serious challenge for researchers and policymakers, but perhaps even more so for the families who live within the borderlands. There is a wealth of border issues that have been researched, particularly macro-level issues related to economics, immigration rates, and trade, but very few studies look at the micro-level impact of border immigration patterns, economic systems, and policies on families who live in the region. Existing research on border families (Ojeda de la Peña 1995; Vélez-Ibáñez 1996; Vila 2000, 2003, 2005) shows that members work in the United States and Mexico, with frequent crossings for visits with relatives, child care, shopping, or entertainment. The border is also an area where some of the poorest families in both countries reside. *Colonias,* or settlements that often lack the basic necessities for family life, are common along the north and south sides. The chapter by Yolanda Padilla and Ana Marie Argilagos in this volume addresses the specific sociodemographic makeup of the border region, with statistics that glaringly illustrate the impact of poverty on families and children.

The concept of family has changed over time to include single parents, extended families, and other nontraditional households, but we affirm the power of families to direct the course of individual lives. We focus on families as important social and economic units of society seriously affected by the border issues of trade, narcotics and prostitution, water rights, unregulated immigration, and labor migration. Much of the existing work on women along the border has been issue driven—for example, female homicides, women working in *maquiladoras* or as prostitutes. These issues obscure the important role of women in the daily economic, cultural, social, political, and family life on the border. Rosa Linda Fregoso (2003: xiv) writes about the shaping of social identities and the "historical, material and discursive effects of contact zones and exchanges among various communities on the Mexico-U.S. border, living in the shadows of more than 150 years of conflict, interactions and tensions." Our perspectives are united in an interactionist framework arguing that what family members say and do and how they are presented take on a reality of their own. The family is not a stock social unit but the creation of its participants as they relate to one another and to the larger society. Families change in response to women's economic strategies, labor market participation, and negotiations with spouses and relatives.

This border area is also grounded in a rich Mexican culture of strong family values, historical legacies, and the engagement and blending of English and Spanish. Women on the border face the impact of differential labor markets based on female work. They negotiate gendered space within social networks and experience different patterns of migration within the course of their lives. Women confront multiple challenges presented by transnational and immigrant labor as domestics, housekeepers, and nannies. The economic conditions on both sides affect the jobs of heads of families and the income and wealth accumulation of border families and their members.

Families on both the U.S. and Mexican sides are similarly affected by negative images and stereotypes that influence adolescents and young children growing up in these areas; moreover, pollution impacts children's health and causes birth defects and other medical problems. *La frontera*, or the extended border, is also where the "grating" of two nations occurs (Anzaldúa 1987). There, two power differentials make contact, producing an environment that may either lack economic opportunities or provide economic advantages for residents of each country. These elements have made and continue to make the borderlands a unique place.

Gender and the Border

The authors contributing to this book are border women who have grown up along *la frontera*. The borderlands are our heritage as well as the heritage of our families who settled this region. As women, we have experienced both the good and the bad in family relationships. Most of us have endured the unequal power arrangements between men and women in the larger society, the disparate power in terms of wealth and capital that women bring to marriage, the dilemmas of finding adequate day care and good schooling for children, and other aspects of family life that relate to gendered discourses about femininity and masculinity, male and female roles, and male dominance.

Women as heads of household in the borderlands are often entrepreneurs in the informal economy that is so vital and central to the prosperity of the region. The contributions made by these women are often omitted from the formal statistics gathered on labor market participation, unemployment, and income. Heads of household may live on one side of the border and work on the other, taking advantage of economic opportunities where they find them. Policies in both countries affect their work, their children, and their families.

Methodological Approach

The scholars included in this volume—Latinas, immigrant women, or academics dedicated to immigrant issues—bring a broad collective knowledge that critically informs their analyses of border dynamics. A major concern as we designed both the research questions and the studies found here was that our scholarship reflect our lifetime of experiences and perceptions about the border. Rather than focus on traditional economic and social categories or common indexes found in the literature and in government reports, we have instead developed indicators reflecting the complexity of border dynamics. Attention to complexity has become the strength of the book, giving it breadth and depth in addressing perspectives from both sides of the border. The thematic threads of gender and family as well as transborder, transnational, and binational issues are interwoven throughout the chapters.

The authors incorporate ethnographic and qualitative approaches, literary and arts analyses, participatory research, and quantitative analyses drawn from various U.S. and Mexican data sets. Our analytical framework examines the border from the nation-state to state, county, and city levels but focuses on the family, or *la familia*. We concentrate on the issues surrounding Latino families because Latinos represent a majority of the U.S. residents along the border (see Padilla and Argilagos, this volume). Additionally, we include normative indicators of the Latino population along the border, such as labor force participation, health, education, and poverty rates—indicators that speak to the issues of immigration, citizenship, language, housing, and family composition. These variables further explain the contexts of Latino border families. We do not pretend to address the totality of issues related to the region, but we do claim to offer a well-rounded portrait of present-day Latino families within the U.S.-Mexico border landscape.

Defining the Border

No relationship between the United States and any other country of the world is perhaps as encumbered by history, geography, economic patterns, culture, and language as that between the United States and Mexico. The shared border extends nearly two thousand miles. If combined, the economies of the northern Mexican states along that border and the U.S. border states of California and Texas would represent one of the largest in the world. More than 11.8 million people (6.3 million in the United States and 5.5 million in Mexico) live along the border, with 90% residing in fourteen "sister city" pairs (Davy and Meyers 2005). The scale of immigration into California (40% of the immigrants in California come from Mexico) is unequaled anywhere else in the United States and represents the principal component of growth in that state's population (McCarthy and Vernez 1998).

In the 1800s the United States annexed a large part of Mexico's northern territory that today comprises the American Southwest and includes California, Arizona, Texas, and parts of New Mexico, Colorado, and Utah. The borderlands reflect an involuntary incorporation of resident Mexicans as well as a continuous process of back-and-forth migration. Free movement of Mexicans to *el norte* occurred when seasonal labor, railroad workers, and agricultural workers were recruited by American labor contractors (Corwin 1978; McWilliams 1967; Montejano 1987), and this movement continues today. Jobs on both sides promote binational commerce, and social gatherings such as weddings, *charreadas, quinceañeras,* and other celebrations involve family members from both countries. Culture and kinship practiced in transborder and transnational interactions and relations help Mexican-origin residents in the United States lessen the strain of racial and class discrimination and foster opportunities for recognition and incorporation.

The U.S. border states with their Mexican culture, Spanish language, Latino institutions, and economic ties to Mexico create a context that promotes transnational lives. World and local events are increasingly linked across nation-state boundaries. Mexicanos along the border use the resources and skills they bring from Mexico to address issues in U.S. communities and family life. Even as they are incorporated into U.S. society, the families we studied maintain ties to Mexico in their work and as they raise children, go to school, vote, and participate in communities in the United States. Instead of loosening their connections or trading one identity for another, Mexican-origin residents of the U.S. borderlands forge social relations, earn their livelihoods, and exercise their rights across borders over many generations.

In this collection of research studies, we propose that the lives of Mexican-origin families in the United States cannot be understood without reference to their ancestral homeland. The transnational social fields in which they live are composed of family relationships and family and community commitments. For example, remittances from workers in the United States often support those relatives left behind in Mexico or contribute to hometown development projects. Children may attend school in both countries as they migrate back and forth with their parents. Adults own or invest in property on both sides of the border. Transnationalism forces us to ask important questions, such as: Will this generation of immigrant children follow the path of earlier waves of immigrants and gradually assimilate into mainstream American life? Or, does the global nature of the contemporary world mean that the trajectory of today's immigrants will be fundamentally different?

Impact of NAFTA and U.S.-Mexico Policy Initiatives

The North American Free Trade Agreement, or NAFTA, signed by Mexico, the United States, and Canada and approved by the U.S. Congress in 1993, represented a dramatic change in U.S.-Mexico relations. Incorporating Mexico into an international "bloc" with its dominant northern neighbor and once hostile enemy, the agreement stimulated employment growth and increased foreign exports, especially along the northern frontier of Mexico that borders the United States. Thus, NAFTA created an economic community, in terms of geography and demographics, that is much larger than the European Union or the Pacific Rim (Davy and Meyers 2005). Guillermo Gómez-Peña notes that this agreement is "based on the arrogant fallacy that 'the market' will solve any and all problems, and it avoids the most basic social, labor, environmental, and cultural responsibilities that are actually [at] the core of any relationship between the three countries" (Gómez-Peña 2003: 752). While NAFTA did not significantly impact problems of poverty, especially in Mexico's southern states, the agreement did bring about dramatic economic changes and internal modernization. Data show that the results of NAFTA include the liberalization and growth of the Mexican economy, more foreign investments in Mexico, and employment growth especially within the northern Mexican border states (Davy and Meyers 2005). Roger Wallace, former U.S. deputy undersecretary for international trade, presented data at a conference on NAFTA held by the Latin American Studies Center at the University of Texas at Austin in February 2007, and he argued that the total value of U.S. trade with Mexico has tripled. It was reported that NAFTA helped to diversify and stabilize the Mexican economy. Those economic results vary significantly by region, however, with the northern states that border the United States benefiting most from NAFTA (Wallace 2007).

Many attribute the successful passage of NAFTA to the efforts of the businessmen in Mexico and in the United States who lobbied legislators, drafted policy papers, and hammered out the differences between the many constituencies involved. Because NAFTA is a trade relationship and not a broader policy, many important issues affecting the border were not addressed in the agreement. For example, nothing in NAFTA promotes macro-level economic stability, such as monitoring exchange rates or long-term interest rates that would avert another devaluation crisis in Mexico, or dramatic interest-rate shifts in the United States (Wallace 2007). NAFTA provided for some infrastructure funds, but certainly not sums sufficient for urban management or the large infrastructure improvements needed in Mexico's southern states.

The NAFTA agreement, moreover, addresses very little on labor issues. Work visas were restricted, and although the requirements were subsequently enlarged and relaxed, there were not enough visas to meet the demand for workers. In addition, many roles in which personnel are greatly needed in the United States were not included, such as physicians and construction workers. Critics of NAFTA claim that the agreement did not go far enough to address labor rights and the existing social order, which includes many very poor and a few very wealthy in both Mexico and the United States. Indeed, many observers argue that more pressure in this area or on core labor standards and the right to unionize and workers' rights enforcement would have jeopardized the passage of the agreement. Thus, while the families living along the border have benefited from NAFTA because of the growth in trade and in employment, in most cases the workers and heads of families have not seen dramatically higher wages or greatly improved working conditions.

In NAFTA, as in other border agreements, there was always the concern that one side would take advantage of the other. It has been difficult for many people with a strong sense of national identity to think about a North American community that extends beyond their own borders. Others have argued that there can never be a free market because one cannot separate economic theory from society. Supporters maintain that NAFTA was revolutionary in terms of U.S.-Mexico relations and has encouraged employment and development in Mexico, particularly in the northern states (Davy and Meyers 2005). Issues of labor mobility, immigration, and citizenship as well as of energy and environmental pollution across the border in all likelihood would have been a "deal breaker" if they had been included in the NAFTA negotiations.

The U.S.-Mexico Partnership Agreement signed in March 2002 (Meyers 2003) attempted to address security issues that have resulted in border crossing bottlenecks that hinder the NAFTA free-trade cooperation between the United States and Mexico. Delayed crossings and border fences continue to be barriers to free trade and open markets as well as to transnational families. The long boundary is certain to play a role in these trade networks, and families in the borderlands will benefit from the improvements in infrastructure for commerce and labor movements.

Key to continued prosperity in Mexico's northern states and in the borderlands is investment in human capital, particularly in border families. The number of children completing higher levels of education in Mexico has risen significantly, but investments in higher education and initiatives in education collaborations are central to the continued and future success of families on the border.

Jim Jones (NAFTA Conference 2007), U.S. ambassador to Mexico from 1993 to 1997, emphasizes how little policymakers know about Mexico and how few of them have even visited the border. Even if policymakers do not recognize the borderless economy shared by the United States and Mexico, a true integration will eventually occur simply by demographics alone. The U.S. population is aging and retiring (many, in fact, to Mexico), and Mexico is producing many young workers who will be attracted to jobs in the United States. As tightened U.S. border security makes it more difficult for workers without documents to cross back into Mexico, they and their U.S.-born children will remain in *el norte*. Thus, a borderless society of North America will probably occur de facto, if not legally, as immigration continues and is encouraged by the social and family networks and economic remittances that extend across borders (Kandel and Massey 2002; Mooney 2003; Pedraza 2006). Certainly, as we can see from the chapters included in this volume, migration is a social and an economic system and the lives of border families are part of a global system. Networks in the border communities are extremely strong and, even with higher wages offered in Mexico, Mexican migration to the United States will continue because of these family ties and the strong labor demands found there.

Experts predicted that NAFTA would reduce immigration pressures in Mexico in the long term but would increase immigration in the short term. According to Dr. Susan Martin, director of the Institute for the Study of International Migration (NAFTA Conference 2007), the majority of Mexican immigrants to the United States have low levels of education (about 40%), but about 25% of these immigrants have levels of education higher than the U.S. average. The greatest surge in immigration from Mexico has been unauthorized immigration, which raises issues about the reform of our immigration system as well as issues of incorporation. The border states are key in the discussion of regulated and unregulated immigration because these states are the major gateways into the United States. Complicating these issues is the fact that many unauthorized immigrants live in households with legal resident-visa holders and U.S.-citizen children.

Additionally, efforts to address immigration reforms failed in 1990 and in 2005. Border enforcement has shifted movements but has not stopped them. Legal assumptions have not kept pace with the realities of immigration and transnational lives on the border, mainly because most Americans are ambivalent about the issue—they have hired housekeepers, nannies, gardeners, and others whom they want to remain in the United States, but at the same time they are fearful of increased waves of immigration. The strong economy in the United States and in northern Mexico has meant a strong demand for workers. The efficiency of immigrant networks continues to meet that demand, and when workers and family members cross the border, their removal is difficult. Border states on the northern side are dependent upon Mexican markets for their goods, and U.S. employers are dependent upon Mexican workers. Whether these neighbors like it or not, the border area will continue to play a pivotal role as the United States and Mexico try to deal with these difficult issues.

Operation Gatekeeper

Operation Gatekeeper is an enhanced border enforcement strategy established on October 1, 2004, to reduce unauthorized migrant crossings into southern California. As a result, the Tijuana-San Diego border area has become "the world's most policed international divide between two nonbelligerent countries" (Nevins 2002). Operation Gatekeeper marked a change of strategy on the part of the United States from apprehension of unauthorized migrants once they crossed the border to one of prevention meant to deter them from entering—the latter through reinforcement of the Border Patrol, increased use of surveillance technologies, and unprecedented levels of enforcement along the U.S.-Mexico boundary. Joseph Nevins (2002) notes that Operation Gatekeeper is somewhat paradoxical since it occurred at a time of rapid economic and demographic growth in the border region and increased interaction and integration between the United States and Mexico with the signing of NAFTA.

This strategy is seen as a reaction to the growing regional integration along the U.S.-Mexico boundary and an effort to enhance separation between the two countries. Operation Gatekeeper, and the general buildup of security and boundaries, has made it more dangerous for undocumented migrants to cross the border and has increased hardships for those transnational or transborder families by restricting where they can go and live and work. In addition to official policies to increase border security, private nativist groups have taken the law into their own hands. In the spring of 2004 the Minuteman Project in Arizona, a group of armed civilians, attempted to seal the border with "a dangerous mix of nativist intolerance, armed and untrained civilians and wild-eyed conspiracy theories" (Buchanan and Kim 2005: 24). Moreover, Claudia Smith, the border project director for the California Rural Legal Assistance Foundation (2004), counted the number of migrant deaths on the rise at the U.S.-Mexican border, including the more than thirty suffocation deaths, among them eighteen people found locked in a truck near Victoria, Texas. More than one hundred migrants have died in the Arizona desert and Operation Desert Safeguard has done little to prevent these tragedies.

In 2006 the U.S. House of Representatives passed a bill that called for a 698-mile wall along the border and that made it a felony to be in the United States illegally. Employers were penalized for hiring undocumented workers. As Congress continues to debate border security, temporary guest-worker programs, and whether or not to allow immigrants to strive for citizenship, families along *la frontera* continue to lead their lives without borders. In addition to the formidable issue of security, the increasing militarization of the border that has accompanied the war on drugs, the persistence of undocumented immigration, and the transnational industrialization of the border region all present unique challenges in the areas of social policy and the study of transnational cultural forms.

Building on Scholarly Research

Research on the U.S.-Mexican border addresses numerous issues on the processes of migration and urbanization as well as on development and ethnic group formation, but it often makes only passing references to women and children or to families, as noted earlier. Attention was given to these topics in a special issue of the *Anthropological Quarterly* published in 1976 that focused on women and migration. Additionally, other women scholars have addressed labor force and family issues faced by Latina immigrant women (Brethel 2000; Fernández-Kelly and Garcia 1998; Gabaccia 1991; Hondagneu-Sotelo 1992; Pessar 1995, 1996; Segura 1994), but little scholarship focuses on the ways that women and families make use of resources on both sides of the border.

　　When scholars do focus on women, they often do so within the family context. Some scholars have argued that women's work lives are best understood as responses to the economy of the family unit within which they live, and as family members dependent upon the unit for their personal well-being (Hondagneu-Sotelo 2001; Zahniser 2000; Zavella 1987). Others have argued that the family unit is particularly patriarchal, and that women must free themselves of the self-sacrifice required of them by family life (Hondagneu-Sotelo 2001). They propose that the lag in adjusting values, behaviors, and institutions to new realities creates problems in contemporary families (Coontz 1997). The absence of husbands through international migration enhances the autonomy of women by making them the sole authority in child rearing and daily household decision-making (Aysa and Massey 2004). Family

solidarity, however, continues to be a theme of considerable importance among Latinos, and it is respected as a positive value benefiting
the individuals who make up the family unit (Lamphere et al. 1997;
Zavella 1987). In kinship and family networks, women exercise considerable authority, and women and children are recognized as resourceful participants (Stack 1974). Moreover, Latinas and their children have strong identifications with their families and often construct
their own identities through relations to others within the family unit
(Hondagneu-Sotelo and Avila 1997; Horowitz 1981; Orellana 2001;
Zavella 1987).

Many of the women on the border confront the same inequities
faced by women of color throughout the United States—earning low
wages, experiencing discrimination and poverty, struggling as single
parents to provide for their children, and making work choices to accommodate family and child care needs (Rothenberg 2007). Many of
these families seek better opportunities in major cities such as Los Angeles and San Antonio, which become extended borders, but they do
not sever ties to the borderlands nor to their home communities in
Mexico (Mooney 2003; Hondagneu-Sotelo and Avila 1997).

Theorizing about the Border

Juan Poblete compiled short essays that elaborated on the benefits and
risks of national/transnational/cross-border frameworks in the Latin
American Studies Association's journal, *Forum* (Fall 2006). The discussion focused on transnational dialogues on globalization and theorizing
contemporary Latin American struggles. Poblete's discussion is relevant as we address the theoretical frameworks appropriate for this
volume.

In addressing the impact of globalization and the emergence of
transnational perspectives for the analysis of border issues, we confront
the multiple angles created by the flows of people, discourses, goods,
and capital across the U.S.-Mexican border. Theories must address the
subnational region that spans the political boundary of the two countries as well as the supranational regional and global dimensions of
migrations, trade, and border economies. Latin American scholarship
raises questions about the consideration of the "nation," which still

defines how people are divided into relations of power and status, especially when a very wealthy nation (the United States) borders a nation (Mexico) with an emerging economy, and when both have long histories of nationalism. We must also consider that the nation-states still play a crucial role in who has the formal rights of citizenship and legal residency. Nicholas De Genova (1998) suggests that rather than envision the border as an extension of Mexico, we see that "the Mexican-ness of the area signifies a permanent disruption of the space of the U.S. nation-state and embodies the possibility of something truly new, a radically different social formation." Others have used the term "transnational community" to characterize this kind of space (Glick Schiller 1999; Glick Schiller et al. 1995; Levitt 2001; Levitt and Waters 2002) and have suggested that parts of transnational communities that participate both in their national country of origin and in their country of settlement create a unique third space that can be called "transnational."

A positive contribution of theorizing about the border in this way is that it encourages us to think differently about the nation-state and the kinds of binary divisions of the two countries that have permeated so much of the social analysis of the border. It is certainly important to consider the "national" when thinking about transnational spaces, because part of the immigrant history and experience has been shaped by the recognition, or lack thereof, of citizenship status and/or basic human and labor rights. We present articles in this volume that address the situations of the border families who have crossed and continue to cross spaces that are much more than "national." Additionally, there are ethnic, cultural, gender, and economic borders within each country that transborder migrants must deal with. Along the border with Mexico, in major sister cities such as San Diego-Tijuana and El Paso-Ciudad Juárez, and in extended border urban regions such as San Antonio and Los Angeles where many transborder migrants concentrate, areas emerge as strategic sites for globalized economic processes and a unique cross-border geography and culture (Sassen 2004). Saskia Sassen argues that transborder migrants can escape the boundaries of the formal polity and create organizations that deal directly with U.S. and Mexican public officials. The increasing number of Mexican immigrants allows these actors to develop a presence that can serve as a precursor to more formal political participation (Stephen 2006).

While there is a consensus that migration from Mexico is changing U.S. border states and other areas, there is no consensus on an interdisciplinary, comparative, and regional framework (Suárez-Orozco 2006). Many scholars are, in fact, assessing the conceptual and political effectiveness of "national/transnational/cross-border frameworks in the analysis of Hemispheric issues" (Yudice 2006). Basch et al. (1994) suggests a framework of transnationalism that defines the ways immigrants build extensive social fields linking their communities of origin to their communities of settlement. Transnationalism extends and challenges the more traditional assimilationist approach to studying border families (Glick Schiller et al. 1995). The past decade has seen an explosion in research on transnationalism, thus making the case that rights need to be extended beyond the national framework, that individuals belong culturally to more than one nation-state, and that new circumstances of migration brought about by globalization processes have an impact on both sending and receiving countries. A major criticism of cultural citizenship and transnationalism is that studies using this perspective have focused mostly on the situations in the receiving country.

Historically, modernization theory has prevailed in discussions of why people migrate, emphasizing the push-pull factors that stimulate movement from poor countries to rich countries. Population movements have often resulted in migration-dependent communities and generation of further migration through the diffusion of consumerism and dependence on remittances (Durand and Massey 2004). Many factors of the push-pull elements of modernization continue to work on the U.S.-Mexico border, but these migration patterns do not result in linear development. The experiences and family lives in the region are much more complex, both for individuals and groups.

The history of U.S.-Mexico relations, the reality that the Southwest was once a part of Mexico, and the extensive shared border suggest that a historical-structural approach, drawing broadly on Marxist thought and world systems theory in the context of global migrations, would be helpful in understanding families on the border (Buchanan and Kim 2005; Buroway 1985). The impact of the global market and national and international economic and political policies have disrupted families, displaced jobs, and attracted new families and single women to the border. Underlying the transnational and transborder patterns and linkages is the position of both the United States and Mexico in a global economy and their unequal positions of power (Basch et al. 1994). Still, there is dissatisfaction with macro-level approaches that portray migrants as passive reactors manipulated by the world capitalist system.

Transnationalism presents a critique of bipolar models of migration and instead suggests a social process whereby migrants operate in social fields that transgress geographic, political, and cultural borders (Basch et al. 1994; Glick Schiller et al. 1992; Pedraza 2006). Transnationalism emerged from the realization that migrants maintain their ties to the communities of origin; they "forge and sustain multi-stranded social relations that link together their societies of origin and settlement" (Basch et al. 1994); they are no longer "uprooted" or "assimilated" into the new society but move freely between home and host communities, back and forth across international borders and within different cultures and social systems (Glick Schiller 1999; Levitt 2001; Levitt and Waters 2002). Immigrants maintain connections through air travel, faxes, electronic mail, digital and video cameras, and cell phones that enable them to keep in close touch with those in their home country and to connect regularly to families left behind. Thus, there may be no bounded units of social analysis or localized communities to study. Spaces may be unbounded, discontinuous, and interpenetrating subspaces or imagined communities or racialized inequalities of power and opportunity (De Genova and Ramos-Zayas 2003; Kearney 1996, 1997; Wood 2004) as they are in the borderlands.

Chapter Contributors

The contributors to this volume represent a multidisciplinary collaboration that reflects our efforts to paint a comprehensive picture of Latino families at the U.S.-Mexico border. Here, the authors employ different theoretical constructs and perspectives in order to analyze the complexity of life at this national boundary. First, a transnational framework helps us understand how families concurrently participate in multiple U.S. and Mexican communities. Second, viewing migration as a process suggests that settling in a receiving country does not necessarily require renouncing allegiance to the sending community, and individuals who lead transnational lives may maintain intricate link-ages across both communities. Third, the role of second-generation youth's participation in transnationalism is often overlooked. Fourth, living in the borderlands includes daily transborder activities and cross-border family negotiations about life decisions. And fifth, economic markets and barriers to entry into these markets do not occur in a vacuum but are the everyday reality of immigrant and ethnic commu-nities.

Chapters 1 and 2 present national-level demographic profiles for each side of the border. The authors discuss the distinctive characteris-tics of the area in relation to the lives of the families and children who reside there. In chapter 1, "A Demographic Profile of Children and Families in the U.S.-Mexico Border Region," Yolanda C. Padilla and Ana Marie Argilagos examine the indicators of social well-being on the U.S. side, using U.S. Census data and variables for the year 2000. In chapter 2, Catalina Palmer, on behalf of La Red por los Derechos de la Infancia en México, offers a profile of Mexican demographics in "An Overview of Children and Youth on the Northern Mexican Border."

Harriett D. Romo suggests in chapter 3, "The Extended Border: A Case Study of San Antonio as a Transnational City," that border influ-ences extend beyond the physical place along the national boundaries. Romo posits that San Antonio, Texas, should be viewed as an exten-sion of the U.S.-Mexico border because of its long history and the eco-nomic, demographic, and cultural links that connect this urban area to the borderlands. Romo further argues that the city of San Antonio, al-though not physically located within the territory traditionally defined as the U.S.-Mexico border, is a transnational border city. For her, in San Antonio, decades of migration support shared cultural beliefs and population movements such that transnational social fields develop and encompass all aspects of social life for families.

Chapter 4 captures changes that are occurring in new and tradi-tional destinations of immigrant families in the United States and brings to the discussion a city- and county-level analysis. Belinda I. Reyes and Amanda G. Bailey, in "The Complex Picture of Cities near the U.S.-Mexico Border: The Case of Southern California," look closely at the changing landscapes of border cities in California. Reyes and Bailey im-plement a typology of cities that highlights emerging trends within the immigrant populations who are settling and living within one hundred miles of California's southern border. The history of the Los Angeles area and the long-term and large-scale Mexican migration along with the high proportion of foreign-born Mexican and other Latin American migrants in the area shape the context of home ownership and the demographics of the receiving communities. Undocumented Mexican immigrant labor in restaurants, domestic work, construction, and landscaping has been institutionalized in the Los Angeles extended border area. Indeed, local Mexicans are well versed in how to circumvent barriers to homeownership due to their legal status, by applying for mortgages in someone else's name or in the names with the Social Security numbers of individuals with legal documents (McConnell and Marcelli 2007).

In chapter 5, "*Maquiladora* or Cross-Border Commute: The Employment of Members of Households in Five Mexican Border Cities," Marie-Laure Coubès investigates the patterns of organization of family economies from the point of view of the participation of different members of the household in the labor market. Coubès focuses on the job and family linkage within a context of economic integration in border cities across the U.S.-Mexican border. Her work demonstrates high levels of cross-border interactions and discusses demand and supply among Mexican cross-border workers (Alegría 2002).

Many families who live in metropolitan areas with sister cities—such as Nuevo Laredo and Laredo, Ciudad Juárez and El Paso, or Tijuana and San Diego—lead their lives as if there were no geopolitical borders. For example, in chapter 6, "Transborder Interactions and Transnational Processes in the Border Community of Laredo, Texas," Raquel R. Márquez examines transborder interactions and transnational processes occurring concurrently within a border setting. Márquez looks at how these phenomena redound to the benefit of families' and women's lives, and she explains how transnational processes allow border families to maintain cultural links and remain intact across national boundaries.

Though many transnational families do not physically cross on a daily basis, Latino families who live farther away from *la frontera* draw from traditions in both the United States and Mexico when they celebrate rites of passage and family celebrations. In chapter 7, "Coming of Age across Borders: Family, Gender, and Place in the Lives of Second-Generation Transnational Mexicanas," Patricia Sánchez studies the ways in which family, gender, and place intersect in the upbringing of transnational youth residing in northern California. Sánchez focuses on familial, social, and religious practices as well as on the gender negotiations of three young women who are U.S.-born but maintain close ties to their parents' rural home communities in Jalisco, Mexico. Her research addresses the parenting strategies of transnational immigrant families as well as the socialization of children in this context.

Mary A. Petrón shifts the discussion from transnationalism to the Mexican side of the border in chapter 8, "'I'm *Bien Pocha*': Borderlands Epistemologies and the Teaching of English in Mexico," where she examines the transnational experience of children of U.S. immigrants who have returned to Mexico and now work there as teachers of English. Petrón's analysis challenges stereotypes of language and cultural practices in identifying how these teachers remain influenced by their experiences on both sides of the border—experiences that ultimately influence and shape their teaching practices in Mexico.

Amelia Malagamba-Ansótegui suggests in chapter 9, "The Real and the Symbolic: Visualizing Border Spaces," that images of the U.S.-Mexico border penetrate the subconscious and imaginations of people who have experienced the borderlands as well as those who have not. The absence of particular images of Latino families, women, and conceptual frameworks sends a powerful message, as strong as the one that comes from other border life images. Images produced by the media and artists often define the border by neglecting the realities of transnational life.

Economist Bárbara J. Robles, in chapter 10, "Latina Entrepreneurship in the Borderlands: Family Well-Being and Poverty Reduction Policies," explores the intersection of Latina entrepreneurial activities and the importance of the cultural competency of community-based organizations in supporting this entrepreneurship. Her work explores the ways in which Latinas contribute to family well-being, and she discusses the pivotal role that public policy plays in grass-roots community development. Robles argues that because of the high concentration of Latinos along the U.S.-Mexico border, Latina entrepreneurs see their biculturalism as an asset and the transnational economic environment of the borderlands as a catalyst for growth.

In the final chapter, "Public Policy Changes on the U.S.-Mexico Border," Irasema Coronado proposes policy recommendations that emerge from the various perspectives of families and children on the border. The author emphasizes the critical importance of bilateral collaboration to address the needs of families on both sides. Her research findings suggest that transnational policies and border families are an integral part of the successful future of U.S.-Mexico relations and of economic and social development in this region.

Families along the U.S.-Mexican border as well as families in the extended border areas and urban cities receiving new immigrants are changing. The ease of transportation and communication as well as the increasing economic collaborations across national borders facilitate living without borders even while terrorism and national security concerns attempt to make those political borders less permeable. As new generations in the borderlands form families, they will have experienced transnational and cross-border living as patterns of socialization. Options for dual nationality may increase the complexity of their lives. The continued growth in population along the U.S.-Mexico border, the demands on scarce resources of water and land, and the continued globalization of work and commerce suggest that the issues addressed in this volume will only increase in importance. Polices and practices affecting families and children on the border will have to be constructed from both sides, from multiple perspectives, and across different academic disciplines. We complete this volume with a full understanding that families will continue to seek resources and relationships from both sides of the U.S.-Mexico boundary despite tightened border security or restrictive immigration policies. Demographic changes, increasing economic regionalism, the continued demand and supply of labor, and the social networks that extend across nation-states and across the lives described in this volume will continue to generate transborder, transnational, and cross-border families.

Glossary

Border Culture: The U.S.-Mexico borderlands at times function as one entity, yet border dynamics are as complex as they are intertwined. Residents of the borderlands recognize the interdependent nature of their relationships. Links between the U.S. and Mexican sides are supported through a strong sense of family unity, social networks, cultural commonalities, and an understanding of the shared binational political and economic interests. Language switching, or code switching, between Spanish and English is an integral part of borderlands culture and occurs daily in a variety of transactions, often without the speakers even being cognizant of the degree of code switching in which they engage. Opportunities to hold dual nationality in Mexico and the United States have encouraged many Mexicans and their family members to become U.S. citizens, which status allows them to participate in the politics, economy, and social fields of the United States.

Borderlands: The area referred to as the U.S. borderlands once belonged to Mexico, and throughout its history the region has continued to receive important migratory flows. The northern Mexican states bordering the United States are densely populated and boast the strongest economies in Mexico. The 1,989-mile boundary along the U.S. states of California, Arizona, New Mexico, and Texas and the Mexican states of Baja California, Sonora, Chihuahua, Coahuila, Nuevo León, and Tamaulipas is the busiest border in the world, with 300 million two-way crossings per year (Migration Policy Institute 2002). If the economies of the border states in both nations were combined, they would represent the third or fourth largest economy in the world. Nearly 12 million people live in the borderlands, with close to 5.5 million on the Mexican side and nearly 6.5 million on the U.S. side, many of whom are Mexican American. The borderlands are disproportionately Latino both in comparison to the rest of the United States and to non-border counties in the border states. Historical and cultural ties with Mexico are evident in the extensive use of the Spanish language, cultural identity and traditions, and daily economic activity.

Extended Border: Despite the physical distance from the official border and a continued accessibility to Mexico, many Mexican and Mexican American residents live in the extended border of their Mexican homeland (Arreola 1987). There, Spanish is spoken regularly across all social classes in stores, restaurants, and social gatherings (Arreola 1995). San Antonio, Texas, and East Los Angeles, California, for example, although not physically located within the territory traditionally defined as the U.S.-Mexico border, have the context and expansive set of relationships produced by decades of migration that support shared cultural beliefs.

Maquiladoras: *Maquiladoras* are assembly plants located in Mexico that are predominantly owned by U.S. corporations taking advantage of low-cost labor, advantageous tariff regulations, and close proximity to northern markets. Employment in *maquiladoras* is characterized by long workdays and rigid schedules (Fernández-Kelly 1983). Daughters and other female relatives dominate the labor force in *maquiladoras,* which are one of Mexico's primary sources of foreign exchange.

Transborder: Sometimes referred to as cross-border, transborder links in the borderlands are characterized by high cross-border mobility. Daily contact between the populations of both countries has facilitated the development of unique transborder social formations. Families and commuters reside, attend school, own businesses, and work on both sides. These families are commonly found in twin border cities such as El Paso and Ciudad Juárez or Tijuana and San Diego or the smaller sister cities all along the international border. In general, persons on the Mexican side must obtain legal documentation, speak a minimum of English, and have a social network to gain entrance into the United States (Alegría 2002).

Transnational: Many Mexicans and Mexican Americans are rooted in the United States, but their lives are integrally involved with resources, contacts, and people on the Mexican side of the border. Basch et al. (1994: 7) formalized the definition of transnationalism by stating that immigrants "take actions, make decisions, and develop subjectivities and identities embedded in networks of relationships that connect them simultaneously to two or more nations." A "transnational social field," or space, is created by the continuous interchanges between a person's sending and receiving community—a space that enables the person to function in both places simultaneously. Transnational social fields encompass all aspects of social life (Levitt and Waters 2002). Moreover, formal and informal institutions promote the established norms and values of the home community in the receiving community and organize social life in ways that promote transnational identities and fields of experience.

Transnational Families: Transnational families live and maintain familial, social, and cultural contacts in both sending and receiving countries simultaneously. Parents often participate in raising children left behind in the community of origin or spend part of the year in one country and the remainder in the other. For transnational families, economic mobility depends upon extended family resources and on economic survival strategies that in turn depend upon social class and community resources. Remittances, that is, money or goods sent by immigrants to their families in their home country, are "a result of migration and also result in migration" by encouraging other relatives to join the migrant (Pedraza 2006: 48).

References

Alegría, Tito. 2002. "Demand and Supply among Mexican Cross-Border Workers." *Journal of Borderlands Studies* 17(1): 37–56.

Anzaldúa, Gloria. 1987. *Borderlands/La Frontera: The New Mestiza*. San Francisco: Spinsters/Aunt Lute Books.

Arreola, Daniel D. 1987. "The Mexican American Cultural Capital." *Geographic Review* 77: 17–34.

_____. 1995. "Urban Ethnic Landscape Identity." *Geographic Review,* Thematic Issue: American Urban Geography 85(4): 518–34.

Aysa, Maria, and Douglas S. Massey. 2004. "Wives Left Behind: The Labor Market Behavior of Women in Migrant Communities." In *Crossing the Border: Research from the Mexican Migration Project,* ed. Jorge Durand and Douglas S. Massey, 131–44. New York: Russell Sage Foundation.

Basch, Linda G., Nina Glick Schiller, and Cristina Blanc-Szanton. 1994. *Nations Unbound: Transnational Projects, Postcolonial Predicaments, and Deterritorialized Nation-States*. Langhorne, PA: Gordon and Breach.

Brettell, Caroline B. 2000. "Theorizing Migration in Anthropology." In *Migration Theory,* ed. Caroline B. Brettell and James F. Hollifield, 99–136. New York: Routledge.

Buchanan, Susy, and Tom Kim. 2005. "The Nativists around the Country, An Anti-Immigration Movement Is Spreading like a Prairie Fire. An Array of Activists is Fanning the Flames." In *The Intelligence Report*. Montgomery, AL: Southern Poverty Law Center.

Buroway, Michael. 1985. *The Politics of Production*. London: Verso Press.

Coontz, Stephanie. 1997. *The Way We Really Are: Coming to Terms with America's Changing Families*. New York: Basic Books.

Corwin, Arthur F. 1978. *Immigrants and Immigrants: Perspectives on Mexican Labor Migration to the United States*. Westport, CT: Greenwood.

Davy, Megan, and Deborah Meyers. 2005. "Immigration Facts: United States-Canada-Mexico Fact Sheet on Trade and Migration." Washington, DC: Migration Policy Institute.

De Genova, Nicholas. 1998. "Race, Space, and the Reinvention of Latin America in Mexican Chicago." *Latin American Perspectives* 102(25:5): 87–116.

De Genova, Nicholas, and Ana Y. Ramos-Zayas. 2003. *Latino Crossings: Mexicans, Puerto Ricans, and the Politics of Race and Citizenship*. New York: Routledge.

Durand, Jorge, and Douglas S. Massey, eds. 2004. *Crossing the Border: Research from the Mexican Migration Project*. New York: Russell Sage Foundation.

Fernández-Kelly, María Patricia. 1983. *For We Are Sold, I and My People: Women and Industry in Mexico's Frontier*. Albany: State University of New York Press.

Fernández-Kelly, María Patricia, and Anna M. García. 1998. "Informalization at the Core: Hispanic Women, Homework, and the Advanced Capitalist State." In *The Informal Economy: Studies in Advanced and Less Developed Countries*, ed. Alejandro Portes, Manual Castells, and Lauren A. Benton, 247–64. Baltimore: Johns Hopkins University Press.

Fregoso, Rosa Linda. 2003. *MeXicana Encounters: The Making of Social Identities on the Borderlands*. Berkeley: University of California Press.

Gabaccia, Donna. 1991. "Immigrant Women: Nowhere at Home?" *Journal of American Ethnic History* 10(4): 61–75.

Glick Schiller, Nina. 1999. "Transmigrants and Nation-States: Something Old and Something New in the U.S. Immigrant Experience." In *The Handbook of International Migration,* ed. Charles Hirschman, Philip Kasinitz, and Josh DeWind, 94–119. New York: Russell Sage Foundation.

Glick Schiller, Nina, Linda Basch, and Cristina Blanc-Szanton. 1992. "Towards a Transnationalization of Migration: Race, Class, Ethnicity, and Nationalism Reconsidered." In *Towards a Transnational Perspective on Migration: Race, Class, Ethnicity, and Nationalism Reconsidered,* ed. Nina Glick Schiller, Linda Basch, and Cristina Blanc-Szanton, 1–24. New York: New York Academy of Sciences.

———. 1995. "From Immigrant to Transmigrant: Theorizing Transnational Migration." *Anthropological Quarterly* 68(1): 48–63.

Gómez-Peña, Guillermo. 2003. "The New World Border." In *The Mexico Reader: History, Culture, Politics,* ed. Gilbert M. Joseph and Timothy J. Henderson, 750–55. Durham, NC: Duke University Press.

Hondagneu-Sotelo, Pierrette. 1992. "Overcoming Patriarchal Constraints: The Reconstruction of Gender Relations among Mexican Immigrant Women and Men." *Gender and Society* 6(3): 393–415.

———. 2001. *Doméstica: Immigrant Workers Cleaning and Caring in the Shadows of Affluence.* Berkeley: University of California Press.

Hondagneu-Sotelo, Pierrette, and Ernestine Avila. 1997. "'I'm Here, But I'm There': The Meanings of Transnational Latina Motherhood." *Gender and Society* 2(5): 548–71.

Horowitz, Ruth. 1981. "Passion, Submission, and Motherhood: The Negotiation of Identity by Unmarried Inner-city Chicanas." *Sociological Quarterly* 22(2): 241–52.

Jones, Jim. 2007. Presentation at NAFTA Conference. Latin American Studies Center, University of Texas at Austin.

Kandel, William, and Douglas S. Massey. 2002. "The Culture of Mexican Migration: A Theoretical and Empirical Analysis." *Social Forces* 80(3) (March): 981–1004.

Kearney, Michael. 1996. "Ethnicity and Class in Latin America." Latin American Perspectives 23(2) (Spring): 5–16.

———. 1997. "Reconceptualizing the Peasantry: Anthropology in Global Perspective." *Journal of the Royal Anthropological Institute* 3(4): 789–90.

Lamphere, Louise, Helena Ragone, and Patricia Zavella, eds. 1997. *Situated Lives: Gender and Culture in Everyday Life.* New York: Routledge.

Levitt, Peggy. 2001. *The Transnational Villagers.* Berkeley: University of California Press.

Levitt, Peggy, and Mary C. Waters, eds. 2002. *The Changing Face of Home: The Transnational Lives of the Second Generation.* New York: Russell Sage Foundation.

McCarthy, Kevin F., and Georges Vernez. 1998. *Immigration in a Changing Economy: California's Experience—Questions and Answers.* Los Angeles: RAND.

McConnell, Eileen Díaz, and Enrico A. Marcelli. 2007. "Buying into the American Dream? Mexican Immigrants, Legal Status, and Home Ownership in Los Angeles County." *Social Science Quarterly* 88(1): 199–221.

McWilliams, Carey. 1967. *Ill Fares the Land: Migrants and Migratory Labor in the United States.* New York: Barnes and Noble Books.

Meyers, Deborah. 2003. *Does 'Smarter' Lead to Safer? An Assessment of the Border Accords with Mexico and Canada.* Washington, DC: Migration Policy Institute.

Migration Policy Institute. 2002. *U.S. in Focus: The U.S.-Mexico Border.* Washington, DC.

Montejano, David. 1987. *Anglos and Mexicans in the Making of Texas, 1836–1986.* Austin: University of Texas Press.

Mooney, Margarita. 2003. "Migrants' Social Ties in the U.S. and Investment in Mexico." *Social Forces* 81(3) (June): 1147–70.

NAFTA and U.S.-Mexico Relations: In Retrospect and Prospect. Conference presented by the Nettie Lee Benson Latin American Collection of the University of Texas Libraries and the Mexican Center of the Teresa Lozano Long Institute of Latin American Studies, February 22–23, 2007, at the Law School, University of Texas at Austin.

Nevins, Joseph. 2002. *Operation Gatekeeper: The Rise of the "Illegal Alien" and the Making of the U.S.-Mexico Boundary.* New York: Taylor and Francis.

Ojeda de la Peña, Norma. 1995. "Familias transfronterizas y trayectorias de migración y trabajo." In *Mujeres migración y maquila en la frontera norte,* ed. Soledad González, Olivia Ruiz, Laura Velasco, and Ofelia Woo, 89–112. México, D.F: El Colegio de México.

Orellana, Marjorie Faulstich. 2001. "The Work Kids Do: Mexican and Central American Immigrant Children's Contributions to Households and Schools in California." *Harvard Educational Review* 71(3): 366–89.

Pedraza, Silvia. 2006. "Assimilation or Transnationalism? Conceptual Models of the Immigrant Experience in America." In *Cultural Psychology of Immigrants,* ed. Ramaswami Mahalingam, 33–54. Mahwah, NJ: Lawrence Erlbaum Associates.

Pessar, Patricia. 1995. "On the Homefront and in the Workplace: Integrating Immigrant Women into Feminist Discourse." *Anthropological Quarterly* 68: 34–47.

———. 1996. *A Visa for a Dream: Dominicans in the United States.* Needham Heights, MA: Allyn and Bacon.

Poblete, Juan. 2006. "Transnational Dialogues on Globalization and the Intersections of Latina/o-Chicana/o Latin American(s) Studies." *Forum* 37(4): 9–17.

Rothenberg, Paula S. 2007. *Race, Class, and Gender in the United States.* 7th ed. New York: Worth Publishers.

Sassen, Saskia. 2004. "The Repositioning of Citizenship: Emergent Subjects and Spaces for Politics." *Berkeley Journal of Sociology* 46: 4–25.

Segura, Denise A. 1994. "Inside the Work Worlds of Chicana and Mexican Immigrant Women." In *Women of Color in U.S. Society,* ed. Maxine Baca Zinn and Bonnie Thornton Dill, 95–111. Philadelphia: Temple University Press.

Smith, Claudia. 2004. "Operation Gatekeeper Fact Sheet." California Rural Legal Assistance Foundation's Border Project. http://www.stopgatekeeper.org/English/facts.html (last accessed July 2007).

Stack, Carol. 1974. *All Our Kin: Strategies for Survival in a Black Community.* New York: Harper and Row.

Stephen, Lynn. 2006. "Some Thoughts on Concepts to Cut Across Latino/Latin American/Chicano Studies." *Forum* 37(1): 10–12.

Suárez-Orozco, Marcelo. 2006. "Some Thoughts on Migration Studies and the Latin American Exodo." *Forum* 37(1): 13–14.

Vélez-Ibáñez, Carlos G. 1996. *Border Visions: Mexican Cultures of the Southwest United States*. Tucson: University of Arizona Press.

Vila, Pablo. 2000. *Crossing Borders, Reinforcing Borders: Social Categories, Metaphors, and Narrative Identities on the U.S.-Mexico Frontier*. Austin: University of Texas Press.

————, ed. 2003. *Ethnography at the Border: Cultural Studies of the Americas*. Minneapolis: University of Minnesota Press.

————. 2005. *Border Identifications: Narratives of Religion, Gender, and Class on the U.S.-Mexico Border*. Austin: University of Texas Press.

Wallace, Roger. 2007. Presentation at NAFTA Conference. Latin American Studies Center, University of Texas at Austin.

Wood, Andrew Grant, ed. 2004. *On the Border: Society and Culture between the United States and Mexico*. Lanham, MD: SR Books.

Yudice, George. 2006. "Linking Cultural Citizenship and Transnationalism to the Movement for an Equitable Global Economy." *Forum* 37(1): 15–17.

Zahniser, Steven S. 2000. "One Border, Two Crossings: Mexican Migration to the United States as a Two-Way Process." In *Immigration Research for a New Century: Multidisciplinary Perspectives*, ed. Nancy Foner, Rubén Rumbaut, and Steven Gold, 242–76. New York: Russell Sage Foundation.

Zavella, Patricia. 1987. *Women's Work and Chicano Families: Cannery Workers of the Santa Clara Valley*. Ithaca, NY: Cornell University Press.

CHAPTER ONE

A Demographic Profile of Children and Families in the U.S.-Mexico Border Region

Yolanda C. Padilla and Ana Marie Argilagos

The U.S.-Mexico border region on the southern margins of the states of Texas, New Mexico, Arizona, and California faces many challenges while possessing a unique vitality. This region contains some of the poorest areas in the United States, especially in Texas and New Mexico. Of the thirty-two border counties examined here, thirteen are among the poorest one hundred counties in the United States, with child poverty rates ranging from 39.7% to 59.5% (Children's Defense Fund n.d.). This chapter focuses on the twenty-four counties contiguous to the Mexican international boundary, plus eight additional ones adjacent to border counties (five in Texas and three in New Mexico) for a total of thirty-two. It takes a closer look at the demographic profile of the counties adjacent to the U.S.-Mexico border based on Census and Vital Statistics data for the year 2000. Data will be provided in four areas: (1) population, geographic distribution, and Latino composition;

(2) immigration, citizenship, and language fluency; (3) child poverty, parental labor-force participation, and family structure; and (4) child and adolescent health and education. Given the high concentration of Latinos living in this region, comparisons are made for Latino and non-Latino white children.

As the data will show, although there exists discernible variability, on the whole, indicators of child and family well-being in border counties reveal greater hardship in comparison both to non-border counties in their respective states and to the rest of the United States. At the same time, other indicators show that families in this region demonstrate patterns of resiliency in spite of a weak economic environment and a variety of factors inherent to this transborder area that affect their well-being. The lack of a strong economic and infrastructural base has meant that the border region has been unable to support the strong population, environmental, and social links that characterize this transborder area. In the context of the vibrant cultural context of the U.S.-Mexico international border, greater attention on the part of policymakers can provide the support necessary for this part of the United States to thrive.

Conditions Affecting the Well-being of Children and Families

In order to make sense of the indicators of well-being in this region, it is important to establish a general understanding of the border context. Children and families who live along the U.S.-Mexico boundary face several unique conditions that put them at risk for poor health and social outcomes. First, the well-being of children and families is intrinsically intertwined with conditions existing on both sides. Environmental, health, economic, and other conditions along the border know no boundaries. Ineffective pollution control, low vaccination rates, or a poor economy on either side, for example, affects residents in both countries. Second, significant resource disparities on opposite sides of the border place children and families in a vulnerable position. Even when the needs of certain sectors of the border population are being met, the presence of pockets of poverty, such as in unincorporated areas known as *colonias,* and limited access to health and human services for some residents mean that often broader problems are not adequately addressed. This transborder region is marked by transactions occurring in close proximity to Mexico across a variety of levels: human, environmental, economic, and found social support. Transborder links here are characterized by a combination of high cross-border population mobility, inadequate oversight of environmental quality, an international border economy that has not effectively helped the area prosper, and a weak binational health and human services infrastructure.

The 1,989-mile United States–Mexico boundary is the busiest border in the world, with 300 million two-way crossings per year (Andreas 2003). In Texas alone, in 2002, there were 22 million pedestrian crossings into the United States from Mexico (DHHS HRSA n.d.). Of the four border states, the lowest volume of crossings occurred in New Mexico, with only 264,000 (U.S. Bureau of Transportation Statistics). Furthermore, in 2002, 3.7 million people moved to the six states in Mexico bordering the United States, with a net in-migration of 2 million people (INEGI n.d.). In the face of severe poverty and inadequate sanitary infrastructure, including the substandard housing, sewage, and electricity services that characterize the area, increased migration to the Mexican border region poses a public health threat (Erickson and Eaton 2002). Such risks include a high incidence of infectious diseases such as tuberculosis and vaccine-preventable illnesses, thus placing children and families at high risk (DHHS HRSA n.d.; Warner and Jahnke 2003).

According to the U.S. Department of Health and Human Services, the border confronts significant sanitation infrastructure deficiencies. Forty-six million liters of raw sewage flow daily into the Tijuana River and 76 million into the New and Rio Grande rivers. The international management of water use does not deal with pollution control issues, such as sewage and pesticide runoff. Due to poor industry compliance with environmental regulations, air pollution is a serious concern in large metropolitan areas such as El Paso/Ciudad Juárez (DHHS HRSA n.d.). Pollution in the region is considered a major cause of greater risk of health problems for children here than for the average child living in either country (U.S. Environmental Protection Agency 2000).

The regional U.S. border economy presents complex challenges because of its connections to an international economy. The U.S.-Mexico border area reflects patterns found in international border economies with large income disparities (Ruiz-Beltran and Kamau 2001). While the U.S. side is one of the poorest regions in the nation, the Mexican side, although characterized by conditions of a developing country, is one of the wealthiest (Erickson and Eaton 2002). As a result, the border region is characterized by large rates of in-migration. People immigrating from Mexico into the U.S. border area experience limited potential due to language differences. Overall, low educational and skills levels in part hamper the ability of the U.S. border populations to take full advantage of economic opportunities. For example, experts estimate that Texas border counties experienced aggregate income losses of approximately $6 billion in 1990 because of lower levels of education compared to the rest of the state (Fullerton 2001 and 2003). In addition, although the Mexican *maquiladora* industry has created a demand for supplier markets, an inadequate reserve of skilled labor has prevented Texas border cities from tapping into that market (Vargas 2001). The poor economic viability of border populations plays an important role in the life chances of children and families.

Despite the fact that problems facing children in U.S. border states are intrinsically interconnected through demographic, environmental, and economic links with Mexico, there is virtually no formal system of international collaboration available to U.S. and Mexican cities on the border in health and human services delivery (Padilla and Daigle 1996). Cooperation has historically been far more extensive in areas other than in human services, such as environmental and land-use management. Initiatives in the health field have been limited to reciprocal data-gathering and research, standardization of health records, use and comparability of officially collected statistics, exchange of information, and joint public education. Nevertheless, many problems faced by children and families in these communities require binational coordination in the actual delivery of health and human services, including client case management, in areas such as public health, child abuse, family problems, domestic violence, and juvenile delinquency (Padilla and Daigle 1996).

Population, Geographic Distribution, and Latino Composition

According to the 2000 Census, nearly one-quarter (23.5%) of all children and a full 58.3% of Latino children in the United States are concentrated in the four southwestern states of Texas, New Mexico, Arizona, and California. The population of this border region is approximately 6.5 million, of whom 1.8 million are children. Nearly 3 million people live in the two border counties of California, while 2 million are spread out across the twenty border counties in Texas. Nearly 1.2 million live in the four border counties in Arizona, and the remaining 300,000 make the six border counties in New Mexico their home. Within the border, four out of five children live in seven urban areas: Brownsville-Harlingen-San Benito, Laredo, and El Paso in Texas; Las Cruces, New Mexico; Tucson and Yuma in Arizona; and San Diego, California.

In order to draw a profile of the population distribution in the border region relative to the rest of the country, Table 1.1 provides data on the total population and on the percentage of the total population that is Latino for the general population and for those under age eighteen. For the population under eighteen, data are broken down for Latinos and non-Latino whites. Aggregate data are presented for the United States, for border and non-border states as well as for each of the four southwestern states, their border and non-border regions, and for each individual county in geographic order from Cameron County in Texas to San Diego County in California.

The border area is disproportionately Latino—primarily Mexican American—in comparison both to the rest of the country and to non-border counties in the border states. As shown in Table 1.1, in the border region, 48% of the total population and 62% of the child population is Latino, which is in sharp contrast to the national figures of 13% and 17%, respectively. In non-border counties, the proportions are 30% and 40%. The highest concentration of Latino children is found in Texas border counties, where 91% of the child population is Latino, followed by New Mexico, Arizona, and California. Every county along the border far exceeds the national average for Latino children. Moreover, although the proportion of children under the age of eighteen is similar for border and non-border counties regardless of race or ethnicity, the Latino population in border counties is very young. A full 36% of the Latino border population is under the age of eighteen, compared to only 19% among non-Latino whites, and this same pattern holds true for all border counties.

Table 1.1. Population Distribution in Border Counties by Age and Race/Ethnicity

	Population	Percent of Population That Is Latino		Percent of Population under 18	
	Total	Total	Under 18	Latino	Non-Latino White
United States	281,421,906	13	17	35	23
46 Non-Border States	219,748,760	7	9	33	23
4 Border States	61,673,146	32	42	37	21
32 Border Counties	6,448,006	48	62	36	19
Non-Border Counties	55,225,140	30	40	37	22
Texas	20,851,820	32	41	36	23
Non-Border Counties	18,832,116	26	34	36	23
Border Counties	2,019,704	85	91	36	19
Cameron	335,227	84	92	37	17
Willacy	20,082	86	93	34	17
Hidalgo	569,463	88	94	38	16
Brooks	7,976	92	95	33	18
Starr	53,597	98	98	38	30
Jim Hogg	5,281	90	92	32	25
Zapata	12,182	85	95	37	10
Webb	193,117	94	95	37	28
Dimmit	10,248	85	89	35	21
Maverick	47,297	95	96	37	25
Zavala	11,600	91	93	35	24
Kinney	3,379	51	68	35	16
Val Verde	44,856	75	83	35	21
Terrell	1,081	49	53	29	23
Brewster	8,866	44	59	30	16
Presidio	7,304	84	91	35	18
Jeff Davis	2,207	35	43	30	21
Culberson	2,975	72	83	37	19
Hudspeth	3,344	75	83	38	23
El Paso	679,622	78	84	35	21
New Mexico	1,819,046	42	51	34	20
Non-Border Counties	1,506,846	40	47	33	21
Border Counties	312,200	54	67	36	19
Otero	62,298	32	43	39	23
Doña Ana	174,682	63	76	36	18
Sierra	13,270	26	45	35	15
Luna	25,016	58	77	40	16
Grant	31,002	49	61	33	20
Hidalgo	5,932	56	64	36	26

Table 1.1.   (cont.)

	Population	Percent of Population That Is Latino		Percent of Population under 18	
	Total	*Total*	*Under 18*	*Latino*	*Non-Latino White*
Arizona	5,130,632	25	36	38	21
Non-Border Counties	3,970,724	23	32	39	21
Border Counties	1,159,908	34	49	37	18
Cochise	117,755	31	42	36	21
Santa Cruz	38,381	81	90	37	17
Pima	843,746	29	43	36	18
Yuma	160,026	50	70	40	16
California	33,871,648	32	44	37	20
Non-Border Counties	30,915,454	33	44	37	20
Border Counties	2,956,194	29	41	37	19
Imperial	142,361	72	82	36	20
San Diego	2,813,833	27	38	37	19

Source: All tables and figures are drawn from the 2000 U.S. Decennial Census or 2000 Vital Statistics records.

Immigration, Citizenship, and Language Fluency

The southwestern border states clearly drive immigration in the United States. In these states, 20% of the population is foreign-born compared to only 8% in the rest of the country. Thus, the rate of immigration in the border states is nearly twice the national average of 11%. Furthermore, as shown in Table 1.2, data on the foreign-born reveal that border counties have only slightly greater proportions of immigrants (22%) than do non-border counties (20%). However, a closer look reveals much variability across states. In Texas, overall, only 14% of the population is immigrant, but a full 28% of the border population is foreign-born compared to only 12% in non-border counties. A similar trend can be observed for New Mexico, although the percentage of immigrants overall is smaller. In California, where one-quarter of the population is immigrant, the foreign-born are concentrated not in the border counties (22%) but in the non-border ones (27%). Arizona has the least variability across the state. There is also a wide variation in immigration rates across individual border counties (not shown here), ranging from a low of 3% in Grant County, New Mexico, to a high of 38% in both Maverick County, Texas, and Santa Cruz County, Arizona.

Not surprisingly, the vast majority of immigrants living in the U.S.-Mexico border area are from Mexico. The proportion of foreign-born and the proportion of the total population born in Mexico in border counties in Texas, New Mexico, and Arizona are very close. For example, in these Texas counties, 28% of all residents are foreign-born and 26% of all residents were born in Mexico, thus indicating that the vast majority of the foreign-born immigrated from Mexico. This is not true for California border counties, where the immigrant rate is 22% and the total proportion of those born in Mexico is only 11%. Except in California, regardless of immigration rates, the data indicate that the vast majority of the foreign-born in each of the border counties are from Mexico. On a national level, as indicated earlier, 11% of the total population is foreign-born, but Mexico is the country of origin for only 3% of the population.

In spite of the extensive activity in terms of the daily movement of people across the U.S.-Mexico international boundary, the immigrant population in the border region is relatively settled. Only 35% report having arrived in the United States since 1990 in comparison to 40% of people living in non-border counties and 42% of the overall U.S. immigrant population. Furthermore, a full 38% of foreign-born residents in border counties are U.S. citizens, a percentage almost identical to that in non-border counties (37%). The same general patterns are observed across border regions of the southwestern states for recentness of immigration and citizenship, although there is more variation across individual counties. Not surprisingly, in general, counties with fewer new arrivals have higher rates of citizenship. The border reflects patterns observed nationally in terms of high rates of naturalization. Overall, rates of citizenship through naturalization are high across the board

Table 1.2. Immigration Characteristics, Citizenship, and Language Fluency

	Percent Foreign Born			Percent Born in Mexico of All Residents	Percent of Latino Adults Who Speak English Fluently	Percent of Latino Children Who	
	Of All Residents	Who Arrived since 1990	Who Are Citizens			Speak a Second Language	Speak English Fluently
United States	11	42	40	3	54	70	73
46 Non-Border States	8	44	43	1	53	68	75
4 Border States	20	40	37	10	55	71	72
32 Border Counties	22	35	38	16	56	80	69
Non-Border Counties	20	40	37	10	55	69	72
Texas	14	46	32	9	57	71	73
Non-Border Counties	12	49	31	7	59	65	75
Border Counties	28	33	35	26	54	86	66
New Mexico	8	39	35	6	76	47	85
Non-Border Counties	7	41	35	4	78	41	88
Border Counties	15	34	33	13	65	66	75
Arizona	13	48	30	8	59	64	74
Non-Border Counties	12	53	27	8	57	62	73
Border Counties	14	36	38	10	64	68	76
California	26	37	39	12	52	73	70
Non-Border Counties	27	37	39	12	51	73	70
Border Counties	22	35	41	11	56	76	69

in the United States, rising from 270,000 in 1990 to over 1 million in 1996, and the share of Mexican naturalization has increased dramatically. Although Mexican immigrants in 1990 accounted for only 6.5% of all immigrants becoming naturalized citizens, the figure jumped to 20.8% in 1996 and to just over 30% in 1999 (Balistreri and van Hook 2004).

Notwithstanding higher immigration in the border region, Latino residents exhibit rates of English fluency equivalent to other parts of the country. According to Table 1.2, about one-half are fluent in English. In Texas border counties, where the proportion of immigrants is twice that of non-border counties, the English fluency rate among Latinos is only slightly lower than in non-border counties (54% compared to 59%). The differential is 13% in New Mexico. As expected, in the state of California, we see the opposite trend. English fluency is somewhat higher in border counties, where immigration is lower compared to non-border counties. Indeed, English-language proficiency has important implications for an individual's economic well-being in the United States. Research on Mexican Americans consistently shows that regardless of nativity, nonproficient workers earn less than proficient workers. In addition, the returns to education and to work experience are lower for nonproficient workers (Kim 2003). It is important to note that the disadvantages posed by the lack of English fluency are also observed in the border region, in spite of the fact that the area extensively utilizes minority languages in business and social interactions. The earnings penalty confronted by Mexican American workers with poor English fluency does not significantly vary between the major cities along the U.S.-Mexico border and the rest of the United States (Davila and Mora 2000).

Latino border children also have English fluency levels similar to the rest of the country, according to U.S. Census data. Overall, 69% of Latino children in border counties are fluent in English, a rate only slightly lower than that found in non-border counties and the rest of the United States, which range from 72% to 75%. A closer look reveals significant variation across border states, however. In Texas and New Mexico, the rate of English fluency is about 10% lower than in non-border areas, whereas in Arizona and California border counties do not differ much from the rest of their respective states. On the other hand, school data reveal that English proficiency is disproportionately low among children in the southwestern states. Data show that over one-half, or 57.2%, of the 1996 national enrollment of Limited English Proficient (LEP) students is concentrated in the five southwestern states, including Colorado. Of the border states, California and Texas were ranked first and second, respectively, with the highest number of LEP students, and Arizona and New Mexico were ranked sixth and seventh, respectively (Hispanic Leadership Border Institute n.d.). Limited English Proficient students are those who are identified as limited in their ability to speak, read, write, and understand English.

Furthermore, a full 80% of Latino border children speak a second language compared to only 69% in non-border counties in the southwestern states. The highest level of Spanish fluency among children occurs in Texas with 86%, and the lowest is in New Mexico with 66%. Such bilingualism places Latino children on the border at an advantage. Although the acquisition of English fluency accelerates the integration of Latino children in terms of educational attainment, a growing body of research shows that bilingualism is positively associated with both cognitive abilities and scholastic achievement. Overall, studies show that proficiency in both English and parental native languages are correlated with higher educational achievement and long-term socioeconomic attainment (García-Vázquez et al. 1997; Zhou 1997). At the same time, however, there are serious concerns that due to racial discrimination and a school system designed for monolingual education, the bilingual skills of Latino children are not developed to their fullest (Valenzuela 1999).

Child Poverty, Parental Labor-Force Participation, and Family Structure

Relative to national statistics, child poverty rates in the border region are extremely high. The national poverty rate is 28% for Latino children and 9% for non-Latino white children. In the border region, however, poverty rates are significantly higher, but only for Latino children. Overall, the Latino poverty rate is about 10% higher in the border region compared to the national rate, at 37%. Non-Latino white children living on the border do not experience significantly higher poverty rates than the general U.S. population. Figure 1.1 compares the poverty rates of Latino and non-Latino white children in each of the southwestern border states. The largest gap between Latino and non-Latino white children occurs in Texas, where the difference between Latino and non-Latino white poverty is 29%. The race/ethnicity differential in the other three states hovers at about 20%.

In addition, every border county, except Jeff Davis in Texas (where it is 1% lower), has a higher Latino poverty rate than that of non-border counties in their respective states, as detailed in Table 1.3. In three counties in Texas (Brooks, Starr, and Zavala) and one in New Mexico (Luna), more than one-half of Latino children are poor. It should be noted that one of the border counties with a lower poverty rate among Latino children is San Diego County, which accounts for nearly one-quarter of all Latino children living in the border region. Aside from Latino poverty, although uniformly lower, poverty rates among non-Latino white children in some border counties are quite high. For example, in the Texas counties of Brooks, Zapata, and Starr—which are also some of the poorest Latino counties—non-Latino white child poverty is above 40%, more than four times the national rate for this population. In every case, however, non-Latino white poverty is

Figure 1.1. Poverty Rate among Latino and Non-Latino White Children in Border Counties Compared to U.S. Rates

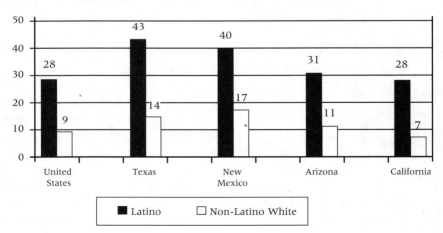

high only in counties where Latino poverty is even higher (except for Zapata, Texas, where both groups approximate 50%).

In the border region, the percentage of Latino children with no parent in the labor force is a very high 20%, yet that rate is identical to that of non-border counties and to the national rate (Table 1.4). Thus, we see that although their parents expend the same work effort as in other regions, Latino child poverty is still much higher in the border area. One factor stands out, however. In Texas, where the overall poverty rate is the highest (43%), the percentage of children with no parent in the labor force among non-Latino whites is double the rate of non-border counties in Texas and non-border states. This suggests that

Table 1.3. Percent of Latino Children in Poverty by County and by the Non-Border Region of Each Respective Southwestern State

Texas		*New Mexico*	
Non-Border Region	27	Non-Border Region	26
Cameron	46	Otero	41
Willacy	43	Doña Ana	40
Hidalgo	47	Sierra	39
Brooks	52	Luna	52
Starr	60	Grant	29
Jim Hogg	32	Hidalgo	51
Zapata	46		
Webb	40	*Arizona*	
Dimmit	43	Non-Border Region	28
Maverick	41	Cochise	39
Zavala	51	Santa Cruz	32
Kinney	36	Pima	29
Val Verde	39	Yuma	35
Terrell	41		
Brewster	28	*California*	
Presidio	46	Non-Border Region	27
Jeff Davis	26	Imperial	32
Culberson	36	San Diego	27
Hudspeth	46		
El Paso	35		

there may be something in the Texas border economy that negatively
affects employment across all groups.

As also seen in Table 1.4, differentials in family structure in Latino
families echo the patterns found in labor-force participation. The proportion of children living with two married parents in border counties,
about 60%, is not much different than that found in non-border regions. The same is true for non-Latino white families, who have rates
averaging about 70%. Moreover, family structure does not seem to be
affected by border residence. There is very little variation between border and non-border counties in each state in the proportions of children in married parent families.

Although the border exhibits comparable rates of working and married parents relative to other parts of the country, Latinos overall are at
a disadvantage both in terms of workforce participation and family
structure compared to non-Hispanic whites. These differences partly
account for higher rates of Latino child poverty (Center for Reproductive Health, Research, and Policy 2002; Lichter and Landale 1995).
However, scholars emphasize that Latino children experience very
high poverty even in two-parent households with working parents. In
the context of Latino working poverty, other factors play a significant
role, including low earnings, concentration in low-paying jobs, limited
human capital (low education and language proficiency), racial discrimination, and gender wage inequality (Chapa and De La Rosa 2004;
Hauan et al. 2000; Lichter and Landale 1995).

Child and Adolescent Health and Education

Table 1.5 shows low birth-weight, infant mortality, and teen birth rates
in the border region by state. Overall, children living in the U.S.-Mexico
border region start life in good health, based on two measures: low
birth weight, and infant mortality. Significantly better outcomes are
observed in the border states compared to non-border states: a low
birth-weight rate of 6.7% compared to 7.6%, and an infant mortality
rate of 5.7% compared to 6.9%. Both of these indicators reveal little
variation between border counties and non-border counties within
each southwestern state, although there is variation across states, with
the best outcomes observed in Texas.

Table 1.4.   Labor-Force Participation and Family Structure

	Percent of Children with No Parent in Labor Force		Percent of Children Living with Two Married Parents	
	Latino	Non-Latino White	Latino	Non-Latino White
United States	20	6	60	75
46 Non-Border States	20	5	57	76
4 Border States	20	6	63	73
32 Border Counties	20	6	62	72
Non-Border Counties	20	6	63	73
Texas	19	5	64	75
Non-Border Counties	19	5	64	76
Border Counties	20	10	64	72
New Mexico	16	6	58	71
Non-Border Counties	15	6	58	72
Border Counties	19	8	59	70
Arizona	20	6	59	71
Non-Border Counties	20	5	60	72
Border Counties	18	6	59	69
California	21	7	62	72
Non-Border Counties	21	7	62	72
Border Counties	19	6	61	74

The healthy birth outcomes evident in the border region are related to the high proportion of Mexican Americans, many of whom are immigrants. Extensive research shows that across the general population, Mexican Americans and in particular immigrants have birth rates similar to, or better than, their non-Hispanic white counterparts, in spite of

Table 1.5.   Low Birth Weight, Infant Mortality, and Teenage Pregnancy in Border Counties of the Southwestern States Compared to U.S. and Non-Border Rates

	Percent Low Birth-Weight Babies[a]	*Infant Mortality Rate*[b]	*Percent of Births to Teenagers*
United States	7.6	6.9	12
46 Non-Border States	7.9	7.3	11
4 Border States	6.7	5.7	13
32 Border Counties	6.6	5.7	14
Non-Border Counties	6.8	5.7	13
Texas	6.7	5.3	17
New Mexico	7.4	6.8	19
Arizona	7.5	5.9	15
California	6.0	5.9	10

[a] Babies weighing less than 5.5 lbs.

[b] Deaths per 1,000 live births.

low socioeconomic status and poor prenatal care (Albrecht et al. 1996; Martin et al. 2001). These outcomes are attributed to positive maternal behaviors such as very low levels of smoking and drug and alcohol use as well as healthier diets (Guendelman and Abrams 1994). On the other hand, some observers speculate that higher birth-weight babies among Mexican American women may be attributed to the very high prevalence of diabetes documented in this population (Centers for Disease Control 2002). However, although mothers with diabetes are two to three times more likely than mothers in the general population to give birth to large babies (American Diabetes Association n.d.), there is currently no research evidence showing that diabetes explains the exceptional low birth-weight rates among Mexican Americans.

In spite of the often extreme poverty in the border region, the percentage of births to teenagers is only slightly higher here than it is in non-border counties or in the rest of the United States. The percentage of births to teenagers in border counties is 14% compared to 13% in non-border counties. There seems to be a relationship between teen birth rate and poverty. The highest teen birth rates are found in New Mexico and Texas border counties, the states where border poverty is the highest, 34% and 40%, respectively. Lower rates are found in Arizona and California, where poverty affects about one-fifth of the population. Research has found that youth in disadvantaged socioeconomic circumstances are more likely than their better-off counterparts to engage in risky behavior and have a child during adolescence (Boonstra 2002). From a national perspective, however, it is important to note that three of the border states—Arizona, New Mexico, and Texas—are among the top five states with the highest teen birth rates in the United States (The Alan Guttmacher Institute 2004), thus indicating the greater risk faced by youth living in the border region relative to the rest of the country.

Despite very high poverty, Latino youth on the border are no more likely to drop out of high school or to be not working and not in school than are their counterparts in other parts of the country (Figures 1.2 and 1.3). However, these figures must be interpreted cautiously. Experts agree that dropout rates in general, and Latino dropout rates in particular, are grossly undercounted. The reasons for such undercounts include errors in school district self-reporting, inadequate student tracking procedures, and reliance on methodology that does not account for significant numbers of students who fail to graduate (for example, not including students who obtain graduate equivalency degrees) (Greene 2001; Hispanic Leadership Border Institute n.d.). To demonstrate the extent of the problem, Jay Greene calculated a graduation rate of 68% in the state of Texas in 1998, although the state reports only a 1.6% annual dropout rate. Thus, the remaining students are unaccounted for. Based on Greene's calculations, in 1998 all four of the southwestern border states ranked in the fourth or fifth quintile in terms of dropout rates (Greene 2001).

Overall, high-school dropout and the proportion not working and not in school among youth sixteen to nineteen years of age show disturbing patterns. Although young people on the border have similar outcomes to those in non-border counties and to the general U.S. population, as shown in Figures 1.2 and 1.3, Latino youth are significantly disadvantaged compared to non-Hispanic whites. Latino youth

Figure 1.2.   High-School Dropout Rates of Latino and Non-Latino Youth (Ages 16–19) in Border Counties Compared to U.S. Rates

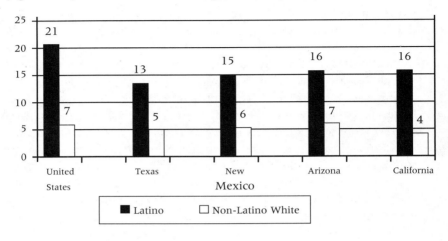

Figure 1.3.   Rates of Latino and Non-Latino Youth (Ages 16–19) Not Working and Not in School in Border Counties Compared to U.S. Rates

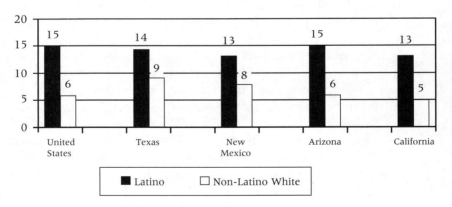

are three times as likely to have dropped out of high school compared to non-Latino white youth. However, this pattern is not unique to the border area but reflects the trends in non-border counties and in the United States as a whole. A similarly significant differential is true for the rates of youth not working and not in school. The greatest disparities occur in the California border region, where Latino youth are four times as likely than are non-Latino white youth not to have finished high school (16% vs. 4%) and not to be working or in school (13% vs. 5%).

Even based on current estimates, ethnic disparities in educational attainment are particularly problematic and have been examined in detail. Some explanations offered for the poor school outcomes of Hispanics include low academic performance, disruption due to school transfers, and language barriers (Vaznaugh 1995). Many scholars believe that relying solely on Hispanic dropout rates without breaking them down according to immigrant status does not accurately capture the problem. An in-depth analysis (Fry 2003) of the immigrant characteristics of Latino dropouts based on 2000 data revealed some significant patterns: (1) one in three Latino high-school dropouts are immigrants who had little or no contact with U.S. schools; (2) nearly 40% of immigrant Mexican sixteen- to nineteen-year-olds are dropouts, while the rate for Mexican immigrants educated in U.S. schools is 20%; and (3) the dropout rate among Latinos who have poor English language skills is 59% compared to an overall Latino rate of 21%. These findings suggest important dynamics that may be associated with the disparities in Latino high-school completion in the U.S.-Mexico border region, in light of significant immigration to the area.

Toward Improving the Quality of Life of Border Children and Families

In sum, the southwestern states and the region along the U.S.-Mexico border are home to the largest concentrations of both Latinos and immigrants in the country. The immigration rate in the border states is twice the national average. Ensuring the successful and rapid incorporation of parents who are new immigrants is one way to improve the well-being of children in this region. Furthermore, one-quarter of all children and fully well over one-half of Latino children in the United States live in these four border states. Moreover, the Latino population in border counties is very young. More than one-third of the Latino population in this region is under the age of eighteen, compared to only about one-fifth among non-Latino whites.

Nonetheless, the indicators of child and family well-being in the U.S.-Mexico border region reveal significant issues facing this part of the United States. Of major concern are the disproportionately high levels of poverty found here, particularly in the counties along the Texas border. However, another outstanding finding is the significant disparity in well-being between children of Latino and non-Latino white backgrounds not only in terms of poverty outcomes but in educational outcomes as well. At the same time, despite the limited resources and a weak economic and public services infrastructure, particularly in Texas, children and families perform similarly or better in other areas relative to groups in non-border regions and in the rest of the country. These include health at birth, the children's ability to speak a second language, and citizenship rates among immigrants.

Overall, the data indicate that attention needs to be placed on children in the border region. However, in addition to meeting the health, educational, and other needs of these children, improving the lot of parents can translate into greater opportunities for their offspring. Clearly, any initiatives to improve the quality of life of children and families along the U.S.-Mexico border must acknowledge the international nature of the region. The context is unique in that it is located on an international border with the single-largest source country of immigration to the United States (Schmidley 2001) and one with extensive social, political, economic, and environmental links to the United States. Issues that must be taken into account are the area's high population mobility, environmental neglect, a weak economy, and a health and human services infrastructure currently not set up to deal with the realities of the area.

Note

Funding for this chapter was provided by the Annie E. Casey Foundation through the Southwest border KIDS COUNT Project and the Institute for Latino Studies/Inter-University Program for Latino Research, University of Notre Dame. The data were compiled by Timothy Ready, research director, Institute for Latino Studies, University of Notre Dame, and Laura Beavers, research associate, KIDS COUNT, The Annie E. Casey Foundation.

The chapter is based on analyses of indicators of child well-being prepared for the Annie E. Casey Foundation's Southwest Border KIDS COUNT project.

The purpose of the project is to inform policymakers, service providers, and other stakeholders concerning the problems facing children in this region. We included all twenty-four counties contiguous to the international boundary, plus eight additional ones adjacent to border counties (three in New Mexico and five in Texas), for a total of thirty-two counties. In order to allow for comparative analyses across counties in the border region and counties in the rest of the state and the country, only indicators available on a county level and across all these geographic areas were included in the analyses. First, we included the ten standard KIDS COUNT indicators; second, we selected indicators that are particularly relevant to this part of the country, including English and Spanish fluency, the percentage of foreign-born, and citizenship. In addition, in light of the high concentration of Latino populations in the border region, all indicators were presented for Latino and non-Latino children.

References

The Alan Guttmacher Institute. 2004. "U.S. Teenage Pregnancy Statistics: Overall Trends, Trends by Race and Ethnicity and State-by-State Information." New York. February 19. http://www.guttmacher.org/pubs/state_pregnancy_trends.pdf

Albrecht, Stan L., Leslie L. Clarke, Michael K. Miller, and Frank L. Farmer. 1996. "Predictors of Differential Birth Outcomes among Hispanic Groups in the United States: The Role of Maternal Risk Characteristics and Medical Care." *Social Science Quarterly* 77(2): 407–33.

American Diabetes Association. n.d. "Diabetes Statistics for Women." Alexandria, VA. http://www.diabetes.org/diabetes-statistics/women.jsp.

Andreas, Peter. 2003. "A Tale of Two Borders: The U.S.-Mexico and U.S.-Canada Lines after 9-11" (May 15). Center for U.S.-Mexican Studies, University of California, San Diego. http://repositories.cdlib.org/usmex/andreas (last accessed August 2007).

Balistreri, Kelly Stamper, and Jennifer van Hook. 2004. "The More Things Change the More They Stay the Same: Mexican Naturalization before and after Welfare Reform." *International Migration Review* 38(1): 113–30.

Boonstra, Heather. 2002. "Teen Pregnancy: Trends and Lessons Learned." *The Guttmacher Report on Public Policy,* vol. 5, no. 1. New York: Alan Guttmacher Institute. February 2002.

Center for Reproductive Health, Research, and Policy. 2002. "Fact Sheet on Latino Youth: Income and Poverty." San Francisco. http://reprohealth.ucsf.edu/publications/internal.html#FactSheets.

Centers for Disease Control. 2002. "National Diabetes Fact Sheet." Atlanta. http://www.cdc.gov/diabetes/pubs/estimates.htm.

Chapa, Jorge, and Belinda De La Rosa. 2004. "Latino Population Growth, Socioeconomic and Demographic Characteristics, and Implications for Educational Attainment." *Education and Urban Society* 36(2): 130–49.

Children's Defense Fund. n.d. "Census 2000: Child Poverty Data for States, Counties, and Large Cities." Washington, DC. http://www.childrensdefense.org/data/census00/states_counties_cities.asp.

Davila, Alberto, and Marie T. Mora. 2000. "English Skills, Earnings, and the Occupational Sorting of Mexican Americans along the U.S.-Mexico Border." *International Migration Review* 34(1): 133–57.

Department of Health and Human Services (DHHS). Health Resources and Services Administration (HRSA). Bureau of Primary Health Care. n.d. "Facts about U.S./Mexico Border Health." Rockville, MD. http://bphc.hrsa.gov/bphc/borderhealth /region.htm.

Erickson, Christopher A., and David W. Eaton. 2002. "Border Finances: Paying for Environmental Infrastructure." In *The U.S.-Mexican Border Environment: Economy and Environment for a Sustainable Border Region: Now in 2020,* SCERP Monograph Series, no. 3, ed. Paul Ganster, 203–49. San Diego: San Diego State University Press.

Fry, Richard. 2003. "Hispanic Youth Dropping Out of U.S. Schools: Measuring the Challenge." Los Angeles: The Pew Hispanic Center. June 12. http://www.pewhispanic.org/site/docs/pdf/high%20school%20dropout%20report--final.pdf.

Fullerton, M. Thomas, Jr. 2001. "Educational Attainment and Border Income Performance—Statistical Data Included." Economic and Financial Review. http://www.findarticles.com/p/articles/mi_m0DKI/is_2001_3/ai_82092013.

———. 2003. "Recent Trends in Border Economics." *Social Science Journal* 40(4): 583–92.

García-Vázquez, Enedina, Luis A. Vázquez, Isabel C. López, and Wendy Ward. 1997. "Language Proficiency and Academic Success: Relationships between Proficiency in Two Languages and Achievement among Mexican American Students." *Bilingual Research Journal* 21(4): 334–47.

Greene, Jay P. 2001. "High School Graduation Rates in the United States." New York: Manhattan Institute for Policy Research. http://www.manhattan-institute.org/html/cr_baeo_t2.htm.

Guendelman, Sylvia R., and Barbara Abrams. 1994. "Dietary, Alcohol and Tobacco Intake among Mexican-American Women of Childbearing Age: Results from NHANES Data." *American Journal of Health Promotion* 8(5): 363–72.

Hauan, Susan M., Nancy S. Landale, and Kevin T. Leicht. 2000. "Poverty and Work Effort among Urban Latino Men." *Work And Occupations* 27: 188–222.

Hispanic Leadership Border Institute. n.d. "Latinos and Education: A Regional Overview of the Southwest." Arizona State University. http://www.asu.edu/educ/hbli/pubs/over.html.

INEGI. n.d. Instituto Nacional de Estadística, Geografía e Informática. "Población inmigrante, emigrante y saldo neto migratorio por entidad federativa." http://www.inegi.gob.mx/est/contenidos/espanol/tematicos/mediano/ent.asp?t=mpob58&c=3235.

Kim, Jongsung. 2003. "Earnings of Mexican Male Workers in the U.S. Labor Market: Role of English Language Proficiency." *Journal of the Academy of Business and Economics.* http://www.findarticles.com/p/articles/mi_m0OGT/is_2_1/ai_113563603.

Lichter, Daniel T., and Nancy S. Landale. 1995. "Parental Work, Family Structure, and Poverty among Latino Children." *Journal of Marriage and the Family* 57(2): 346–54.

Martin, Joyce A., Brady E. Hamilton, Stephanie J. Ventura, Fay Menacker, and Melissa M. Park. 2001. "Births: Final Data for 1999." *National Vital Statistics Report* 49(1): 1–100.

Padilla, Yolanda C., and Lesley E. Daigle. 1996. "Social and Economic Interdependence in the U.S.-Mexico Border Region: Critical Implications for Social Welfare." *New Global Development* 12: 65–77.

Ruiz-Beltran, Martin, and Jimmy K. Kamau. 2001. "The Socio-Economic and Cultural Impediments to Well-Being along the U.S.-Mexico Border." *Journal of Community Health* 26(2): 123–32.

Schmidley, A. Dianne. 2001. U.S. Census Bureau, Current Population Reports, Series P23-206, "Profile of the Foreign-Born Population in the United States: 2000." Washington, DC: U.S. Government Printing Office.

U.S. Bureau of Transportation Statistics. "Table 12, Incoming Pedestrian Crossings, U.S.-Mexican Border." http://www.bts.gov/programs/international/ border_crossing_entry_data/us_mexico/table_12.

U.S. Environmental Protection Agency. "2000 Annual Report: Region 9, The Pacific Southwest." http://www.epa.gov/region9/annualreport/00/border.html.

Valenzuela, Angela. 1999. *Subtractive Schooling: U.S.-Mexican Youth and the Politics of Caring.* Albany: State University of New York Press.

Vargas, Lucinda. 2001. "Maquiladoras: Impact on Texas Border Cities." *The Border Economy* 8: 25–29. http://www.dallasfed.org/research/border/tbe_vargas.pdf.

Vaznaugh, Adriana. 1995. "Dropout Intervention and Language Minority Youth." *ERIC Digest*. Washington, DC: ERIC Clearinghouse on Languages and Linguistics. http://www.ericdigests.org/1996–1/dropout.htm.

Warner, David C., and Lauren R. Jahnke. 2003. "U.S./Mexico Border Health Issues: The Texas Rio Grande Valley." San Antonio: Regional Center for Health Workforce Studies, Center for Health Economics and Policy, The University of Texas Health Science Center at San Antonio.

Zhou, Min. 1997. "Growing Up American: The Challenge Confronting Immigrant Children and Children of Immigrants." *Annual Review of Sociology* 23: 63–95.

CHAPTER TWO

An Overview of Children and Youth on the Northern Mexican Border

Catalina Palmer

Border areas, between any countries, present complexities due to particular social, economic, and cultural dynamics. Because of these particularities, it is crucial to consider them when trying to understand a country's society and structure. When we think of the border, particularly between Mexico and the United States, what first comes to mind is a constant going back and forth of those who inhabit these regions, but this is not true for all border residents. Many live in the borderlands without actually crossing the boundary. Before attempting to examine the complexities of children and youth at the northern Mexican border—a place where people may straddle both sides, a place of bright social prosperity and dark deprivation, a place of economic development and commercial risks, a place where there is a present and a future—we offer a brief overview of its basic geography, population, and family structure. In this chapter, data were collected on the thirty-seven Mexican municipalities along the border between the United States and Mexico, which are referred to as "border municipalities."

Due to the availability of data, during the discussion the reader will notice that sometimes reference is made to border municipalities and at other times to border states.

The border between Mexico and the United States extends more than three thousand kilometers, from the Pacific Ocean to the Gulf of Mexico. A varied topography includes a mountain range, extensive deserts, the Río Bravo, which itself has been used as a division line two thousand kilometers long, and several reservoirs. Six Mexican states are located across the border from the United States: Baja California, Sonora, Chihuahua, Coahuila, Nuevo León, and Tamaulipas. In these states are the thirty-seven border municipalities noted above. Prominent among them for their population size or economic development are Tijuana, Mexicali, Nogales, Piedras Negras, San Luis Río Colorado, Agua Prieta, Ciudad Juárez, Matamoros, Nuevo Laredo, and Reynosa.

Although the border states together comprise a large territory, most of the population is centered in a few cities, which results in an overall low state population density. In these Mexican border states, there are 16.6 million inhabitants, or 17% of the total Mexican population of 97.5 million (INEGI 2000a: IRIS 2000). Of those, 10.8% (1.8 million) are four years old or less. The thirty-seven border municipalities have a population of 5.5 million, which accounts for 33% of the population of the border states; of those, 11.4% (0.6 million) are under the age of four, a percentage slightly higher than that observed in the border states and nationally (10.9 %). (See Table 2.1.) It is worth mentioning that in northern Mexico, the city of Monterrey, which is the capital of the state of Nuevo León, is the largest center of population and economic activity, where 1.1 million live; in fact, it is considered the second most important city of the country because of its industrial role in the nation's economy. Although Monterrey is not located on the contiguous border, its economic activity heavily influences the extended northern Mexico border region. Approximately 6.2 million people in the border states are less than eighteen years old and make up 37% of the total regional population, a proportion less than the national rate of 40% (see also Table 2.1). This youthful potential workforce represents a rich human resource both in the short and long term.

A particular characteristic of the region is the predominance of the *mestizo* (those of Spanish and Mexican indigenous blood) with a very small indigenous population. About 1.23% (INEGI 2000b: SIMBAD 2000) of the border population are indigenous, which is significantly lower than the same population levels in central and southern Mexico. There are eleven indigenous languages registered for the northern states of Mexico. Most of the indigenous populations (93.25%) of northern Mexico, however, speak Spanish as a first or second language, unlike other indigenous populations, specifically those in southern Mexico that are not as likely to be bilingual and therefore have fewer opportunities to be part of the general national development. In the 2000 Census, in the thirty-seven northern border municipalities, there were 8,244 children ages 5–17 who were speakers of indigenous languages within the total of 51,699 children in this age range in the border states. It is believed that most residents on both sides of the border are bilingual; they speak Spanish and are often fluent in English. Also, although there are no available data, there is a growing cultural influence and use of English on the Mexican side, particularly among young people. This area calls for immediate attention as language competency is known as a predictor of economic success. In fact, people who migrate in search of skilled or professional jobs to northern Mexico or to the United States know in advance that they should be able to speak English in order to find and keep a good job.

Immigration and Internal Migration

Mobility of the population is evidenced by the proportion of foreign-born in this zone. While only 0.4% of the total adult population in Mexico were born in another country, according to the 2000 Census, in the border municipalities some 1.2% of the population age eighteen and above were born in a foreign country (INEGI 2000c). Meanwhile, the population less than eighteen and born in another country is 0.7% at the national level, 2.0% at the border state level, and 4.8% for border municipalities. In particular, 4.7% of those younger than eighteen who live in the border municipalities were born in the United States and comprise almost all of the foreign-born. In total, in the thirty-seven border municipalities, there are 95,337 inhabitants below the age of eighteen who were born in the United States. This group represents the 38% of all those born north of the boundary but who are residents

Table 2.1. Population in the Northern Mexican Border States and Municipios (Municipalities)

Name of State	Municipality	Total Population	Population 0–4	% of Population 0–4	Population 0–17	% of Population 0–17
México	Total	97,483,412	10,635,157	10.9%	38,710,777	39.7%
Baja California	State Total	2,487,367	268,682	10.8%	885,457	35.6%
	Mexicali	764,602	79,232	10.4%	270,775	35.4%
	Tecate	77,795	8,745	11.2%	28,505	36.6%
	Tijuana	1,210,820	135,181	11.2%	428,343	35.4%
Coahuila	State Total	2,298,070	253,171	11.0%	881,265	38.3%
	Acuña	110,487	14,307	12.9%	43,816	39.7%
	Guerrero	2,050	205	10.0%	732	35.7%
	Hidalgo	1,441	173	12.0%	570	39.6%
	Jiménez	9,724	1,166	12.0%	3,911	40.2%
	Nava	23,019	3,082	13.4%	10,095	43.9%
	Ocampo	12,053	1,432	11.9%	5,100	42.3%
	Piedras Negras	128,130	15,336	12.0%	50,471	39.4%
Chihuahua	State Total	3,052,907	334,521	11.0%	1,158,645	38.0%
	Ascensión	21,939	2,786	12.7%	9,619	43.8%
	Guadalupe	10,032	1,301	13.0%	4,067	40.5%
	Janos	10,214	1,272	12.5%	4,629	45.3%
	Juárez	1,218,817	137,342	11.3%	439,677	36.1%
	Manuel Benavides	1,746	160	9.2%	598	34.2%
	Ojinaga	24,307	2,580	10.6%	9,024	37.1%
	Praxedis G. Guerrero	8,905	1,091	12.3%	3,640	40.9%
Nuevo León	State Total	3,834,141	396,563	10.3%	1,357,497	35.4%
	Anáhuac	18,524	1,981	10.7%	7,129	38.5%
Sonora	State Total	2,216,969	244,619	11.0%	850,937	38.4%
	Agua Prieta	61,944	8,077	13.0%	25,515	41.2%
	Altar	7,253	891	12.3%	2,845	39.2%
	Caborca	69,516	7,584	10.9%	27,503	39.6%
	Naco	5,370	702	13.1%	2,313	43.1%
	Nogales	159,787	21,290	13.3%	61,581	38.5%
	Puerto Peñasco	31,157	3,479	11.2%	12,509	40.1%
	San Luis Río Colorado	145,006	17,322	11.9%	57,416	39.6%
	Santa Cruz	1,628	204	12.5%	642	39.4%
	Sáric	2,257	237	10.5%	873	38.7%
	General Plutarco Elías Calles	11,278	1,401	12.4%	4,688	41.6%
Tamaulipas	State Total	2,753,222	296,314	10.8%	1,022,557	37.1%
	Camargo	16,787	1,839	11.0%	6,195	36.9%
	Guerrero	4,366	474	10.9%	1,659	38.0%
	Gustavo Díaz Ordaz	16,246	1,692	10.4%	5,923	36.5%
	Matamoros	418,141	49,446	11.8%	160,250	38.3%
	Mier	6,788	720	10.6%	2,460	36.2%
	Miguel Alemán	25,704	2,940	11.4%	9,684	37.7%
	Nuevo Laredo	310,915	37,396	12.0%	118,482	38.1%

Table 2.1.   (*cont.*)

Reynosa	420,463	49,634	11.8%	155,750	37.0%
Río Bravo	104,229	12,135	11.6%	40,821	39.2%
Total among Border States	16,642,676	1,793,870	10.8%	2,017,810	36.9%
Total in 37 Border Municipalities	5,473,440	624,835	11.4%	6,156,358	37.0%

Source: XII Census of population and Housing 2000, Instituto Nacional de Estadística, Geografía e Informática (National Institute of Statistics Geography and Informatics), INEGI, México. Data processed by La Red por los Derechos de la Infancia en México.

of border municipalities (a total of 250,722). This point calls to attention that even in smaller border municipalities, the population below age eighteen and born in the United States can reach levels of more than 10%, as in Guadalupe and Manuel Benavides in Chihuahua, and Guerrero in Tamaulipas. Thus, there exists a group of children and youth who live in Mexico, have dual nationality, and may likely claim services (such as health care) on either side.

In terms of composition, border families exhibit some important characteristics. Most of the estimated 4 million (INEGI 2000b: SIMBAD 2000) families (approximately 80% of families) along the northern border maintain the traditional Mexican male-headed family structure. Similarly, at the national level, 20.6% of the households in Mexico are headed by a female (INEGI 2000a: IRIS 2000). Several smaller border municipalities, however, have low percentages of households headed by females. The percentage of children in single-parent homes is similar between border municipalities and the national index, with both recording 17% of the population younger than age eighteen living in single-parent homes.[1] In the border states, this percentage lies a little lower at almost 16%. In the border municipalities, there are 1,154,790 children younger than eighteen in single-parent homes. These two indicators about families headed by women and single parents reveal that border municipalities and states reflect a structure similar to the national average in Mexico. Therefore, it can be said that communities along the border are similar in family types to the rest of Mexico. It can further be argued that those who migrate to northern Mexico in search of work will likely be migrating with a family or will settle family members there.

The northern Mexican border is the natural land bridge most frequently crossed by those seeking undocumented entrance into the United States, including Mexicans, Central Americans, South Americans, and immigrants from other continents. Those trying to enter by way of the land border are evading the severe immigration controls now imposed at American airport entries. Furthermore, this northern Mexico border region acts as a center of large internal immigration, as seen in the great number of people from other areas of Mexico who have settled there. An average of 25% (Sin Fronteras 2005) of border residents were not born in this region. These residents who have come from other places in Mexico primarily work in the maquiladora industry, or assembly-line factories, and the service sector (Centro de Estudios Fronterizos y de Promoción de los Derechos Humanos AC, 2000). It is important to recognize that the border functions as an important passageway for migratory traffic. Contrary to what many people believe, most of the Mexicans who emigrate to the United States are not originally from the border region. They are, in fact, from Mexico's non-border states. Approximately 62% (XIPN Canal ONCE TV 2000) come from states that have produced the majority of Mexico's migratory emigrants, namely, Guanajuato, Jalisco, Michoacán, and Zacatecas, and, more recently, Hidalgo, Oaxaca, Puebla, and Querétaro (Woo Morales 2004).

Table 2.2, with indicators drawn from the 2000 census,[2] shows migration indicators of Mexico's thirty-two states. Coahuila, Nuevo León, Sonora, and Tamaulipas are below the median percentage of homes receiving remittances. Of all the border states, only Chihuahua is above the median among those receiving remittances, and Baja California has the median proportion. More important, the border states have a medium level of migration, except for Nuevo León and Sonora, which have a low level of migratory intensity.

To address the structural causes of immigration at the Mexican border, the American authorities have implemented several initiatives (Operation Guardian, Safeguard, Crossroads, and others) that have not decreased the number of immigrants who come into the United States. Instead, such efforts have shifted access routes over to high-risk zones such as the Arizona desert, which has resulted, in turn, in a large number of immigrant deaths (over 2,500 people died between 1995 and 2003) (Stop Gate Keeper 2004). It is particularly interesting that there

Table 2.2. Indicators about Migration to the United States by States of Mexico: Level of Migratory Intensity, 2000

State	Total of Homes	% of Homes that Receive Remittances	% Homes with Some Emigrant to the U.S. in the five Years Previous to Census 2000	Level of Migratory Intensity (Internal)
México (Total)	22,639,808	4.35	4.14	
Aguascalientes	207,327	6.69	6.66	High
Baja California*	613,602	4.02	2.38	Medium
Baja California Sur	107,536	1.08	1.03	Low
Campeche	163,451	1.02	0.88	Very Low
Coahuila*	555,793	3.38	2.23	Medium
Colima	136,926	7.34	5.62	High
Chiapas	832,111	0.76	0.79	Very Low
Chihuahua*	767,679	4.32	3.70	Medium
Distrito Federal	2,203,741	1.72	1.60	Very Low
Durango	331,242	9.70	7.31	Very High
Guanajuato	990,602	9.20	9.55	Very High
Guerrero	677,731	7.86	6.79	High
Hidalgo	507,225	5.06	7.14	High
Jalisco	1,457,326	7.70	6.53	High
México	2,978,023	2.11	2.63	Low
Michoacán	893,671	11.37	10.37	Very High
Morelos	376,140	6.44	7.46	High
Nayarit	222,714	9.64	6.82	Very High
Nuevo León*	925,493	2.46	1.91	Low
Oaxaca	762,517	4.13	4.76	Medium
Puebla	1,098,409	3.28	4.02	Medium
Querétaro	311,896	3.71	4.81	Medium
Quintana Roo	219,671	0.99	0.71	Very Low
San Luis Potosí	509,582	8.20	7.43	High
Sinaloa	586,245	4.60	3.58	Medium
Sonora*	539,528	3.16	1.59	Low
Tabasco	426,653	0.64	0.58	Very Low
Tamaulipas*	690,067	3.64	3.02	Medium
Tlaxcala	203,259	2.24	2.70	Low
Veracruz	1,649,332	2.74	3.20	Low
Yucatán	387,434	1.41	1.02	Very Low
Zacatecas	306,882	13.03	12.18	Very High

Source: Estimations of Consejo Nacional de Población, CONAPO (National Population Council), based on the 10% sample done in the 2000 Census.
* Indicates one of Mexico's six Border states.

is an ever-growing number of emigrant women and children, to the point that this change in migration, which includes families (women, children, and the elderly) represents a pattern not seen before in the movement of Mexicans to the United States (Ceballos 2005). Ofelia Woo Morales (2004) reveals that there are two main reasons for the increased migration of women: family reunification and the search for work opportunities.

Estimations of the Mexican Migration Surveys by the National Population Council (CONAPO, Consejo Nacional de Población), El Colegio de la Frontera Norte, and the Labor Ministry identify the patterns of female migration. In the period 1994–1995, the migrating female population consisted of 112,632 women. For the period 1998–1999, it was calculated that 348,570 were migrating; and in 2000–2001, 329,142 women migrated. During the period 1994–1995, 82% of the female migrants had northern Mexico as their destination and 18% identified the United States. The latest estimations reveal an increase of the numbers that have as their destination the United States—approximately 30%. The remaining 70% migrate to Mexico's northern borderlands. Interestingly, the surveys do not show a similar increase in migrating youth ages 15–19. Estimations indicate that between 20% to 30% of migrants are youth who have been moving to the United States. Each year more than 40,000 adolescents and children try to cross to the other side. It is also important to mention that these northern border migration surveys focus on populations age 12 and over, and younger children are not included. Estimations of children ages 12–14 are unreliable and vague as sometimes these ages are not reported (see Table 2.3).

Risks Facing Children on the Border

Just as relevant as the number of children who cross to the United States is the number of children who return to Mexico. In 2002, Mexico's National Institute of Migration recorded 47,585 children under age eighteen formally returned by demonstrating how at times U.S. agencies work in collaboration with Mexican authorities. A total of 52,535 children under eighteen were returned to Mexico in 2003, and 39,690 in 2004. Although there is a 24% decrease in ordered returns,

Table 2.3.   Estimations of Migrating Population in the North of Mexico:
Total and 15–19 Age Group

Estimated Number of Migrating Population in the North Border of Mexico by Period	*Destination*					
	Mexico's North Border			*United States*		
	Total	*Male*	*Female*	*Total*	*Male*	*Female*
1994–1995						
Total	695,895	603,348	92,547	458,212	438,128	20,085
15–19	137,098	118,326	18,772	43,967	42,153	1,814
% 15–19	19.70%	19.61%	20.28%	9.60%	9.62%	9.03%
1996–1997						
Total	670,233	591,152	79,081	493,465	465,804	27,661
15–19	93,708	73,904	19,804	47,377	43,670	3,707
% 15–19	13.98%	12.50%	25.04%	9.60%	9.38%	13.40%
1998–1999						
Total	1,204,857	974,156	230,701	606,369	488,500	117,869
15–19	139,267	104,685	34,583	55,165	46,617	8,548
% 15–19	11.56%	10.75%	14.99%	9.10%	9.54%	7.25%
2000–2001						
Total	1,116,225	897,937	218,287	484,685	373,830	110,854
15–19	119,360	92,708	26,652	28,735	20,942	7,793
% 15–19	10.69%	10.32%	12.21%	5.93%	5.60%	7.03%

Source: Encuesta de Migración en la Frontera Norte, EMIF (Migration Survey in the North Border), Colegio de la Frontera Norte, COLEF (North Border University), Consejo Nacional de Población, CONAPO (National Population Council), and Secretaría del Trabajo y Previsión Social, STPS (Labor and Social Provision Ministry of Mexico).

there are specific localities where these returns have increased. Throughout Chihuahua, returns of child immigrants increased at a rate of 52% for males and 32% for females; in Sonora the returns of males increased 11% and in Coahuila, 2% (INAMI 2005).

Thus, whenever policy discussions turn to returned children, special attention should be devoted to the Chihuahua border. These data portray the crude reality of the border region. While it can be argued that housing conditions, nutrition, and education of those who settle at the border are better there than in other parts of Mexico, an important passing-through population suffers numerous threatening risks and situations that violate human rights. Based on his interactions with children, Diego Ceballos portrays the situation for children on the border by quoting Oscar Escalada of the Tijuana YMCA: "The minors are the ones that suffer the most this story of migration, because they are exposed to maltreatment and great problems, especially young girls that are frequently raped" (Ceballos 2005). He goes on to explain that many of the children migrate in order to reunite with their parents, who have gone before them. Other relatives migrate to look for a job or to escape from domestic violence.

There are some very difficult situations that children and youth have to face in the border region, for which there is no exact information, due to the nature of the problem. Shirk and Webber (2004) address the expansive growth of the commercial sex industry in their study of Tijuana, described as the most important destination cited by tourists seeking prostitutes and sex. In addition, the authors point out that many of the sexual predators who come to Mexico specifically to exploit children originate in the United States and Canada. The authors cite evidence that suggests that children are trafficked into the United States through Mexico for illegal adoptions. They explain that even though U.S. and Mexican laws require minors traveling between the two countries to be accompanied either by both parents or with a notarized parental permit, these requirements are enforced in air travel but not always at land points of entry.

There are no good estimations of how many illegal adoptions may be occurring through the trafficking of children, and only very vague ones of how many children are victims of sexual exploitation in Mexico. The reality of migrating children, however, is explicitly clear in part because of the numbers of ordered returns. To address this problem, the Mexican government has established a network of *albergues*, or shelters, to care for migrating children at the northern border. Today there are eighteen homes, thirteen of which work in municipalities through the Sistema Nacional para el Desarrollo Integral de la Familia, DIF (National System for the Integral Development of the Family) and five privately. From 1998 to 2002, these *albergues* assisted an annual average of 8,000 migrating or returned children and adolescents (Salud y Apoyo al Migrante 2005). The DIF financially supports the relocation of these children with their families in their places of origin.

Quality of Life

For families in general, border-state housing indicators demonstrate better conditions than at Mexico's national levels; nevertheless, there are several municipalities along the border where housing conditions are very poor. While 27% of the Mexican population below the age of eighteen live in housing without any system of sewage, in the northern border states this lack occurs only in 19% of the population of that same age group. In the border municipalities, it stands at 18%. However, when examining the data at the local level, great variability appears. In seventeen municipalities, the percentage of children living in homes without drainage is higher than at the national level. The highest occurs at Jiménez, Coahuila (82%). Also, in five other municipalities this percentage is higher than 40%: Hidalgo, Coahuila, at 70%; Guerrero, Coahuila, at 55%; Práxedis G. Guerrrero, Chihuahua, at 47%; and Guadalupe and Janos, Chihuahua, at 43%.[3]

Another important indicator of the quality of life for Mexican border families comes is access to electricity. Electrical services statistics have only one exception among the northern border states, which is Chihuahua, with lower rates of electrical services than at the national average, perhaps due to its vast and varied territory (Chihuahua is the largest state in the Republic). Otherwise, 2.9% of the population below age eighteen in the border municipalities do not have electricity in their homes in comparison to the national average of 5.8%. In the six border states the rate is 3.7%, and in the state of Chihuahua, in particular, it is 7.5%. Yet, the border municipality with the highest percentage of children and youth not having electricity is in Ocampo,

Coahuila, where 10.4% of children do not live in homes with electricity. Nowadays, not having access to electricity also means not having access to computers, the Internet, and other electronic devices that support the learning process.

Most important of all housing services probably is the access to water, the determinant of basic hygiene. We found that 18.1% of the Mexican population younger than age eighteen do not have piped water or access to water in the immediate vicinity of their homes. The situation in the northern border states is quite different, given that only 8.2% of the population of that age lacked this access to water. Of the border municipalities, only five have percentages higher than the national average: Jiménez, in the state of Coahuila, 52.9%; Ocampo, in Coahuila, 36.9%; Nogales, in Sonora, 22.8%; Tecate, in Baja California, 21.3%; and Manuel Benavides, in Chihuahua, 19.9%.

Home ownership is also more favorable in the border states compared to the rest of Mexico, with approximately 4 million private residences, of which more than 3 million are owned by the family who lives there; and most of them, about 75%, are fully paid for (INEGI 2000a: IRIS 2000). Nevertheless, home ownership at the border municipalities is slightly lower than the national mean, showing figures from 60.3% to 76.5% in twenty-eight municipalities; and in nine, the percentage is higher than 78%, which is the mean in Mexico. On the other hand, the percentage of rental housing tends to be higher in the border municipalities than the national or the state average. However, home ownership in Mexico may not be as strong an indicator of an economically stable condition as it is in the United States. Reviewing the types of families in Mexico, we see that it is common for an extended family—grandparents, parents, children, and even several brothers and sisters with their own spouses and children—to reside in one housing unit. It is also common to see a house continually in a state of construction, waiting for the next generation to finish it. So, when the Census asks about home ownership, it finds that indeed the house is owned, but it may be in the name of one of the grandparents or one of the heads of several families living together.

Family ties are strong in Mexico, and, in fact, these ties usually work as "unemployment insurance" or as "social security." Because of this and other factors, Mexico uses a measurement of overcrowding, *Hacinamiento*, defined by INEGI as having more than three persons in one room. In all border municipalities, the population below age eighteen who live in overcrowded conditions is less than the national index of 42.6%. Only Jiménez, Coahuila, has a percentage similar to the national value, 42.4%. At the same time, the municipality of Manuel Benavides, Chihuahua, shows the lowest percentage of children living in overcrowding, 15.2%. So, in general, we see a little less ownership of homes and a higher percentages of rented houses in the border area, accompanied by a little less overcrowding, which may reflect the impact of families who have migrated to those regions. Yet, for those same families who may have moved north in search of jobs, these figures might also represent an improvement in housing conditions compared to their previous residence. Border housing conditions also reflect the challenge faced by local governments in creating the infrastructure needed during the growth of their cities and towns.

On a positive note, we found a significantly lower level of illiteracy at the northern border, which was estimated at 9.5% in the last Census, and is actually reported by the Education Ministry at 8.5% (INDISEP 2005). Regardless of the source or the year, illiteracy at the border states is significantly lower than the national average. Furthermore, school achievement of the population age fifteen and older is higher than the 7.9 grade-level national average.

Even though the primary school coverage—the percent of corresponding age children for a school level that attends school—is lower in the northern states, as reported by the Education Ministry for the cycle 2003–2004, a greater percentage of students complete primary school. The coverage of secondary and high school is greater in the border states as well, with both factors contributing to the higher school achievement levels for the border population in general. Dropouts at the secondary level (grades 7–9) are near the national average, except for the state of Chihuahua, where it was one point higher in 2003–2004. However, the number of dropouts during the high school years is higher than the national average of 14.7%, except for the state of Tamaulipas. This figure is in keeping with a lower completion index in border-state high schools, except again for Tamaulipas. (See Table 2.4.)

In the area of health care it is estimated that public health services at the border area for the population ages 0–19 are not accessible only to four out of every ten people, whereas the national average reflects that

Table 2.4. Indicators of Education for the Northern Border States of Mexico during the School Cycle, 2003–2004

School Cycle 2003–2004	*Secondary, 7–8–9 Grades*					
	Coverage		*Completing*		*Dropouts*	
State	*%*	*Rank*	*%*	*Rank*	*%*	*Rank*
Baja California	87	19	80	21	6.6	21
Coahuila	91	11	82	11	5.9	12
Chihuahua	81	30	77	25	7.6	25
Nuevo León	92	7	90	2	3.1	2
Sonora	87	18	80	20	6.4	20
Tamaulipas	90	12	83	10	5.4	9
Mexico (Total)	88	.	80	.	6.4	.

School Cycle 2003–2004	*High School, 10–11–12 Grades ("Bachillerato")*					
	Coverage		*Completing*		*Dropouts*	
State	*%*	*Rank*	*%*	*Rank*	*%*	*Rank*
Baja California	44	25	60	17	15.7	14
Coahuila	48	16	59	18	17.6	25
Chihuahua	47	18	55	30	19.5	32
Nuevo León	39	30	60	16	18.9	30
Sonora	54	7	58	21	16.5	20
Tamaulipas	48	15	71	5	10.9	5
Mexico (Total)	48	.	62	.	14.7	.

Source: INDISEP, System of Indicators of the Secretaría de Educación Pública (Education Ministry), Dirección General de Planeación, Programación y Presupuesto, DGPPP (General Direction of Planning, Programming, and Budget of the Education Ministry).

six out of ten people do not have access to these benefits (INEGI 2000b: SIMBAD 2000). Consequently, the northern border population has a life expectancy of seventy-eight years of age, while the national average is only seventy-seven. The lower rate of children and youth without health services might be related to the job opportunities available within the region.

A factor directly related to health is a person's nutritional condition. Researchers (Roldán et al. 2004) in Mexico in the area of nutrition have created a municipality index that measures the risk of undernourishment. This index rates levels from Low, Medium, High, Very High, to Extreme. We find that the border municipalities fell in a Low or Medium level of risk. Nevertheless, it should be mentioned that the state of Chihuahua has four High, five Very High, and ten Extreme municipalities. Nuevo León has two municipalities falling in the High category and five in Very High, while Tamaulipas has three rating at High and four at Very High. These individual high ratings show that even in the northern states of Mexico there are places where poverty affects the well-being and physical development of children.

In sharp contrast to the relatively high quality of life found on the northern border of Mexico is the proliferation of illicit activities at the border, in particular those that are profitable, harmful, complex, oblique, and cruel—trafficking in drugs, weapons, and migrants, kidnapping, prostitution, and human exploitation. The border environment with the presence of illegal migration, a large floating population, and illicit drug traffic fosters the development and growth of criminal behavior. This environment jeopardizes the safety and well-being of the families who live there. Even though the infrastructure might be better at the border than in other regions of Mexico, the lack of safety may translate into an uncomfortable perception of border life. It calls attention to the reality that the border states, with the exception of Coahuila, occupy the first eight places of Mexico in numbers of children under the age of eighteen who have been placed under arrest. The state of Baja California leads with more youths under eighteen in conflict with the law, even though its population is much lower than the state of México, or the Federal District (SSP 2004).

In contrast to the extreme violence in the larger cities, the vast rural areas at the border are peaceful. But the crime rates alone in the border cities of Tijuana, Baja California, and Ciudad Juárez, Chihuahua, place these two states among the top five for criminality (Centro de Estudios Económicos del Sector Privado A.C. 2002) in the entire country. A lamentable phenomenon that must be mentioned because of its size and significance in the northern border region is the murder of 370 women in Ciudad Juárez between 1993 and 2003 (Amnistía Internacional 2003). More than one-third of the victims were younger than nineteen. This tragedy has profound legal, social, and political implications, since the authorities have not yet solved these crimes, nor have they taken concrete actions to end this wave of murders. Indeed, similar types of murders have begun to happen in the capital of the state of Chihuahua and in other border towns.

An economic boom at the border has occurred thanks to the high volume of imports and exports in the commercial area, the significant size of the *maquiladora* industry, and the growth of the service sector. Other contributors to this economic prosperity are the remarkable industrial activity in Monterrey, Nuevo León, and the port and oil trade in the state of Tamaulipas. Lately, however, the increasing relocation of border manufacturing jobs to Asian countries, particularly to China, and the illegal import of clothes-assembly components at the border area seriously threaten the regional and national economies (González 2003).

This threat has been promoted by the constant turnover of manufacturing jobs and the continued creation of new employment in the *maquiladora* and service sectors. As a matter of fact, of the forty-eight cities in the country that are surveyed to assess the unemployment rate, Ciudad Juárez, Mexicali, Nuevo Laredo, and Tijuana are among the top ten for employment rates (STPS 1994–2000). The income of those border cities with the presence of long-term jobs, on average, is the equivalent of twice the minimum regional wage. Furthermore, in most of the border cities, minimum wages are among the highest in Mexico. Interestingly, from the 2000 Census, it is observed that the percentage of youth ages 16–19 in the border states who do not study or work stands at 12%, more than one point higher than the national mean of 10.7%; and in the border municipalities an average 12.4% of youth ages 16–19 do not work and do not go to school. These percentages speak to the lack of opportunities found by young people throughout the border region and the neighboring states. The same data at the individual municipal level indicate that there are five municipalities where this percentage is significantly higher than 20%: 34.8% in Manuel Benavides, Chihuahua; 29.3% in Sáric, Sonora; 22.6% in Santa Cruz, Sonora; 21.4% in Hidalgo, Coahuila, and Práxedis G. Guerrero, Chihuahua. Twelve other municipalities reflected a rate of 15% of the percentage of youth ages 16–19 not working and not going to school. So, while traditional employment indexes pursued by decision makers and politicians are better in several big cities at the border, in reality an important sector of young people from small border municipalities is losing a crucial time to prepare for the future by studying or getting work experience.

Generally, in Mexico, it is important to understand the correlation between the percentage of youth ages 18–19 not working and not studying with the level of migration from states and the respective percentage of homes that receive remittances. (See Figure 2.1.) The states with higher migration, or receiving more remittances, are also the states that have a higher proportion of teenagers not working and not going to school—a statistic that points to lack of opportunities and helps to explain the level of migration. The data tell us that the reality of small border municipalities is quite similar in many ways to most poor places in other areas of Mexico.

If the previous data created a concern about youth in northern Mexico, the findings about teenage mothers further confirm these worries. (See Table 2.5.) The national proportion of teen mothers ages 18–19 encompasses 21.9% of the population of females of that age, while in the border states it is 23.5% and in the border municipalities, 27.7%. A total of 28,490 females ages 18–19 in the thirty-seven border municipalities have had a child born alive, which is 6.5% of the mothers of that age for all of Mexico. In ten border municipalities, more than 35% of young females ages 18–19 have had a born-alive child: in Guadalupe, Chihuahua (51.1%); Naco, Sonora (42.2%); Guerrero, Tamaulipas (41.9%); Ascención, Chihuahua (39.6%); Manuel Benavides, Chihuahua (39.3%); Mier, Tamaulipas (39.2%); Altar (37.6%) and Agua Prieta (36%), Sonora; and Hidalgo, Coahuila (35.3%). On the other hand, teen mothers ages 15–17 are 8.2% of the border municipalities' similar-age female population, 6.7% at the six border states, and 5.7% at the national level. At all age levels, the patterns indicate that the risk of a teen pregnancy is higher at the northern border.

Figure 2.1.   Percentage of Youth 18–19 Years Old Who Do Not Work and
Do Not Go to School vs. Percentage of Homes That Receive Remittances,
by States of Mexico, 2000

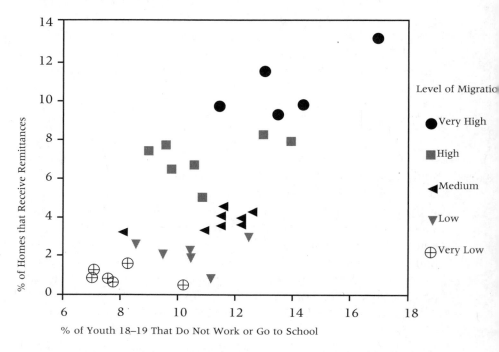

Source: Based on data from XII Census of Population and Housing 2000, INEGI.

Even though, in general, school achievement for the population in
northern Mexico is higher than in the center and south, the high-
school dropout rate in the border states is higher than the national average of 14.7% in five of these states; the exception is Tamaulipas,
which shows an index of 10.9% in the school cycle 2003–2004. The
state of Chihuahua ranked the highest in high-school dropout levels
among the thirty-two states of Mexico in the same cycle, and Nuevo
León, the third, with levels of 19.5% and 18.9%, respectively. Although the dropout indicators are not available by municipality, this

Table 2.5.   Number and Proportion of Teenage Girls 15–19 Who Have Had a Child Born Alive in the Northern Border States of Mexico, 2000. Showing Highest and Lowest Border Municipalities of Each State, by % of Females 18–19 with a Child Born Alive.

State	Name of Municipality	Females 15–17 with Child Born Alive 2000	% Females 15–17 with Child Born Alive 2000	Females 18–19 with Child Born Alive 2000	% Females 18–19 with Child Born Alive 2000
Baja California		5076	7.96%	12040	26.8%
	Mexicali	1554	7.76%	3559	26.3%
	Tecate	147	7.41%	409	28.9%
	Tijuana	2324	7.77%	5781	26.3%
Coahuila		4670	6.92%	10788	24.5%
	Guerroro	9	19.15%	5	16.1%
	Hidalgo	7	16.28%	12	35.3%
Chihuahua		6683	7.72%	15974	28.2%
	Guadalupe	31	11.79%	93	51.1%
	Janos	12	3.60%	42	22.6%
Nuevo León		5856	5.32%	14243	18.6%
	Anahuac	49	8.57%	118	33.1%
Sonora		4368	6.70%	10337	24.1%
	Caborca	175	7.93%	401	27.6%
	Naco	28	17.39%	38	42.2%
Tamaulipas		4985	6.15%	12040	21.7%
	Guerroro	22	17.05%	39	41.9%
	Reynosa	730	6.19%	1942	21.2%
Total Border Muns.		11891	8.20%	28490	27.7%
Total Border States Mexico		31638	6.67%	75422	23.5%
TOTAL		176219	5.71%	436036	21.9%

Source: XII Census of Population and Housing 2000, National Institute of Statistics, Geography and Informatics, INEGI, Mexico 2000. Data processed by La Red por los Derechos de la Infancia en México.

finding is congruent with the two previous factors that have been discussed. High-school dropout rates that are among the highest in Mexico should be related to a higher proportion of youth not working and not going to school, to a greater risk of teenage pregnancy, and a substantial number of children less than age eighteen who are in conflict with the law.

Conclusion

The marginalization index, which is calculated by CONAPO in Mexico, is a composite index based on statistical techniques, which summarizes variables that describe housing conditions, income, illiteracy, and other basic indicators of poverty. Higher marginalization rates show that there is a majority of the population who lack, or are at the fringes of, employment, social services, and other social benefits. The rates of marginalization in the country are lower for the border region and put all six border states among the second- and tenth-best places for marginalization, in a total of thirty-two states in the entire nation (CONAPO 2000). Looking at the proportion of families with very low income in Mexico illustrates clearly this basic difference. The percentage of children less than age eighteen in homes where the income consists of two minimum salaries or less (but there is an income) in Mexico overall is 29.2%, in the border states 16.9%, and in the border municipalities 11%. Those numbers show that in the northern region, the poverty level is less than in the rest of the country. Similarly, from the 2000 Census, 13.4% of the population ages 0–17 were part of a household declared not to have any income; in the border states this percentage was 6.6%, and in the border municipalities, 4.3%. Nevertheless, in three municipalities of the border this percentage is higher than at the national level: Santa Cruz, Sonora (15.7%); Sáric, Sonora (14.8%); and Manuel Benavides, Chihuahua (14%). Again, even along the northern border, differences and disparities exist in a localized way. So when talking about the richness of the north of Mexico, there are gaps where this description cannot be applied.

If we narrow our view to this index only, it really looks as though the border region of Mexico is a paradise in comparison to the south or center of the country. We have one image of the population and families settled in big cities with economic development, another image of small towns where lifestyles and difficulties are very much like those found in other small communities in Mexico, and a third image of the floating moving population that is an intrinsic part of the region and whose risks, difficulties, and desperation are reflected in their everyday lives. So, we may say that the northern border is an indistinct boundary that encompasses the well-being of those who find it there, and the aspirations for a better life of those who live along it and experience its discrepancies as well.

Notes

Special thanks to the Instituto Nacional de Estadística, Geografía e Informática (INEGI) for its advice to La Red por los Derechos de la Infancia en México and to the Annie E. Casey Foundation (AECF) for its support to important projects of the Network, as well as to the Fundación para la Protección de la Niñez, I.A.P. I am also grateful to Ana Marie Argilagos, who invited me to be part of Las Fronterizas, and to all Las Fronterizas, especially Raquel Márquez, Harriett Romo, and Criselda Rivas, who encouraged me and patiently corrected my English; and to my colleagues of the Network, particularly Patricia Ezeta, who was technical assistant for the data process, and César R. Núñez, who participated in the initial phase of the research for this chapter.

1. Calculated as homes with a head of household but without a spouse or partner.

2. The 2000 Population and Housing Census of Mexico included a special questionnaire about migration, asked of 10% of the population. This is the "10% sample" referred to in the source for Table 2.2.

3. It may be useful to the reader to know that these data come from the 2000 Census, with one of the following possibilities of drainage: (1) connected to the public drain network; (2) connected to a septic tank; (3) connected to a pipe that goes to a ravine or trough; (4) connected to a pipe that goes to a river, lake, or sea; (5) does not have any drainage; (6) not specified. The data reported correspond to option 5.

References

Amnistía Internacional. 2003. Informe "10 años de desapariciones y asesinatos de mujeres en Ciudad Juárez y Chihuahua." August 11, 2003.

Ceballos, Diego. "EEUU Inocencia perdida en la frontera." InterPress Service News Agency. http://www.ipsnoticias.com/print.asp?idnews=31374 (last accessed March 6, 2005).

Centro de Estudios Económicos del Sector Privado A.C. 2002. La Inseguridad Pública en México, Octubre de 2002.

Centro de Estudios Fronterizos y de Promoción de los Derechos Humanos AC. 2000. Estudios Fronterizos, Globalización, Migración y Explotación en la Industria Maquiladora, Enero-Febrero, 2000. http://www.derecho-shumanosenmexico.org/ informesenword/infglbl.doc.

CONAPO, Consejo Nacional de Población. 2000. Database of Marginalization Levels, Based on XII General Population and Housing Census, 2000, INEGI, Mexico. http:// www.conapo.gob.mx.

González, Román. 2003. "La sombra de China en la industria maquiladora." *Cimacnoticias*, May 21, 2003. http://www.mujereshoy.com/secciones/736.shtml.

INAMI, Instituto Nacional de Migración. 2005. http:// www.inami.gob.mx (last accessed August 2005).

INDISEP. 2005. System of Indicators of the Education Ministry, General Direction of Planning, Programming, and Budget of the Education Ministry, "DGPPP," Mexico.

INEGI, Instituto Nacional de Estadística, Geografía e Informática. 2000a. IRIS (Información Referenciada Geoespacialmente Integrada en un Sistema), Version 2.0, Database of the XII General Population and Housing Census, Mexico, 2000.

————. 2000b. SIMBAD (Sistema de Información Municipal de Bases de Datos), Database of the XII General Population and Housing Census, Mexico, 2000.

————. 2000c. Database of the XII General Population and Housing Census, Mexico, 2000.

Roldán, Antonio, Abelardo Ávila, Adolfo Chavez, Marsela Alvarez, Miriam Muñoz, and Teresa Shama. 2004. "Regionalización de la Situación Nutricional, en México a través de un índice de riesgo por municipio." Edited by Instituto Nacional de Ciencias Medicas y Nutrición Salvador Zubiran and the Latin American Society of Nutrition.

Salud y Apoyo al Migrante, Interinstitucional de Atención a Menores Fronterizos, Programa Interinstitucional de Atención a Menores Fronterizos. 2005. http://www.saludmigrante.salud.gob.mx/directorios/resumen.htm (last accessed March 6, 2005).

Shirk, David, and Alexandra Webber. 2004. "Slavery without Borders: Human Trafficking in the U.S.-Mexican context." *Hemisphere Focus* II:5. Center for Strategic and International Studies.

Sin Fronteras I.A.P. 2005. "Migration and Refugees." Questions about Migration. Available at http://www.sinfronteras.org.mx/mi.htm (last accessed September 23, 2005).

SSP, Secretaría de Seguridad Pública. 2004. Consejo de Menores. Registro Nacional de Menores Infractores: Instituciones para menores infractores del país, citado en *Mujeres y Hombres de México*. INEGI, México.

Stop Gate Keeper. 2004. Proyecto Fronterizo. "California Rural Legal Assistance Foundation." http://www.stopgatekeeper.org/Espanol/index.html.

STPS, Secretaría del Trabajo y Previsión Social (Labour and Social Provision Ministry). 1994–2000. Labor Statistics, Table I.2 "Tasa de Desempleo Abierto 48 Áreas Urbanas, 1994–2000," *Encuesta Nacional de Empleo Urbano e Indicadores de Empleo y Desempleo*. INEGI, México.

Woo Morales, Ofelia. 2004. "Las mujeres en la migración mexicana hacia Estados Unidos y su condición de género." Forum "Las Mujeres y la Migración en México" (Women and Migration in Mexico), Guanajuato, Gto., December 2004, General Direction of Promotion and Linkages, Direction of Human Development, National Institute of Women, Mexico.

XIPN Canal ONCE TV del Instituto Politécnico Nacional. 2000. Investigación y Serie Televisiva "México, Tierra de Migrantes," México, 2000. http://www.oncetv-ipn.net/migrantes/.

CHAPTER THREE

The Extended Border

A Case Study of San Antonio as a Transnational City

Harriett D. Romo

This chapter considers San Antonio, Texas, the eighth largest city in the United States, as an extension of the U.S.-Mexico border. I argue that San Antonio, although not physically located within the territory traditionally defined as the border, is a transnational border city and an important area in which to study transnational children and families. Transnationalism in San Antonio is created by the social fields or sets of multiple interlocking networks of social relationships through which ideas, practices, and resources are exchanged, organized, and transformed (Levitt and Glick Schiller 2004). As the urban gateway of South Texas and a short two-hour drive from the official boundary, San Antonio has a large, long-established Mexican-origin population and has also historically been a destination for Mexican immigrant workers, much like Chicago and Los Angeles. However, unlike Chicago or Los Angeles, the Latino population in San Antonio is the majority group, and there are no other major ethnic groups competing with the dominant Mexican culture. It is within this cultural context and the expansive set of relationships produced by decades of migration that San Antonio is able to "diminish the importance of movement as a requirement for engaging in transnational practices" (Levitt and Waters 2002: 10).

Living in a transnational city such as San Antonio blurs the boundaries between those recent immigrants who have many connections with Mexico and the second- and third-generation Mexican Americans who may never have even been to Mexico (Alba 2005). According to the 2000 U.S. Census, Bexar County, where San Antonio is located, has a population of almost 800,000 Hispanics, representing 58.7% of the population, of whom 41.4% are of Mexican origin and predominantly second- or third-generation Mexican Americans. Census predictions project that number growing to over 1.2 million Hispanics by the year 2040. At the same time, Census analysts note that the non-Hispanic white population in the San Antonio and Bexar County area is decreasing. The 2000 Census identified 44% of the population in San Antonio who speak Spanish. Commonly, a large percentage of Mexican American families who speak English very well also use a mixture of Spanish and English in their homes and communities. This majority Latino population fosters a way of life, a culture, and a language that is the borderlands, despite the physical distance of San Antonio from the official U.S.-Mexico border.

Transnationalism is defined in this study as events, communities, and lives linked across borders and includes the economic and cultural transformations that result from the frequent and widespread movement of Mexicans back and forth between their communities of origin and San Antonio as well as the social networks and social fields in which day-to-day activities are carried out. Many San Antonio residents travel regularly between San Antonio and communities in Mexico, especially to Nuevo Laredo and Monterrey. Others have lived in San Antonio for generations and seldom cross over, but their lives are integrally involved with resources, contacts, and people from the Mexican side of the border.

In considering various migration patterns, Luis Guarnizo (2000) makes a distinction between "core transnationalism," which is a part of the everyday life of people who regularly go back and forth to Mexico and their U.S. communities, and "expanded transnationalism," which involves occasional participation in transnational activities. As noted above, San Antonians of Mexican descent often engage in both types. In addition, the city's large Mexican American population, many of whom have resided in San Antonio for three generations or more, continue to construct their identities, pursue economic mobility, and maintain social and family networks in both countries. These patterns have been the norm for some families since the incorporation of Texas, formerly a Mexican territory, into the United States. Furthermore, we are beginning to see in San Antonio an increasing Mexican population that consists of American citizens, by birth in the United States, by birth to Mexican parents who became naturalized American citizens, or by birth in Mexico to an American parent. Many of these young people grew up in Mexico or spent a good deal of time there during key periods of their social and emotional development. As a result of their American citizenship, they can move freely across the border and take part fully in the economic, social, and cultural life of both the U.S. and Mexican communities. When these youths live, attend school, and work in San Antonio, they are embedded in a community of Mexican immigrants and Mexican Americans that supports their Mexican identity and culture, encourages the use of the Spanish language, promotes Mexican cultural norms, and allows them to interact with others as both Mexicans and Americans.

The term "transnational social field" encompasses the social, economic, and political processes in which the migrating populations are embedded and to which they react and includes all aspects of social life (Basch, Glick Schiller, and Blanc-Szanton 1994; Levitt and Glick Schiller 2004; Levitt and Waters 2002: 10). This explanation focuses on human interaction, personal social relationships, and the simultaneous connections to two or more nation-states. Levitt and Glick Schiller (2004) have expanded the definition of social fields to include ways of being and ways of belonging in that field. There is a "simultaneity"— leading lives that incorporate daily routines and institutions in the destination community and connect to a homeland. This includes dispersed networks of family compatriots or persons who share a religious or ethnic identity. These processes "occur at the same time and reinforce one another" (Levitt and Glick Schiller 2004: 1003). It is this definition of social field that helps us to look at San Antonio as a transnational extended borderlands community.

Methodological Approach

Comments and case studies presented in this chapter are drawn from 250 extensive, tape-recorded interviews conducted with adults and high-school students in San Antonio as part of a larger project funded by the Rockefeller Foundation to explore transnational lives in that city.[1] Adult working-class and elite subjects were contacted using the snowball technique. High-school students were contacted through English as a Second Language courses and regular English classes at two high schools: one a working-class, inner-city school, and the other a middle-class high school located in a Westside neighborhood. A sample of twenty interviews with residents of Monterrey, Nuevo León, Mexico, who have lived in or frequently visit San Antonio, provided insights from the Mexican national perspective about transnational lives. All interviews were conducted by bilingual interviewers and were transcribed and coded with Atlas ti qualitative software.

The open-ended interview guide used in this study was adapted from one used by Mary Waters and her colleagues in their study of West Indian migrants in Boston and New York. Topics covered in the interview included descriptions of the home community; background of parents; immigration status; friendship and family networks across borders; child-rearing practices; language use; political participation; identity; transnational experiences; work and schooling; and philosophical questions about stereotypes, dual nationality, what it means to be an American, and what it means to be successful. The quotes and case studies found in this chapter are drawn from these interviews.

To place contemporary experiences in historical context, this chapter draws on historical research that documents the ties between San Antonio and Mexico even before Texas became a part of the United States and illustrates the powerful influences of transnational social fields on the lives of contemporary Mexican-origin residents of San Antonio (Arreola 1987, 1995, 2002; Jones 1992, 1994, 1995, 2003; Montejano 1987; Mora-Torres 2001). A brief review of recent research on migration documents the cultural, social, economic, political, linguistic, and familial ties that have been established between cities such as San Antonio and the Mexican border.

Historical Context

Juan Mora-Torres, in *The Making of the Mexican Border* (2001), describes the U.S.-Mexican boundary as "both a link and a barrier." He points out that the two countries have different economic and political systems, different cultural values, and vast differences in "plenty" and "want." An official boundary between the nations was not firm until the 1848 signing of the Treaty of Guadalupe Hidalgo, which ended the U.S.-Mexican War. San Antonio, a former northern settlement of Mexico, and Monterrey, once the economic capital of Mexico's northern frontier, both had weak ties to the central economy and government of their respective nations and both were frontier settlements sharing a physical space now recognized as the borderlands. Mora-Torres explains that neither the government of Mexico nor the government of the United States had the capacity to police and administer the societies at the edges of their territories. As a result, among the most important features that distinguish the north of Mexico from the rest of the country are its proximity to the United States as well as an evolving economic relationship with it (Richardson 1999). Thus, northern Mexico and San Antonio became one permanent zone in which the economies and cultures of two nations engaged each other and created a region different from either Mexico or the United States.

San Antonio has been described as the "Mexican American cultural capital" and the primary focus of Mexican culture in the United States (Arreola 1987: 17). Daniel Arreola attributes this cultural dominance to the founding of San Antonio in the early eighteenth century on the eastern frontier of New Spain with the settlement of five missions, a presidio, and a civilian colony located along the San Antonio River. "The concentration of these varied institutions," he emphasizes, "made San Antonio unique along the Spanish borderlands" (Arreola 1987: 18). The long history of relations between South Texas and Mexico, the economic interdependence of the subregion, the extended length of the Texas-Mexico border, and the concentrated Mexican-origin population make this borderland distinct from others in the Southwest (Arreola 2002).

The first U.S. Census, taken shortly after the annexation of Texas, enumerated approximately 14,000 Mexicans in Texas. They "were the most numerous, . . . next the Anglo-Americans, and then the Germans" (Montejano 1987: 31). Texas boasted a 39% Mexican population in 1850, and their prominence in political office and numbers signaled an important distinction between Mexicans in Texas and Mexicans in other southwestern states (Arreola 1987). In 1912, 1913, and 1916, Mexican residents of border cities fled to San Antonio to escape attacks by Pancho Villa and his Villistas. Communities of families from the northern state of Coahuila became established in San Antonio and Laredo at that time (Jones 1995). After the Mexican Revolution, migrants from the interior of Mexico streamed northward and displaced workers from the border state of Coahuila. Many then crossed into the United States, attracted to agricultural jobs in the Texas Lower Valley and urban jobs in San Antonio. In 1928, people of Mexican origin made up 81% of the manufacturing workforce in San Antonio (Jones 1995). Continued proximity and accessibility to Mexico bound many of the Mexican residents in San Antonio to their homeland "well beyond the 20th century" (Arreola 1987: 19).

Monterrey was once one of Mexico's most commercialized cities and the regional trading center for most of northeastern Mexico. Mexican merchants routinely crossed the border and traveled to San Antonio to conduct business (Arreola 1987). The International and Great Northern Railroad extended from San Antonio to Laredo on the Mexican border and connected in Nuevo Laredo with the Ferrocarril Nacional Mexicano, which stretched from Laredo to Monterrey and into the heart of central Mexico. As Monterrey became more industrialized and a center of northern Mexico's commerce, merchants in San Antonio saw Monterrey residents as an extension of their commercial markets and opened branches in Monterrey (Jones 1995, 2003; Mora-Torres 2001). One Mexican-born San Antonio businessman whom we interviewed explained that his family always spent the summers in Monterrey, where he also ran a business. During the early twentieth century, San Antonio was the destination of Mexican migrants recruited to pick Texas cotton crops. Texas became the residence of more than half of all foreign-born Mexicans in the United States during those early decades, and San Antonio served as the primary point of dispersal of Mexican laborers (Durand et al. 2000). Perhaps the success of Mexican Americans in continuing a distinctive Mexican culture and persisting as an ethnically distinct people resulted from American racism and the Mexican Americans' de facto subordinate status in the Southwest, which encouraged them to identify as Mexicans in a way they had never done before (Gutiérrez 1995). Because of both longtime segregation and the growing Mexican population in San Antonio, many Mexican-origin residents in the city still live, go to school, and work in predominantly Mexican social and cultural fields.

As a result of these historical patterns, international migration is so deeply rooted in San Antonio that transnational movement has become the norm. Kandel and Massey (2002) suggest that young people in Mexico "expect" to live and work in the United States at some time in their lives, making it highly probable that residents in San Antonio will live and work among Mexicans. Mexican policymakers have led efforts to make Mexicans in the United States (*los mexicanos de afuera*) nationals once again, a status entitling them to most social, economic, and civil rights enjoyed by Mexican citizens, including the right to carry a Mexican passport and vote in Mexican elections (Shain 2000). This policy has encouraged many of those Mexican nationals who have legal residency in San Antonio to naturalize as U.S. citizens as well. Debra Weber (1999) argues that current work on transnationalism should be couched in broader historical perspectives. She suggests that contemporary Mexican migrations are a recent manifestation of very old processes, and she notes that studies of working-class immigrants and transnationals have helped to shift the historical perception from the "uprooted" to a more complex understanding of immigrants' experiences and their ongoing connections with their home communities.

San Antonio has always been attractive to Mexican nationals seeking economic opportunities and to Mexican residents unhappy with conditions in their homeland. These emigrants brought with them their language, political ideologies, business skills, and institutions and rose to prominence in the San Antonio business community. Their influence laid the foundation for the Spanish-language media, cultural traditions, bilingual education, and political leadership that exist in the city today.

Culture and Transnational Lives

Approximately 25,000 political refugees fleeing the Mexican Revolution between 1900 and 1910 settled in San Antonio, thus increasing the city's intellectual networks with Mexico (Areola 2002). These exiles established an influential Spanish-language newspaper, *La Prensa,* and organized the headquarters of the Los Angeles Spanish-language newspaper, *La Opinion.* David Gutiérrez (1995: 35) notes that these and other Spanish-language publications promoted a strong sense of ethnic solidarity among members of what the newspapers variously described as "*la población mexicana* (the Mexican population), *nuestros compatriotas* (our compatriots), or *nuestra raza* (our people)." These newspapers, in addition, asserted an American identity. An article appearing in *La Prensa* in San Antonio in 1954 declared that Mexicans had earned a legitimate place in American society through their work, contributions, and sacrifices. Moreover, this loyalty had been "sealed with their own blood" in brave military actions defending the United States (Gutiérrez 1995: 176).

The Spanish-language media continue to support San Antonio's cultural links with Mexico. *La Prensa* still covers the social and political life of Mexicans and Mexican Americans in the city. A growing number of elite Mexican residents and professional Mexican American residents who want to enhance their Spanish skills provide a thriving market for a new Spanish-language newspaper, *Rumbo,* which began publication in San Antonio in 2003. *Rumbo's* Mexican and Mexican American writers target the middle-class, well-educated Spanish speakers in the city. Responding to the growing competition from the Spanish-language newspapers, the *San Antonio Express-News,* the main English-language newspaper in the city, added a bilingual weekly in 2003 that includes columns written by Mexican American journalists and Mexican guest columnists. The *Express-News* further changed its regular format to include a section called "Culturas" and a page featuring news and sports in Mexico. These publications allow residents of San Antonio to maintain close contact with daily events in Mexican communities as well as with cultural and social trends throughout Mexico.

The Spanish language is an important aspect of Mexican cultural identity. Bilingual educational programs in the city's public schools help to maintain the Spanish language in San Antonio. Texas, unlike California and Florida, has not passed an English Only initiative (Macedo 1997). San Antonio's community-based organizations have historically protested segregation and promoted bilingual education (Garcia 1997). Spanish is taught in bilingual programs in the San Antonio Independent School District, Southside School District, Northeast

School District, and Northwest School District as well as in the Alamo Heights School District, which is located in one of the traditionally Anglo American upper-class neighborhoods. Currently spoken across all social classes, Spanish persists in San Antonio by way of continued immigration, the Spanish-language newspapers mentioned above, major Mexican cultural events in the city, and Spanish-language television and radio stations.

The Spanish-language programming that originates in Mexico enables immigrants to follow their favorite music and entertainment programs and strengthens a sense of identity among Mexican Americans with their place of origin. Today, San Antonio hosts two major Spanish-language television stations, Telemundo and Univisión. Worth nearly $10 billion, Univisión is the fifth-largest television network in the United States, behind Fox and ahead of WB, reaching some 98% of U.S. Spanish-speaking households through its sixty affiliate stations and more than twelve hundred cable affiliates (Ross Sorkin 2006). The Mexican media giant Grupo Televisa provides much of Univisión's programming. Live interviews, *novellas* or soap operas, local interest stories, and national news from both sides of the border are carried in Spanish; local radio stations play *tejano conjunto, ranchero, banda, bolero,* and *mariachi* music.

In addition to language and music, San Antonio continued the tradition of political opposition begun by the Mexicans fleeing the Mexican Revolution. San Antonio residents gave birth to civil rights organizations such as the Mexican American Legal Defense and Educational Fund (MALDEF) and hosted the landmark First Chicano/Latino Conference on Immigration and Public Policy in 1977. They also supported La Raza Unida, a political party, in the 1970s and initiated several key court cases that ended the legal segregation of Mexican students (Gutiérrez 1995). With gains made in the political arena as a result of the efforts of many of the civil rights groups, Mexican-origin residents of San Antonio now hold prominent leadership positions. Currently, Mexican Americans are the majority on the San Antonio city council and on several public school-district boards. For example, a Mexican American businessman chairs the San Antonio Independent School District board, which has predominantly Mexican American members. Two previous mayors, three presidents of four-year universities, the president of the San Antonio Health Science Center, state legislators, local congressmen, physicians, lawyers, judges, and the Catholic arch-bishop in San Antonio are Texas Mexicans. Thus, Mexican-origin residents influence important policies in the city, and many of these leaders forge vital social and political links with Mexico.

Mexican government institutions located in San Antonio, such as universities and the consulate, have played a significant role in promoting intellectual and political links across the border. San Antonio has a permanent extension campus of the Universidad Nacional Autónoma de México (UNAM), the major public university system in Mexico that came to San Antonio in 1944. The San Antonio UNAM campus enrolls students in cultural heritage courses in the Spanish language and literature and in Mexican architecture and history. Also, the UNAM campus offers a GED in Spanish that is equivalent to the Mexican *secundaria* diploma. The campus recently accepted a large grant to install modern-language laboratories to teach both English and Spanish. The UNAM organizes visiting lecturers, cultural tours to Mexico, and other intellectual activities in San Antonio. Another major private Mexican university, the Universidad Autónoma de Guadalajara, also has a campus in San Antonio, and many graduates of its medical program complete internships and residencies in San Antonio's health facilities.

The consulate offices help Mexican nationals to solve problems encountered in the United States, register Mexican citizens for dual nationality and for voting in elections in their homeland, promote Mexico's interests, and make contacts in the United States for business and investment opportunities. San Antonio hosts one of the largest Mexican consulates in the United States. Twelve *clubes regionales,* similar to hometown associations, are supported by the consulate, which helps them to organize and promote cultural events representing their respective Mexican states or regions. These *clubes regionales* maintain social and economic networks between San Antonio and the home communities in Mexico. Another large Mexican government office in San Antonio, the Mexican Cultural Institute, sponsors art exhibits, *salsa* dancing, special events, lessons, and speakers. By providing ideological and institutional support, these institutions promote close cultural ties with Mexico and strengthen a sense of Mexican identity in the city.

The cultural dimensions of transnational lives have inspired creative and powerful cultural manifestations on both sides of the border. As we know, culture is a part of everyday life and gives life meaning. A range of cultural forms and practices are embedded in transnational spaces such as San Antonio (Arreola 2002). The intermingling of spaces and practices along the U.S.-Mexican border is a product of globalization and consumption, but its effects are experienced and organized in culturally distinct ways at the individual and institutional levels (Herzog 2000).

The San Antonio Museum of Art, for example, has one of the largest Mexican folk art collections in the United States, which was donated to the museum by the Rockefeller family in 1985, and the $11-million, 30,000-square-foot Nelson A. Rockefeller Center for Latin American Art. The museum has hosted major shows of Mexican and Mexican American art as well as exhibitions featuring the collection of a Monterrey family and the work of cutting-edge contemporary Mexican artists. The McNay Art Museum, housed in a Mexican-style mansion, has featured major exhibits by three local Mexican American artists—Cesar Martinez, Kathy Vargas, and Vincent Valdez. The new Museo Americano sponsors Mexican-heritage exhibitions.

Religious institutions also play a dominant role in San Antonio in preserving Mexican culture, particularly Roman Catholic beliefs and practices, although congregations in both Protestant and Catholic churches in the city span across the border. San Fernando Cathedral, one of the earliest structures in the city, anchors the main downtown plaza. Live broadcasts on Sundays of the Spanish-language mass from the cathedral reach into Mexico and Latin America. The cathedral organizes traditional celebrations at Christmas and dramatic religious pageants at Easter. The Spanish missions that formed the original settlements of San Antonio still conduct mass in Spanish and have active congregations.

Hispanic architectural influences have been a part of San Antonio since the founding of the missions and San Fernando Cathedral. The Alameda, one of San Antonio's oldest Mexican movie theaters, is under renovation to return it to its glory days of the 1920s and 1930s when popular Mexican movie stars and singers performed regularly there. The Guadalupe Cultural Arts Center, located in the Westside, the oldest Mexican-origin neighborhood in the city, is a community-based organization recognized throughout the United States for its programming in theater, film, dance, and visual arts. It is housed in the remodeled Guadalupe Theater with its colorful Mexican tilework.

Although the increasing influence of Mexican culture has encountered some resistance among a few residents of San Antonio, its impact has been significant in the identity of the city. A large statue of the Virgin of Guadalupe, sculpted by the Mexican American artist Jesse Trevino, graces the outside of the Guadalupe Cultural Arts Center's theater. Several newspaper editorials questioned the appropriateness of a religious icon as a nonprofit site funded by the city, but an overwhelming number of both Anglos and Mexican-origin residents defended the Virgin as an important cultural symbol. One of Mexico's most famous architects, Ricardo Legorreta, designed the "enchilada red" San Antonio Central Library, criticized by some as being "too colorful." Sandra Cisneros, a successful writer and resident of San Antonio, stirred up a controversy when she painted her home in the historic King William neighborhood a bright Mexican purple. The San Antonio Historic and Design Review Committee determined that the color was not a legitimate one for the neighborhood. The debate sparked national media attention, but Cisneros prevailed and persuaded the committee that the color was indeed a part of San Antonio's Mexican cultural identity. A large sculpture, "The Torch of Friendship," designed and constructed by the Mexican artist Sebastian, has become a symbol of downtown San Antonio despite arguments between conservationists who thought the public art was too contemporary and the Mexican entrepreneurs who sponsored it. Together these institutions play an important role in promoting Mexican culture and in featuring the Texas Mexican culture that characterizes the city. Mexicans and Mexican Americans have used art, popular culture, literature, and other artistic means to protest unjust treatment of Mexicans and to explore and promote Mexican identity (Maciel and Herrera-Sobek 1998).

Transnational Social Ties

The educational, social, and cultural institutions in San Antonio are embedded in networks that span the Mexican-U.S. border and interact to shape perceptions, interests, and decisions in the community. Residents of Mexico travel to San Antonio to shop, see friends, attend cultural and social events, and conduct business. Many of the well-to-do families of Monterrey have developed permanent ties in San Antonio by sending their children to San Antonio public schools to learn English or enrolling their adolescents in the Catholic or public universities in the city. Mexican nationals buy homes and settle in enclaves in both the wealthiest and the poorest neighborhoods there. In fact, one of the gated subdivisions in San Antonio is referred to locally as "Monterrey North." A Mexican resident of that community labeled a recent event at the complex's country club as "a replication of the social affairs of Monterrey's upper-middle-class and elites." Moreover, a recent Mexican immigrant professional described the local ethnic community in San Antonio as "mini-Mexico."

Transmigrants are part of the fabric of daily life in Mexico and San Antonio. They often participate in the economic and social processes of their home communities, as well as in the workforce, neighborhood activities, and the cultural, religious, and educational life of San Antonio. In interviews conducted with people who live transnational lives, we learned that some Mexican-origin residents make short trips to San Antonio to live with relatives or friends in order to earn investment money for property they already own in Mexico, to buy or repair a home, or to buy a new property or a business in Mexico. Other Mexican residents live part of the year in San Antonio and part of the year in Mexico and fly back and forth on short commuter flights between San Antonio and Monterrey or Mexico City. These patterns signify a solid base of membership in the community of origin, even if the investors continue to make migration trips (Goldring 1998; Mooney 2003). Our interviews demonstrate that, increasingly, Mexican-origin immigrants are investing in homes, property, or businesses in San Antonio as well as in communities in Mexico. For example, San Antonio hosts a large organization of *empresarios,* or Mexican entrepreneurs, who run businesses that operate both in San Antonio and in Mexican cities. A professional whom we interviewed recognized the transnational aspects of San Antonio as he described the city: "I think San Antonio wouldn't be San Antonio, the town that it is today—one of the largest cities, highly respected for having accomplished a good deal of integration of many of the business and social things without the constant interaction with Mexico. What makes San Antonio unique is the fact that there's so much rich Mexican culture and so many rich traditions, and the people here in San Antonio can come from Mexico, interact here, buy homes, open bank accounts, do business here."

As noted earlier, dual nationality encourages Mexicans residing in San Antonio to become U.S. citizens without giving up their Mexican identities (Castañeda 1995). Ignacio, who was born in Mexico, attended school in San Antonio and is currently a bilingual sales representative at a major San Antonio bank. He recently became a naturalized U.S. citizen and explained his reasons for doing so: "I identify more with the issues in the United States because they affect my life and it was important for me to do it. . . . As a citizen you get to participate in a lot of different things that as a non-resident you don't . . . and I better do it now, before I can't do it later. . . . When I became an American citizen, they did not say, bring in your Mexican passport so we can shred it or anything like that, so I didn't do anything. And in Mexico, they haven't told me anything either." Not long ago, he traveled to Mexico and boarded the airplane as an American in order to confirm that he could return to San Antonio, so he showed his U.S. passport. But he "came back with the Mexican passport because the line was shorter." When asked if he felt more or less Mexican now, he said, "I feel the same . . . living in San Antonio is great because you have the best of both worlds, friends that are from Mexico, good food from Mexico, and Mexico is 140 miles away if you really, really need to go to Mexico."

Differences in socioeconomic position and English-language proficiency, of course, influence the ability of Mexican residents in San Antonio to live outside ethnic enclaves and make investments and ties that strengthen their positions in the San Antonio community (Alba et al. 2000). In San Antonio, much as in other large cities, Mexican-origin residents whose physical appearance, language, or customs differ radically from the dominant Anglo residents are most likely to experience discrimination and residential segregation (Rosales 2000). Many of the Mexicans living in San Antonio know English well, have attended schools in the United States, or have family members living in the city. Although they are well off and integrated into the social life of San Antonio, many choose to remain clustered in majority Latino neighborhoods out of ethnic pride and a desire to speak Spanish with friends and neighbors. The changing demographics of San Antonio and the emergence of a dominant Latino population appear to have lessened segregation and afforded Mexican-origin residents those amenities found in Anglo-dominant communities, but within a context of familiar Mexican institutions (Jones 2003).

Defining San Antonio as an extended border city does not imply that all residents view it in that way, or that policies and legal boundaries established by the nation-states do not affect personal lives. Many Mexican Americans use nationality to detach themselves from Mexicans and to distinguish themselves from Anglos (Vila 2000). The more than 44,000 Mexican nationals who live in San Antonio daily confront the emigrant reality dealing with legal issues, U.S. institutions, and immigration policies and restrictions (Waldinger and Fitzgerald 2004). However, San Antonio's context allows those who wish to maintain family, cultural, and economic ties with Mexico to do so rather easily.

Constructing Identities

In the following pages, I present two case studies and comments from Mexican-origin residents of the city who view San Antonio as a major center of the extended border. These interviews show that the Mexican and Mexican American residents of San Antonio foster the continued presence of Mexican culture and institutions in both societies. In the first case study, the Saenz family has invested in houses in both San Antonio and Monterrey. Instead of experiencing a sense of lost Mexican identity, this transnational family sustains the culture and social networks of their homeland at the most basic level—the nuclear family (Jones 1994). In the Saenz family, the mother stays at home to care for her son, but she volunteers in her son's school as a translator and assistant. She and her husband help newly arrived Mexican students adjust to school by tutoring them, and they assist new immigrant parents to incorporate into the school community. The family retains a strong sense of Mexican identity but is comfortably integrated into the San Antonio community as well.

In the second case study, the family of Stephanie, a Mexican American high-school student, has resided in San Antonio for three generations. Stephanie sometimes struggles with her Mexican American culture, the Spanish language, and Anglo interactions, but she continues to live in a very Mexican cultural milieu and strongly identifies with her Mexican heritage. Both case studies exemplify San Antonio's transnationalism through family ties, cultural and language practices, and self-identities. These individuals see themselves as both Mexican and American.

A Transnational Nuclear Family

The Saenz family illustrates the complexity of national identity and immigration status within families. The interviews conducted in this research project revealed many Mexican households in San Antonio like that of the Saenz family, with members who are Mexican citizens, U.S. citizens, undocumented immigrants, or individuals who have dual nationality. In this family, Mirium Saenz was born in the United States but raised in Mexico; her husband, Tirzo Saenz, is a Mexican national born and raised in Monterrey. Their son was born in San Antonio and is being raised in a Mexican American neighborhood and a predominantly Mexican American school.

Mirium and Tirzo recently moved to a new subdivision about thirty miles north of downtown San Antonio, where the houses sell for about $70,000. Important to Mirium is that her mother and brothers live nearby. (Her father was a construction worker and a U.S. permanent resident.) Tirzo boasted that their new home has a Mexican flag in the window; and because they are so patriotic, they married on Mexican Independence Day.

Mirium has dual U.S. and Mexican citizenship. She and four of her brothers were born in the United States, but when she was seven months old, her parents returned to Mexico where she lived until returning to San Antonio at age twenty-six with her husband. At the time, she was five months pregnant. The couple moved in with Mirium's brother, and Tirzo took a job as a dishwasher in a restaurant. They lived frugally, and when Tirzo was promoted to the position of cook, they rented their own apartment. They managed to save enough to pay cash for a new car and for the down payment on their home.

When they first arrived in San Antonio, Tirzo recalled, he frequently walked long distances to the grocery store and carried heavy grocery bags home because he could not afford a car or taxi. The couple claims that they are better off in San Antonio than in Mexico, but they feel even more like Mexicanos in San Antonio than in Mexico. When asked whether she felt more or less Mexican now, Mirium explained, "More Mexican; because of the traditions that we follow, we continue feeling

Mexican, but now, with a little English, we continue feeling Mexican, and at the same time, we are trying to accept American policies. But as far as possible, we follow much of the Mexican culture" [translation].

In keeping with traditional Mexican values, Mirium and her husband see her major role as caring for their son and keeping house. She fixes tortillas, a Mexican staple, everyday for the family. She volunteers at her son's school tutoring children, helping teachers, and translating notes and flyers from English into Spanish. Mirium's work at the elementary school is highly valued by those teachers who cannot communicate with the Spanish-speaking children. Both she and Tirzo attend free English classes at their child's school, and their seven-year-old son, Tirzo Osvaldo, has learned English well. Mirium speaks some English, but Tirzo's is poor. It is difficult for him to learn English because everyone at his worksite is Mexican and speaks Spanish. Mirium was able to acquire Mexican nationality for their son since Tirzo is a Mexican citizen; the boy already is an American citizen because he was born in the United States.

Mirium's kitchen pantry is filled with Mexican products—pinto beans, rice, *leche, Maria's Gamesa* cookies, *salsa*—and Cokes bottled in Mexico "because it tastes better." In fact, the family prefers to shop in Monterrey where Tirzo grew up, a five-hour drive from San Antonio. When they cannot go to Monterrey, they travel to Laredo, a border city two hours from San Antonio. They have built a small house in Monterrey, and Tirzo proudly pointed out to me that Mirium painted the house herself. They have no immediate plans to return to Mexico, but they maintain active roles in the community where Tirzo was born. When a small border town near his home experienced a bad flood, Tirzo helped to gather clothing for the refugees who fled the storm.

The Saenz family is investing in both the San Antonio community and the father's community of origin, Monterrey, where the majority of Tirzo's family remains. They send remittances to relatives in Mexico by mail and through friends who are making return trips. The family's cash investments in their homes in both communities are considerable, even though Tirzo is the only family member working and holds a traditionally low-wage job. Mirium explained that she and her husband had only a few clothes that she washed and ironed regularly to keep them presentable, and that they saved their money for larger purchases.

Even with traditional institutional barriers to participation in the U.S. community (that is, limited English skills and low income), this transnational family is incorporating well into San Antonio. Tirzo's ethnic work environment allows him to succeed even though he speaks only Spanish. Mirium's skills in Spanish have become an asset as the school accepts greater numbers of Mexican students. Their son is learning English well and is excelling in his studies. Their network of family and friends from Mexico and their property investments help them to maintain connections with their Mexican community.

Transnational Attachments across the Generations

Stephanie's family represents three generations born in San Antonio. She has never traveled to Mexico, but she is immersed in Mexican culture and relationships in San Antonio and identifies herself as Hispanic or Mexican American. Stephanie currently lives with her mother and a younger sibling and attends an inner-city high school that enrolls 98% Mexican-origin students. Her neighborhood is also predominantly Mexican in origin. Her peers are mostly Mexican American, but sometimes, if there are new students from Mexico in her school, Stephanie interacts with them. She does not socialize with recent immigrants outside of school, although she noted, "There's a big percentage of kids here at school from Mexico, so, like, just going to school with them, it's, like, doing things with them."

Stephanie does not know much about her family's history in Mexico, but she acknowledges her Mexican heritage. She told me, "I've always tried to find out who was from Mexico." In addition, she learns about Mexico through her life experiences in San Antonio, "the restaurants, the traditions. The library is bright orange. The parades, the downtown [area, and] the music." Stephanie is definitely Americanized; she stated that she prefers San Antonio and would not consider living in Mexico because she has never been there. Nonetheless, she clings to her Mexican culture. She struggles with her Spanish, but she is trying to learn more of the language. When she tries to read it, she says, "It sounds funny, like I'm white." She prefers what she considers the "professional" Spanish heard in Mexico: "The Spanish is different here. They will just be talking Spanish and English mixed. They don't talk professional Spanish. It's slang. It's mixed. I feel like stuck between. I feel like I have some Spanish but I know more English. I wasn't brought up hearing Spanish. I was brought up hearing rock and roll music. That's my mom. It's also partly the color of the skin. . . . The way we look. Regular brown eyes, black hair, brown skin." Stephanie acknowledged with her dark features that she looked Mexican, but when asked what term she would use to refer to herself, "I would say Hispanic 'cause Mexican is kind of different. They [Mexicans] would know Spanish and know the culture and be born in Mexico, and I really don't know Spanish and I wasn't born in Mexico. I really don't know the culture, so I would say I'm Hispanic. I'm of Mexican descent but it's different."

In some cities in the United States, race raises barriers against Mexicans, especially those of indigenous phenotype, but those barriers are lowered in San Antonio because of the majority Mexican-origin population. Stephanie sometimes identifies herself as Mexican American because she was born in San Antonio, but she claims that "Chicano," a word associated with an activist identity, . . . "is only used around 'old people.'" She never uses the word white in reference to herself, and she cannot recall the last time when someone commented about her ethnic group. However, "Teachers will bring it up when they talk about us finishing high school or going to college. They'll say it like how they have the statistics, how they're having white people, black people, Mexican people, who is rated higher, who is going to college, finishing college more. That's when they bring it up, for us to not be a statistic. For us to go to college, to do better." Her teachers made more references to ethnic boundaries than Stephanie, but she also reported that her Mexican American teachers emphasized her ethnicity by exposing the students to books about Mexican culture and to Mexican American literature. On her own initiative, she used the library to learn about Mexican pottery, the Spanish language, and her Indian heritage.

Stephanie receives considerable reinforcement of her Mexican culture and identity through her relationship with her grandparents who live nearby. She visits them daily, and in their home she watches Spanish-language television and talks with them in Spanish about school. Her grandmother tells her about Mexico, "over there how it is different, the food. The way they do things." Stephanie also tries the ways of cooking handed down from her grandmother, but with some modifications: "The food, my mom must have gotten it from her mom, the enchiladas and stuff like that. Refried beans. I can't make tortillas, it's hard. But I can make everything else."

Stephanie told me that her family sometimes returns to Mexico for health care, but she was skeptical about some of her grandparents' practices. She described her grandmother's reliance on a folk healer, or *curandero*:

> Grandmother has bought medicines in Mexico. It was like magic, like witch doctors. They sell little bottles of white stuff. That's what she bought. It's like spells. She said they bless the house. It's like white and red. It's weird. She used to read the cards. You know how they have the cards and read them? She told me some stories. There was like a ghost in the house and she called some lady and she used to do good and bad stuff and she came over and spread some stuff. And she made that ghost go away. She knew it was gone because she couldn't feel the spirit anymore.

Certainly, Stephanie's grandparents maintain some traditional Mexican folk beliefs and practices, and often Stephanie contrasts those experiences with her own. She describes the *limpia* or cleansing of the ghost as "weird," but she acknowledges that the rite worked for her grandmother and "made that ghost go away." Stephanie's beliefs and traditions transcend national boundaries, and she recognizes that in San Antonio, there is a significant preponderance of Mexican culture. She said, "I think they [Mexicans] are most of the population here."

Stephanie's case study demonstrates that although she has lost some of her Mexican traditions, such as fluency in Spanish, she is constructing her Mexican identity through family relationships, as she speaks Spanish with her grandparents and mother; through institutional relationships, as she interacts in her school and neighborhood with other Mexicans; and through transnational social fields, as she takes the initiative to learn about her culture. Her Mexican American teachers have assigned tasks to help students explore their heritage. Her grandparents tell her about traditional ways of doing things in Mexico. She attends a predominantly Mexican-origin school and lives in a predominantly Mexican neighborhood. She does not need to travel to Mexico itself to encounter transnational fields.

These two case studies clearly illustrate the different types of transnationalism that recent Mexican immigrants and second-generation and beyond Mexican Americans may experience. Mexican Americans engage in transnational fields that reinforce their "Mexican-ness." The experiences of both Stephanie and the Saenz family are not distinct from the many others whom we interviewed in the larger study of San Antonio as a transnational community. Stephanie is proud of her heritage but is struggling to maintain it. Although she looks Mexican, she is not fluent in the Spanish language. She sees the importance of Spanish and cultural traditions in her interactions with her grandparents, but she remains skeptical of her grandmother's *curandero*. Still, she acknowledges that these traditions worked for her grandmother. She is immersed in border culture in her daily life through her family, her neighborhood, her school, the media, and health and religious practices. She continues to feel most comfortable around Mexican-origin people and identifies herself as an Hispanic of Mexican descent.

The Saenz family has strong family and cultural roots in Mexico and represents the more conventional definition of transnationalism. Its members maintain ties with their community of origin in Mexico, have strong Spanish skills, and interact primarily with social networks of other Mexican nationals. They have not incorporated negative stereotypes of being Mexican into their identity construction. The experiences of their second-generation son may be more similar to those of Stephanie, but that remains to be seen. The cultural milieu in San Antonio may become even more Mexican.

Mexican Influences and the Anglo Community

Philip Deloria (1998) identified the role of ethnicity within the construction of an American identity in the early history of the United States. Whites often formed clubs, associations, and social groups that took on aspects of Native American identity, as they played out scenarios in American politics and history.[2] Perhaps the same could be said for taking on a Mexican identity in San Antonio. Arreola (1995: 518) suggests that "one of the strongest measures of American urban identity is the association of a city with a specific ethnic group and its landscape." He argues that in San Antonio, with its long-term Mexican cultural presence and its majority Mexican population, Mexican cultural identity remains unchallenged. Arreola (2002) further notes that San Antonio, which is especially famous for its lively fiestas, is host to some eighteen Hispanic celebrations annually, thus making the city the recognized capital for such events.

The Mexican cultural presence in San Antonio is perpetuated by Mexican residents and families and also by the Anglo, German, and other non-Hispanic white residents. Many of these Anglo residents of San Antonio maintain transnational relations in their economic enterprises across nation-state borders. Arreola (1995) refers to El Mercado, or Market Square, a large enclosed Mexican craft market, and documents how "the modern Hispanic identity of the city is linked to ideal landscapes conceived, created, and sustained by local non-Hispanic city patrons." Each spring the entire city of San Antonio celebrates its Mexican cultural roots in a weeklong fiesta of débutante parties, parades, art, entertainment, and food. Bright colors, flowers, and *cascarones* (eggshells filled with confetti) are seen everywhere, but especially along the Paseo del Rio, or River Walk, and La Villita, or Little Town— historic recreations of the city's early Mexican landscape. Tourists and local residents, such as Stephanie and the Saenz family, enjoy the Texas-influenced Mexican foods such as *tacos, fajitas, chalupas,* and *chile con queso.* The Mexican marketplace in the center of town features popular Mexican music groups and crafts that rival the markets in Guadalajara or Mexico City.

The Mexican population organizes events that parallel those of the Anglos. San Antonio's Mexican American *Rey Feo* (ugly king) candidates compete to raise money for scholarships. The winner is honored at a ball with his court officials and princesses. Young people of both Anglo and Mexican origin construct their identities in these transnational fields as they portray the images of what it means to be Mexican and American. Deloria (1998) claims that these festivals break down the boundaries between upper and lower classes, law and custom, and past and present. In these celebrations, Anglos become "white Mexicans" for the duration of the holiday festivals.

San Antonio: The Extended Border

In this chapter, I argue that the definition of the border and the borderlands must remain flexible. Transnational fields of social relationships, ideas, practices, and resources organize and transform San Antonio into a border transnational community. The city's Mexican-origin residents' attachments to Mexico can be reinforced relatively easily through the range of contacts and services provided by Mexican institutions in the city. At the same time, large segments of the Mexicano and Mexican American populations have successfully integrated into American society. The case studies and the history of San Antonio demonstrate that economic, social, political, and cultural borders fall in different socially constructed places (Rouse 1992). Border phenomena are experienced far from the international boundary in U.S. cities and, in Mexico itself, as far away as Sinaloa, Durango, Jalisco, and Mexico City (Lorey 1999). In San Antonio, people of Mexican origin—both recent immigrants and Mexican Americans—have influenced the city with their distinctive cultural characteristics and growing economic and political power.

The first case study in this chapter, that of Mirium and Tirzo Saenz, is an example of first-generation transnationalism and the integration of families in both Mexico and San Antonio. The couple's son has dual nationality and is growing up in San Antonio, but he visits family in Mexico frequently and attends school with primarily Mexican-origin students. In the second case study, Stephanie and her family exemplify the transnational fields that continue to promote traditions, Spanish-language media, a variety of the Spanish language, and Mexican identification beyond the second generation. Both of these families behave socially and politically in ways that cannot be explained within the framework of the nation-state order or traditional assimilation theories. Moreover, San Antonio's Anglo community has embraced the Mexican culture (albeit an Anglicized version of it), as seen in the city's fiesta celebrations, architectural styles, and arts presentations. The extended border phenomena are not new, but I argue that they are more intense and more interconnected than in previous decades. In these and many other San Antonio families, social networks and cultural patterns continue to extend the boundaries of the border world both north and south. Arreola (2002) argues that Mexican South Texas is a distinctive borderland, unlike any other Mexican American subregion, and demographically, economically, and culturally, San Antonio is the capital of south Texas. A Mexican American resident of San Antonio explained, "I am here because I am inspired here. Because my roots are here, because the flavor of my life, my essence, my spice, my everything is here in San Antonio. Here is where culturally I am accepted. Here is where my culture, my life, my people's language, the language of my parents is celebrated, is expressed, is not negative, is not bad, is not poor, is everything. I can't be anywhere else but here. It's very, it's like, my mom says, 'It's so like Mexico.'"

These two case studies demonstrate the interconnectedness of societies through flows of Spanish-language media, capital, social networks, and people. These particular residents of San Antonio, and the residents interviewed in the larger study, illustrate the importance of social relations and social context in the study of transnational communities. The lives of Stephanie and the Saenz family are based on a concept of social field that distinguishes between ways of being and ways of belonging. San Antonio represents a "network of networks" that extends beyond the study of the individual. Moreover, as an extended border social field, San Antonio represents multiple interlocking networks of Mexicans and Mexican Americans through which ideas, practices, and resources are exchanged, organized, and transformed.

Some of the Mexican Americans in San Antonio may have little direct connection to Mexico, but their daily lives are acted out in a city dominated by Mexican culture and by the Mexican-origin population. Contact with transnational formal and informal institutions—such as the Spanish-language media, the Catholic religion, and other institutions characterized by solid intercultural ties—are part of the complex interconnectedness of contemporary reality in San Antonio.

It is unclear to what extent the second generation, and later generations of Mexican-origin youth such as Stephanie, will continue to participate in transnational social fields. However, extended border communities such as San Antonio suggest that transnational social fields may be more extensive and more widely distributed among contemporary immigrants and descendants of immigrants than proposed by previous accounts, especially when contextual factors of the settlement community are considered. If we shift to a more inclusive definition of transnationalism that is sensitive to contextual conditions and consider the formal and informal institutions that promote transitionalism in an extended border city, we may suggest a broader scope of transnational lives. Core transnationals, such as the Saenz family, who physically travel back and forth between San Antonio and their Mexican communities of origin, stay closely involved in their home country. Other later generations may only become active in transnational activities at special junctures, such as in Stephanie's relationship with her grandparents, her interaction with the Spanish language media, and her involvement in traditions and practices passed from earlier transnational generations. Transnational engagement varies by generation, gender, migrant's age, human capital, social capital, and by social context, as is evident in the families featured here in San Antonio. It is hoped that the experiences of these families shed light on the scope and determinants of transnational practices and expand our understanding of transnational fields in extended border communities.

Notes

Research for this paper was part of a larger study, "Knowledge, Culture, and the Construction of Identity in a Transnational Community: San Antonio, Texas," that was funded by a grant from the Rockefeller Foundation, Arts and Humanities Division. The author would like to acknowledge the work of interviewing, transcribing, and coding on the part of the staff and students of the University of Texas, San Antonio, particularly Marcela Becker, Tamara Casso, Carino Hurtado, Olivia Lopez, Sophia Ortiz, Carmen Rivas, Maria Rodríguez, Crissy Rivas, and Martha Stiles. The interview guide used in the study was adapted with permission from one used by Mary Waters in her study of transnational identity with valuable input from Raquel Márquez and Ellen Clark, professors at UTSA. This paper is based on interviews conducted by the author.

1. The Rockefeller Foundation funded the project, "A Study of Transnational U.S.-born Mexican Origin Families in San Antonio," from 2002 to 2005. The project focused on how people lead transnational lives, and the ways language and culture interact with assimilation processes in a city with a Mexican identity. The results of the study suggest a reversal of the traditional assimilation trajectory. People in San Antonio are constructing new, complex transnational identities that are both Mexican and American.

2. The Boston Tea Party is perhaps the most famous example. American colonists dressed as Native Americans dumped tea into Boston Harbor in protest of British taxes. These "true Americans" took on the identity of "Indians," the first natives of the land.

References

Alba, Richard. 2005. "Bright vs. Blurred Boundaries: Second-generation Assimilation and Exclusion in France, Germany, and the United States." *Ethnic and Racial Studies* 28(1): 20–49.

Alba, Richard E., John R. Logan, and Brian J. Stults. 2000. "The Changing
Neighborhood Context of the Immigrant Metropolis." *Social Forces* 79(2):
587–621.

Arreola, Daniel D. 1987. "The Mexican American Cultural Capital." *Geographic Review* 77: 17–34.

———. 1995. "Urban Ethnic Landscape Identity." *Geographic Review*, Thematic
Issue: *American Urban Geography* 85(4): 518–34.

———. 2002. *Tejano South Texas: A Mexican American Cultural Province*. Austin:
University of Texas Press.

Basch, Linda G., Nina Glick Schiller, and Cristina Blanc-Szanton. 1994. *Nations Unbound: Transnational Projects, Postcolonial Predicaments, and Deterritorialized Nation-States*. Langhorne, PA: Gordon and Breach.

Castañeda, Jorge G. 1995. "U.S. Policy Shifts Wake Up Neighbors' Immigration: Mexicans Are Seeking U.S. Citizenship in Record Numbers, Now the
Motherland Is Mulling Dual Citizenship for Them." *Los Angeles Times*, August 28, 1995.

Deloria, Philip J. 1998. *Playing Indian*. New Haven: Yale University Press.

Durand, Jorge, Douglas S. Massey, and Fernando Charvet. 2000. "The Changing Geography of Mexican Immigration to the United States, 1910–1996."
Social Science Quarterly 81: 1–16.

Garcia, Mario. 1997. "Education and the Mexican American: Eleuterio Escobar and the School Improvement League of San Antonio." In *Latinos and
Education*, ed. Antonia Darder, Rodolfo D. Torres, and Henry Gutierrez,
398–419. New York: Routledge.

Goldring, Luin. 1998. "The Power of Status in Transnational Social Fields." In
Transnationalism from Below, ed. Michael Peter Smith and Luis Eduardo
Guarnizo, Comparative Urban and Community Research V-6-1998,
165–95. New Brunswick, NJ: Transaction Publishers.

Guarnizo, Luis. 2000. "Notes on Transnational." In *The Changing Face of Home:
The Transnational Lives of the Second Generation*, ed. Peggy Levitt and Mary C.
Waters, 11. New York: Russell Sage Foundation. Paper also presented at
the Conference on Transnational Migration: Comparative Theory and Research Perspectives, Oxford, England, June.

Gutiérrez, David G. 1995. *Walls and Mirrors: Mexican Americans, Mexican Immigrants, and the Politics of Ethnicity*. Berkeley: University of California Press.

Herzog, Lawrence A., ed. 2000. *Shared Space: Rethinking the U.S.-Mexico Border Environment*. La Jolla: Center for U.S.-Mexican Studies, University of California, San Diego.

Jones, Richard. C. 1992. "U.S. Migration: An Alternative Economic Mobility Ladder for Rural Central Mexico." *Social Science Quarterly* 73(3): 496–510.

———. 1994. "Spatial Origins of San Antonio's Mexican-born Population." March. Report RE-06. University of Texas at San Antonio: Hispanic Research Center.

———. 1995. *Ambivalent Journey: U.S. Migration and Economic Mobility in North-Central Mexico*. Tucson: University of Arizona Press.

———. 2003. "The Segregation of Ancestry Groups in San Antonio." *Social Science Journal* 40: 213–32.

Kandel, William, and Douglas S. Massey. 2002. "The Culture of Mexican Migration: A Theoretical and Empirical Analysis." *Social Forces* 80(3): 981–1004.

Levitt, Peggy, and Mary C. Waters, eds. 2002. *The Changing Face of Home: The Transnational Lives of the Second Generation*. New York: Russell Sage Foundation.

Levitt, Peggy, and Nina Glick Schiller. 2004. "Conceptualizing Simultaneity: A Transnational Social Field Perspective on Society." *International Migration Review* 38(3): 1002–39.

Lorey, David E. 1999. *The U.S.-Mexican Border in the Twentieth Century*. Wilmington, DE: SR Books.

Macedo, Donaldo. 1997. "English Only: The Tongue-tying of America." In *Latinos and Education*, ed. Antonia Darder, Rodolfo D. Torres, and Henry Gutierrez, 269–78. New York: Routledge.

Maciel, David R., and Maria Herrera-Sobek. 1998. *Culture across Borders*. Tucson: University of Arizona Press.

Montejano, David. 1987. *Anglos and Mexicans in the Making of Texas, 1836–1986*. Austin: University of Texas Press.

Mooney, Margarita. 2003. "Migrants' Social Ties in the U.S. and Investment in Mexico." *Social Forces* 81(3): 1147–70.

Mora-Torres, Juan. 2001. *The Making of the Mexican Border: The State, Capitalism, and Society in Nuevo León, 1848–1910*. Austin: University of Texas Press.

Richardson, Chad. 1999. *Batos, Bolillos, Pochos, and Pelados: Class and Culture on the South Texas Border*. Austin: University of Texas Press.

Rosales, Rodolfo. 2000. *The Illusion of Inclusion: The Untold Political Story of San Antonio*. Austin: University of Texas Press.

Ross Sorkin, Andrew. 2006. "Univision Considers Going on the Block." *New York Times*, Business, February 8, C1.

Rouse, Roger. 1992. "Making Sense of Settlement: Class Transformation, Cultural Struggle, and Transnationalism among Mexican Migrants in the United States." In *Towards a Transnational Perspective on Migration: Race, Class, Ethnicity, and Nationalism Reconsidered,* ed. Nina Glick Schiller, Linda Basch, and Cristina Blanc-Szanton, 25–52. New York: New York Academy of Sciences.

Shain, Yossi. 2000. "The Mexican-American Diaspora's Impact on Mexico." *Social Science Quarterly* 114(4): 661–91.

U.S. Census Bureau. Census 2000. Table DP-1. Profile of General Demographic Characteristics: 2000. Geographic area: San Antonio City, Texas.

Vila, Pablo. 2000. *Crossing Borders, Reinforcing Borders: Social Categories, Metaphors, and Narrative Identities on the U.S.-Mexico Frontier.* Austin: University of Texas Press.

Waldinger, Roger, and David Fitzgerald. 2004. "Transnationalism in Question." *American Journal of Sociology* 109(5): 1177–95.

Weber, Debra. 1999. "Historical Perspectives on Mexican Transnationalism: With Notes from Angumacutiro." *Social Justice* 26(3): 39–58.

CHAPTER FOUR

The Complex Picture of Cities near the U.S.-Mexico Border

The Case of Southern California

Belinda I. Reyes and Amanda G. Bailey

The intent of this chapter is to examine the conditions of the Southern California cities in which immigrants are living. We look at cities because people's chances for success are dependent not only on their characteristics but also on the opportunities available in the communities in which they reside. Evidence provided in this chapter suggests that strong links with Mexico exist in cities within one hundred miles of the border and that the foreign-born are an important and growing part of the population in many of these cities. In California, the region over fifty miles from the U.S.-Mexico border is one of the fastest growing in the state, and in many cities the foreign-born population are leading this growth. Data throughout the chapter indicate that those cities nearest the border are, for the most part, stagnating. The analysis presented here underscores the complexity faced by these communities in terms of poverty and prosperity, growth and stagnation; yet, it is a situation in which the border and the foreign-born play a critical role in the growth and diversification that the region is experiencing.

The California-Mexico border is one of the most transited and populated regions in the entire two-thousand-mile boundary.[1] We look at cities one hundred miles from the border and differentiate between cities in the border counties of San Diego and Imperial and those in the extended border counties of Riverside and Orange. We look at the extended border as a comparison to cities along the California-Mexico line. But they are also affected by the flow of people to and from the border. For instance, many residents of Southern California go to Mexico for medical care. In Riverside County, over sixty miles from the border, 6% of Latinos bought medicines across the border and 5% sought dental care there (California Health Interview Survey 2005).

The chapter begins by examining the cities in Southern California and then focusing on the characteristics of the population: the foreign-born population, household structure, age distribution, and ethnic makeup. Next we look at growth and development in these cities, with a concentration on housing, population, and economic growth. The final section explores critical policy issues facing the region.

Cities in Southern California

We look at the incorporated cities with at least 10,000 residents in Riverside, Orange, San Diego, and Imperial counties.[2] These four counties have a land area larger than Rhode Island, with five times the population. There were 7.4 million residents in the region, with 5.4 million in the cities under analysis.[3] This large population tends to be concentrated in a few clusters, since the Mojave Desert occupies a significant part of the region. In Imperial County and in most of Riverside County there are less than five inches of rain per year, and about half of the San Diego-Mexico border is in the mountains. For this reason, most of the border population is near the San Diego coast, and most of the extended border population resides at the coast and in the mountains near Los Angeles.

Figure 4.1 shows the location of the fifty-seven cities under study and the concentration of the population in the region.[4] One of the most populated counties of Southern California is Orange County. There were twenty-five cities that met our restriction in Orange County; eight of them had more than 100,000 people, and the population density was about twice that of the state median in four of every five cities in the county.[5] The other large population center is the San Diego metro area. Cities such as Oceanside, Chula Vista, San Diego, and Escondido each have over 100,000 people, with a density of over 3,500 people per square mile. On the other hand, Imperial and Riverside counties are underpopulated. Imperial County only had three cities incorporated that met our conditions, and two-thirds of the cities in Riverside had less than 1,500 people per square mile.

Demographics of Cities on the Southern California Border

In this section, we examine the characteristics of the population in border cities. We address the proportion of foreign-born residents, the ethnic makeup of their population, and the structure of their households. This should give us an idea of the characteristics of the families living in Southern California. Later, we will look at their economic conditions. What is clear from this section is that the foreign-born residents, many of whom are Latinos, are a large and growing part of the population of these cities. New immigrant destinations are emerging with large numbers of families and children.

Foreign-Born Population

In spite of being near the border, few residents in Southern California in 1980 were born abroad. In San Diego, the largest urban center less than fifteen miles from the border, only 15% of the residents were born abroad in that year. In the extended border region, only a few cities ranked above the state median of 11% foreign-born. Immigrants were a significant share of the population only in Imperial County.

However, there was tremendous growth in the foreign-born population since 1980. Some 500,000 immigrants lived in Southern California in 1980, and by 2000 the number approached 1.5 million. At the

Figure 4.1.   Location and Population of Incorporated Cities in Southern California

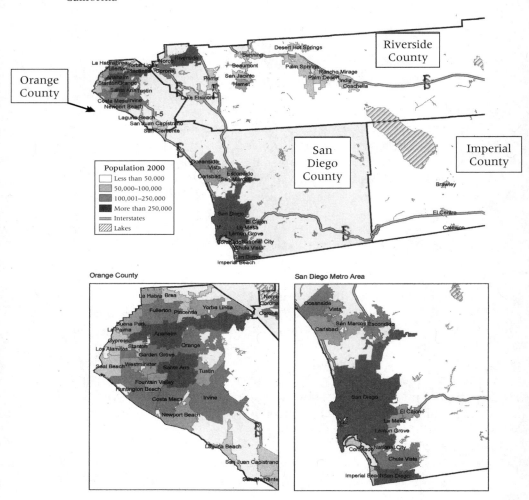

extended border, the foreign-born population increased more than at the border. They grew by 270% in the median city in Riverside County (see Table 4.1), but in cities such as Perris, Corona, Lake Elsinore, and Palm Desert, the growth was over 400%.[6] In eleven of the twenty-five cities in Orange County, the foreign-born population tripled in size from 1980 to 2000. By 2000, Santa Ana was 53% foreign-born, and Garden Grove, Westminster, and Stanton were over 40% foreign-born.

At the border, Imperial County cities had some of the highest shares of immigrants in the state. At least one in four Imperial County urban residents was born abroad in 2000, and in Calexico one-half of the population was born abroad. Growth was also significant in San Diego, where the numbers of foreign-born rose from 15% to 26%, and there was considerable immigrant growth south of the city of San Diego and north around Highway 215 (see Figure 4.1).

Many of these cities are also becoming new immigrant destinations. Recent immigrants are increasingly choosing Southern California over more established immigrant destinations in Los Angeles.[7] In 1980, 20% of recent immigrants headed for Los Angeles County and 19% for Southern California. While the share of recent immigrants going to Los Angeles declined to 18% in 2000, it increased in Southern California to 25%.

Since few of the cities in Southern California had high proportions of immigrants in 1980, the growth in the foreign-born population is creating challenges and opportunities at new destinations. In order to capture these patterns, we divided cities in Southern California among Traditional Destinations, New Immigrant Destinations, and Low/Stable Immigrant cities.[8] There were only seven Traditional Destinations, the largest of which was Santa Ana, at the extended border in Orange County. In 2000, Santa Ana had 340,000 residents, 53% of whom had been born abroad, and 42% of them were recent arrivals. The largest category was New Immigrant Destinations, which numbered thirty, and they were primarily located at the extended border or around the city of San Diego. There was only one New Immigrant Destination, Chula Vista, within five miles of the border. The remaining cities in the region (twenty of the fifty-seven) are Low/Stable Immigrant cities, and they were either high-income communities along the Southern California coast or stagnant communities in the deserts.

Table 4.1. Foreign-Born Population in Southern California Cities by Their Respective County

	Border Cities		Extended Border	
	Imperial	*San Diego*	*Orange*	*Riverside*
Number of Cities	3	13	25	16
Total Population All Cities 2000	86,996	2,194,513	2,328,416	784,731
Total Foreign-Born All Cities	32,828	533,847	756,386	159,957
% Foreign-Born City (Median)				
1980	20	11	11	11
2000	34	21	27	18
Median Immigrant Growth 1980–2000	104%	175%	190%	273%
Total Recent Immigrants[a]	10,585	194,352	303,197	51,475
Median Growth Recent Immigrants	59%	129%	138%	269%
Immigrant Categories				
Traditional Destinations	3 cities	1 city	1 city	2 cities
New Destinations	0	7 cities	15 cities	8 cities
Stable/Low Immigrant Cities	0	5 cities	9 cities	6 cities

Source: Author's calculations from 1980 and 2000 data from the U.S. Census Bureau.
Note: To generate the median, all the cities in each county are combined, thus generating the median growth among the cities in that county.
[a] New immigrants are immigrants who arrived in the last ten years.

Table 4.2.   Ethnic Distribution in Southern California Cities by Their Respective County

	Border Cities				Extended Border			
	Imperial		*San Diego*		*Orange*		*Riverside*	
Number of Cities	*3*		*13*		*25*		*16*	
Ethnic Distribution	1980	2000	1980	2000	1980	2000	1980	2000
% White	38	18	78	52	82	57	73	52
% Hispanic	58	75	15	30	12	22	18	37
% African American	2.7	2.1	1.8	5	1	1.4	1.6	4.3
% Asian and Native American	1.5	1.9	3.2	5.2	4.6	11	1.5	2.6

Source: Author's calculations from 1980 and 2000 data from the U.S. Census Bureau.
Note: To generate the numbers in this table, cities in each county were aggregated.

Ethnic Distribution

Large immigration combined with natural increase (births minus deaths) led to an ethnic transformation in Southern California, as it did in the rest of the state. On average in 1980, 69% of California's urban population was white non-Hispanic, 21% Latino, and 4.8% Asian and Native American.[9] By 2000, white non-Hispanics were 48%, Latinos were one-third, and Asians and Native Americans were 11% of the state's urban population.

Ethnic diversity varies throughout Southern California (see Table 4.2). Although the proportion of white non-Hispanics has been declining throughout the region, the median city in Orange, Riverside, and San Diego counties was still over 50% white in 2000. But many cities in the region are no longer majority white. There was increasing diversity in the cities nearest to the border and in New Immigrant Destinations. For example, whites were less than 40% of the population in Anaheim, Westminster, La Palma, and Buena Park in Orange County; in Coachella, Indio, and Perris in Riverside; and in National City and Chula Vista in San Diego.

Table 4.3.   Households and Children in Southern California Cities by Their Respective County

	Border Cities		Extended Border	
	Imperial	San Diego	Orange	Riverside
Number of Cities	3	13	25	16
Household Characteristics				
Household Size (median)	3.3	2.8	3	2.9
% of Household That Are				
Families	79	70	74	71
% Married Couples				
1980	82	83	83	82
2000	70	74	78	74
% Female-Headed				
Households				
1980	11	7	6	6
2000	14	11	8	12
Age Distribution				
Age < 16				
1980	31	22	24	25
2000	31	25	23	29
Age > 65				
1980	8	13	8	19
2000	10	11	10	10

Source: Author's calculations from 1980 and 2000 data from the U.S. Census Bureau.
Note: To generate the numbers in this table, cities in each county were aggregated.

The share of Hispanics grew throughout the region to become the majority in cities along the border in Imperial County. The median city in Imperial County was 75% Latino in 2000, and in Calexico the population was 95% Latino. Even at the extended border a number of cities were majority Latino, especially at New Immigrant Destinations. For example, Coachella in Riverside County was 97% Hispanic, Santa Ana in Orange County was 76% Hispanic, and National City in San Diego County was 59% Hispanic.

Households of Families and Children

The cities nearest to the California-Mexico border had more people per household, more households composed of families (as opposed to single individuals or roommates), and more children than other cities in California (see Table 4.3). The growth in the foreign-born population has resulted in an increase in the number of families and children in the region. In the extended border, the cities with a high proportion of immigrants and New Immigrant Destinations are those with large numbers of families and children. In Buena Park, Santa Ana, and Garden Grove, over 78% of households were families and over 26% of the residents were children. Many of these households likely were attracted to the region by housing and/or employment opportunities. This is explored in the next section.

Growth and Development in Southern California

Southern California is one of the fastest-growing regions in the state. Housing, population, and employment have been rising dramatically in the last twenty years, and new urban centers are being created with large proportions of foreign-born residents. However, most of this growth is taking place at the extended border.

Housing and Population

The urban population in Southern California cities increased by almost two million people between 1980 and 2000. Foreign-born residents accounted for 44% of the growth at the border and 60% at the extended border. Cities in Riverside County experienced some of the most dramatic population and immigrant growth in the region (see Figure 4.2). Orange County did not undergo a large population growth, but it did have a significant immigrant growth—78% of the growth in Orange County was in foreign-born residents, which could imply that while white non-Hispanics left the region, they were being replaced by the foreign-born.

An important factor behind this growth is that more than 500,000 new homes were built in the urban areas under study. This number is more than the total units in ten states, including Delaware, Rhode Island, and Montana. Most of the construction took place in the extended border and north of the city of San Diego. In Riverside County there were 80% more homes in its cities in 2000 than in 1980. In nine cities, among them Perris, Corona, and San Jacinto, the housing stock doubled since 1980. Although in the extended border there was limited housing development in Orange County, 69% of the homes in that county's incorporated cities were built before 1980, compared to 56% of the units in Riverside County. The smaller increase in housing stock in Orange County decreased vacancy rates and raised high-density rates. In studying residential overcrowding in Southern California, Myers and Lee found that Hispanics are more likely than other groups (Asians and non-Hispanic whites) to experience overcrowding, especially in major urban areas such as Orange County (Myers and Lee 1996). Among border counties, San Diego had some expanding cities,

Figure 4.2. Median Growth in the Cities' Population, Foreign-Born Residents, and Number of Housing Units by County, 1980–2000

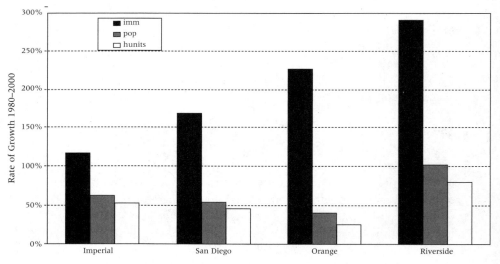

Source: Author's calculations from 1980 to 2000 data from the U.S. Census Bureau.
Note: These figures were generated by calculating the growth in each city and determining the median level of growth for all the cities in a particular county.

but they were concentrated north of the city of San Diego, more than forty miles from the border. As mentioned above, the only border city to experience significant growth was Chula Vista.

This housing development is mostly taking place in New Immigrant Destinations. About 80% of the new construction in Southern California took place at what became New Immigrant Destinations. Some 60% of New Immigrant Destinations were growing above the average (eighteen of the thirty cities), while only eight of the twenty Low/Stable Immigrant cities had significant housing development. But many of the fast-growing Low/Stable Immigrant cities may become the New Immigrant Destinations of the future, since they are also undergoing significant immigrant growth, even if they still had a small percentage of immigrants as compared to the rest of the state. So the dramatic growth taking place in Southern California is being fueled by the foreign-born population.

Families may be choosing these cities because they are escaping crime and violence in urban centers and are looking for better schools, more affordable places to live, or opportunities for homeownership. Housing prices in California were among the highest in the nation, just behind Hawaii (U.S. Census Bureau 2000). If we look at cities incorporated prior to 1980, the median house value in California was $198,000, while the median for the nation was $119,600.[10] In Los Angeles County the median house cost $203,000. In Southern California, housing values were lower than in Los Angeles, especially in the counties away from the coast—Riverside and Imperial—and the cities nearest the border (see Figure 4.3). Myers and Lee (1999) explain that purchasing a house is a goal for many immigrants who are renters, and these lower prices enable Latinos and immigrants to become homeowners. Myers and Lee, for example, also find that Latino home purchases began at a lower rate than that of other race and ethnic groups but have been increasing since the 1980s in Southern California. Even if families cannot afford to buy a house, rents were also lower on average in Southern California ($791 per month) than in Los Angeles County ($817 per month), but especially away from the coast and near the U.S.-Mexico border. Almost all cities in Imperial and Riverside counties, except for Norco and Corona, had a median rent below the state median of $764 per month.

Figure 4.3.   Average Median Home Value and Rental Prices for All Cities in
Each County, 2000

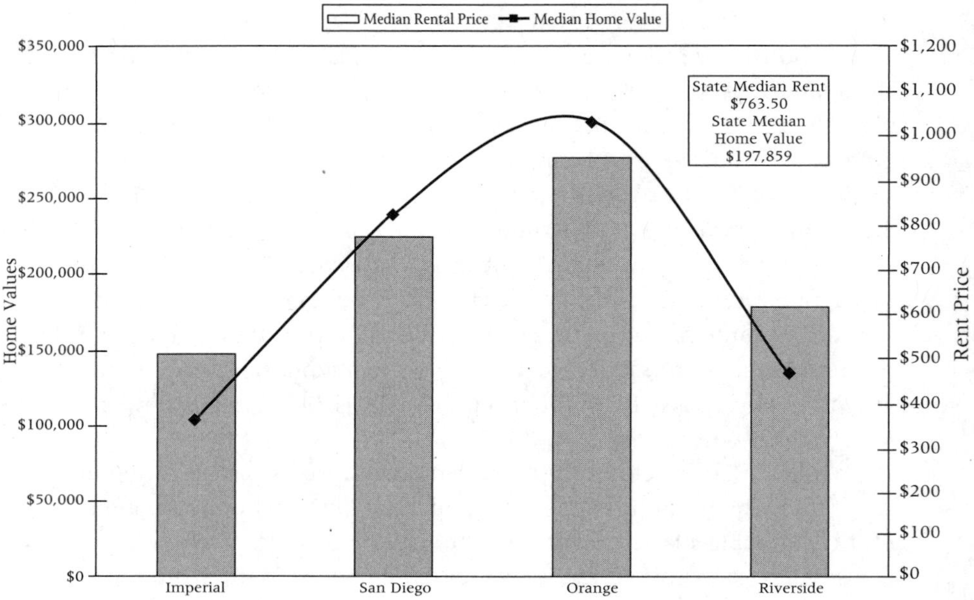

Source: Author's calculations from 2000 data from the U.S. Census Bureau.
Note: These figures were generated by calculating the median home and rental value in each
city, aggregating cities within each county, and estimating the average of the median prices for
all the cities in a county.

Employment and Occupational Distribution

Housing development and low prices may be attracting many families
to the region, but, in addition, Southern California has experienced
substantial employment growth. (See Figure 4.4.) Even when employment declined in almost 40% of California cities during the 1990s, employment increased in two-thirds of Southern California cities. Employment growth was especially high in Riverside County, where it
was three times the state median. However, in Orange County there
was limited employment growth in seventeen of its twenty-five incorporated cities, and employment declined in the 1990s, especially in La

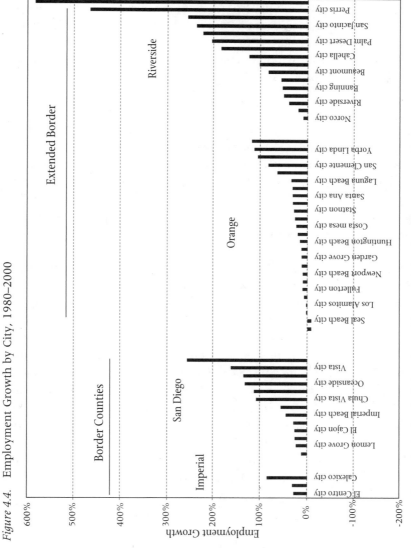

Figure 4.4. Employment Growth by City, 1980–2000

Source: Author's calculations from 1980 to 2000 data from the U.S. Census Bureau.

Palma and Seal Beach, where a smaller percentage of residents was employed in 2000 than in 1980. Among the border counties, employment growth was significant in cities with considerable housing development north of the city of San Diego and in Chula Vista.

In addition to growth in employment, there were changes in the occupational distribution of workers. The number of professionals more than doubled in cities in Riverside and San Diego counties, while agricultural employment declined in all counties except for Imperial. Figure 4.5 shows the occupational distribution in the average city in each county in 1980 and 2000. As it makes clear, the occupational distribution of these cities improved in the last twenty years. The proportion of professionals increased, as did those in service occupations, but sales, agriculture, and construction declined. By 2000, 37% of workers in cities in Southern California were professionals (27% in Imperial, 39% in San Diego, 37% in Orange, and 30% in Riverside).

A substantial part of this growth is taking place north of the California-Mexico border, in Riverside County and north of the city of San Diego. Border cities, especially those along the Imperial County–Mexico border, although affordable, have experienced limited growth. Still, the foreign-born population has impacted conditions even at the extended border. When we look at the foreign-born population throughout the extended border region and our typology of immigrant cities, most cities in the region are becoming New Immigrant Destinations (Loveless et al. 1996). Over 60% of the cities with employment growth above the state median were New Immigrant Destinations. They all have experienced occupational improvements in the last twenty years. But construction, although declining in most places, still constitutes an important share of employment in New Immigrant Destinations. This points to the importance of looking at cities beyond the U.S.-Mexico border that are also linked to it with a large immigrant population and increasing economic opportunities.

Challenges Facing Southern California Cities

For children and families, the growth and development described in the prior sections offer great opportunities in Southern California. Not only is home ownership possible because of new housing construction ˙

Figure 4.5. Occupational Distribution for the Average City in Each County, 1980 and 2000

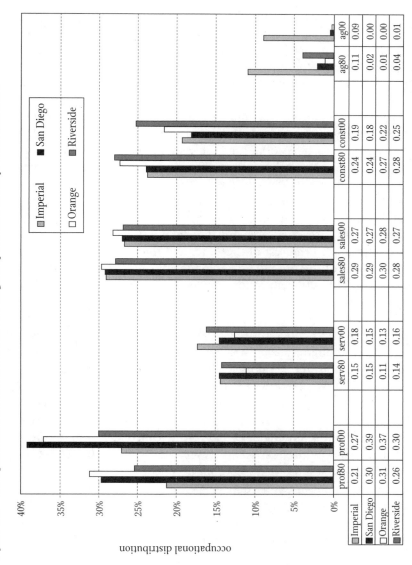

	prof80	prof00	serv80	serv00	sales80	sales00	const80	const00	ag80	ag00
Imperial	0.21	0.27	0.15	0.18	0.29	0.27	0.24	0.19	0.11	0.09
San Diego	0.30	0.39	0.15	0.15	0.29	0.27	0.24	0.18	0.02	0.00
Orange	0.31	0.37	0.11	0.13	0.30	0.28	0.27	0.22	0.01	0.00
Riverside	0.26	0.30	0.14	0.16	0.28	0.27	0.28	0.25	0.04	0.01

Source: Author's calculations from 1980 to 2000 data from the U.S. Census Bureau.

and lower purchase prices, but job opportunities appear to be expanding. However, there are critical challenges facing children and families in Southern California. On the one hand, most of the growth is concentrated in the northern part of San Diego County and within the extended border in Riverside County. Families at the border are still at a significant disadvantage. Notwithstanding the cheaper housing, the proportion of households spending more than 35% of their income in rents has increased, more than doubling in many cities. Commuting patterns have also deteriorated in the region. More people must go outside their city and even county of residence to work, which has lengthened commuting times in the region and increased the need for affordable public transportation. Furthermore, although the occupational distribution appears to be improving and the number of workers is growing in the area, per capita income did not rise as much in Southern California as in the rest of the state, and there was an increase in poverty. Many of the immigrant residents are still trapped in low-end jobs because of limited education, inadequate training, or lack of fluency in English.

A measure used by scholars when looking at affordability is the proportion of the population that spends over 35% of their income in rent. Even though housing was expanding in many cities in Southern California, this number doubled in two-thirds of the cities between 1980 and 2000 (see Figure 4.6). The increase was especially large in Orange and San Diego counties. There was less of an increase in cities in Riverside and Imperial counties, although there was still a large proportion of families spending over 35% of their income in rent in these cities. For example, in Perris and Desert Hot Springs, over 45% of the residents spent more than 35% of their income in rent. Also at the U.S.-Mexico border in Calexico, over 45% of the residents spent more than 35% on rent. This implies that in spite of the development, many families in Southern California spend a significant part of their income on rent, thus reducing the sums available for expenses such as food, schools, and medications.

Furthermore, residents' pursuit of more affordable housing may affect commuting patterns and the need for reliable public transportation in the region. As shown in Table 4.4, commuting time rose in Southern California, but especially in the extended border. In 2000 over one-half of the cities in Riverside County and 64% of the cities in Orange County had a commuting time above the state average because many residents

Figure 4.6. Proportion of Population Spending over 35 Percent of Income on Rent in the Average City by Their Respective County, 1980 and 2000

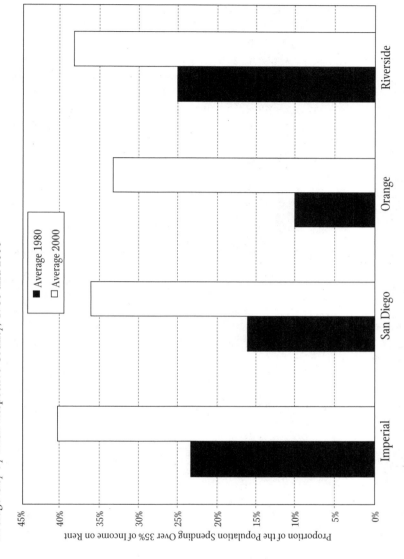

Source: Author's calculations from 1980 to 2000 data from the U.S. Census Bureau.
Note: To generate the numbers in this table, cities in each county were aggregated.

travel outside of their city and even their county of residence to work. In Riverside, Orange, and San Diego counties, over two-thirds of the residents commute beyond their city of residence to their jobs. Within the extended border region, one in five residents go outside their county of residence to work. The longer commutes mean less family time and more child care issues if both parents are employed.

Not only are more people commuting, but it is especially important to note that the proportion of city residents without a car increased in 60% of the cities, and those using public transportation increased in 72% of the cities. In the median city in Imperial County, 14% of house-holds had no car, a statistic typical of retirement communities, as can be seen in Seal Beach in Orange County and Hemet in Riverside. But

Table 4.4. Commuting and Public Transportation in Cities in Southern California

| | Border Cities | | Extended Border | |
| | Imperial | San Diego | Orange | Riverside |
Number of Cities	3	13	25	16
Average Travel Time (minutes)				
1980	15	19	24	20
2000	20	26	27	28
% Cities with High Commute Time	0	46%	64%	57%
Commute Outside the City for Work				
1980	40%	67%	78%	56%
2000	49%	71%	79%	67%
Commute Outside the County for Work				
1980	4%	6%	26%	13%
2000	5%	4%	23%	20%
No Car 2000	14%	8.8%	5.9%	8.8%
Growth Public Transportation	154%	188%	49%	565%
% Cities High Use of Public Transportation	33%	85%	40%	6%

Source: Author's calculations from 1980 and 2000 data from the U.S. Census Bureau.
Note: In the median city in California, the average resident travels 27 minutes to work, and 2.2% of its workers used public transportation to get to work.

this is also the case in many New Immigrant and Traditional Destinations. In Santa Ana, 10% of households did not have a car, and it was over 10% in Stanton and Desert Hot Springs, two New Immigrant Destinations. The share of residents using public transportation doubled in 21% of the cities, which speaks of a need to expand public transportation systems in many New Immigrant and Traditional Destinations.

Many families in these cities are facing serious financial difficulties. In Table 4.5, we see income, poverty, and unemployment rates in cities in Southern California. In Orange County, families appear to be doing better than the median city in the state overall: family incomes, per capita income, poverty, and unemployment were better than in the median California city. Only in Stanton and Santa Ana are unemployment and poverty rates above the state median. On the other hand, families in Imperial County are facing serious disadvantages—some of the highest rates of poverty and unemployment and some of the lowest incomes in the state. The median city in Imperial County was at the bottom quartile of the state income distribution and at the top quartile in terms of family poverty. In San Diego County the two border cities of National City and Imperial Beach had twice the poverty rate as the state median.

If we combine poverty, unemployment, and income, we come up with three categories of cities: those with serious disadvantages, those prospering, and those near the state median. Figure 4.7 shows the distribution of cities by their respective counties. Some 76% of the cities in Orange County are prosperous, and only two, Stanton and Santa Ana, had serious disadvantages. In San Diego County, about half of the cities were at or above the median in terms of economic outcomes, but in six—National City, El Cajon, Imperial Beach, Vista, Escondido, and Lemon Grove—families face significant disadvantages. All of them, except for Escondido, a New Immigrant Destination, were within fifteen miles of the U.S.-Mexico border. Riverside and Imperial counties had even more cities at serious disadvantage than Orange and San Diego counties. In Riverside, the fastest growing county in the region, over 60% of cities had low family incomes, high poverty rates, and high unemployment rates. In Imperial County all the cities were at serious economic disadvantage in 2000.

Part of the problem stems from the fact that although there has been an improvement in the educational level reached by city residents, many individuals still lack a high-school education and many are not

Table 4.5. Income, Poverty, and Unemployment in Southern California Cities by Their Respective County, 1979 and 1999

	Border Cities		Extended Border	
	Imperial	*San Diego*	*Orange*	*Riverside*
Number of Cities	3	13	25	16
Median Income per Capita[a]	$12,881	$18,556	$25,932	$15,820
Median Family Income	$35,514	$50,136	$68,423	$39,889
Growth Family Income	-14%	8.7%	1.5%	7.4%
Distribution of Income				
% Households < $25,000 a year	42%	26%	16%	35%
% Households > $75,000 a year	15%	22%	37%	14%
% Families Poor [b]				
Median City 1979	12.8%	8.4%	4.7%	8.5%
Median City 1999	23%	9%	6%	15%
Cities Top Poverty	3	1	2	9
Median Unemployment[c]				
1979	10.5%	7.3%	4.1%	6.6%
1989	14.8%	6.5%	4.3%	7.5%
1999	14.1%	6.2%	4.8%	8.6%
Cities above Median	3	6	4	12

Source: Author's calculations from 1980 and 2000 data from the U.S. Census Bureau.

Note: To generate the numbers in this table, cities in each county were aggregated.

[a] In 1999 the median California city had a per capita income of $20,084 and a family income of $52,502; the latter grew by 6.7% between 1979 and 1999. Also in 1999, in the median California city, 24.2% of the households made less than $25,000, and 25.5% earned over $75,000.

[b] The median city in California had 8% of its families in poverty, the city at the top quartile had more than 14.7% of its families in poverty, and the cities at the bottom quartile had a family poverty rate below 4% in 1999.

[c] The median unemployment rate in California's incorporated cities was 6% in 1979 and 1989, and 6.3% in 2000.

Figure 4.7. Categories of Cities Based on Poverty, Unemployment, and Income Level

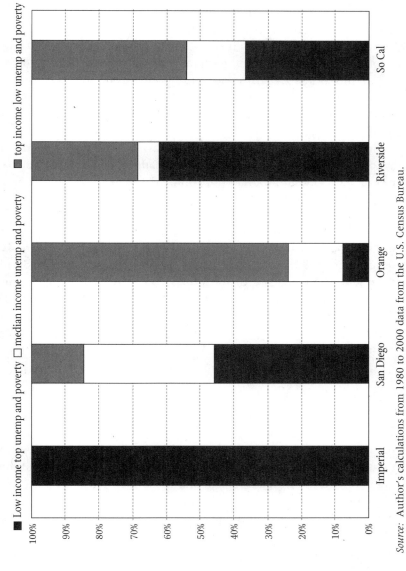

■ Low income top unemp and poverty □ median income unemp and poverty ■ top income low unemp and poverty

Source: Author's calculations from 1980 to 2000 data from the U.S. Census Bureau.

proficient in English. As shown in Figure 4.8, there has been an improvement in the educational attainment of adults throughout the region: a lower percentage of adults have less than a high-school education, and there has been an increase in the percentage of residents with a college education. But in the average city in Imperial County, 45% of adults still lacked a high-school education in 2000. In Calexico, 53% of the adults lacked a high-school education. The case is similar for 29% of the adults in the average city in Riverside County. In two Traditional Destinations of immigrants in Riverside County, Coachella and Indio, 68% and 44% of adults do not have a high-school degree, respectively. In Orange County, 56% of the adults in Santa Ana and 37% of the adults in Stanton had not completed high school, while in San Diego County, high-school dropout rates were especially high in National City.

In addition, language acts as a constraint. In 2000 many residents did not speak English well, especially in Imperial County, where 41% of residents in the average city did not speak English well. All counties experienced an increase in the proportion of residents not fluent in English. In cities such as Calexico, in Imperial County, Santa Ana in Orange, and Coachella in Riverside—three traditional cities of immigrants—over half of the population did not have a high-school degree or did not speak English well in 2000.

Conclusion

Throughout this chapter, we have seen tremendous growth and development in Southern California, especially in New Immigrant Destinations and in cities along the extended border. We have found that there are strong links between Mexico and the United States in this region, even among cities one hundred miles from the border. The critical aspect is that the foreign-born have been an important and growing part of the population in many of these cities. In California the region over fifty miles from the U.S.-Mexico border is one of the fastest growing in the state, and in many cities the foreign-born population are leading this growth. On the other hand, cities nearest the border are for the most part stagnating. What emerges from this analysis is a complex picture of poverty and prosperity, growth and stagnation, that makes simple characterizations difficult.

Figure 4.8. Educational Attainment of Adults and English Proficiency in the Average City by Their Respective County, 1980 and 2000

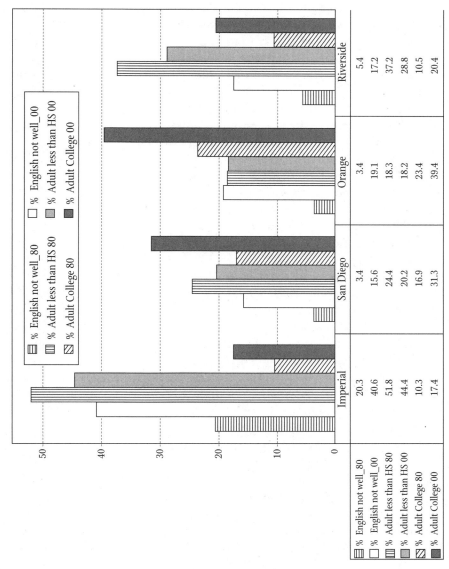

	Imperial	San Diego	Orange	Riverside
▤ % English not well_80	20.3	3.4	3.4	5.4
▢ % English not well_00	40.6	15.6	19.1	17.2
▤ % Adult less than HS 80	51.8	24.4	18.3	37.2
▥ % Adult less than HS 00	44.4	20.2	18.2	28.8
▨ % Adult College 80	10.3	16.9	23.4	10.5
▩ % Adult College 00	17.4	31.3	39.4	20.4

Source: Author's calculations from 1980 and 2000 data from the U.S. Census Bureau.

Although there has been tremendous housing development in the region and many families have been able to purchase a home, many more have to spend a significant part of their income on housing because their incomes are so low. This leaves them with less money for other expenses. The need for more affordable housing will soon be critical in the area, especially in the growing regions in the extended border. Moreover, although employment has been growing, many residents have to go outside their cities and counties to work, which has lengthened commuting time, increased pollution and congestion, and reduced the time that workers spend with their families, thus requiring child care. Furthermore, an increasing number of residents rely on public transportation systems, which are already strained.

Language limitations, low educational attainment, and a shortage of high-paying jobs have led to low incomes and high poverty rates. English classes, living-wage measures, the Earned Income Tax Credit, and improvements in job skills are good routes out of poverty, but many obstacles stand in the way, especially for immigrant families (Loveless et al. 1996; Peralta 2001; Office of Human Relations Citizenship and Immigrant Services Program 2000). Immigrants cannot obtain accreditation, take classes, or access job-training programs without some mastery of the English language. Many of them take multiple jobs, and conflicts between their work schedules and classtime make course attendance difficult. Job-training programs often are not given for immigrants in their native language or in their line of work, or overcrowded classes cannot admit them (Office of Human Relations Citizenship and Immigrant Services Program 2000).

These problems are especially severe at the Southern California–Mexico border. Cities in Imperial County are some of the poorest in the state, and even some of the cities at the San Diego–Mexico border are facing serious disadvantages. In the extended border, expanding opportunities show some promise for families, but in order for progress to be made in the region, programs such as the ones mentioned above need to be implemented. Addressing language limitations for children and adults, providing access to affordable public transportation, engaging the foreign-born in their communities, and improving economic opportunities through training, education, and access to credit could be critical for these families and for the future of these Southern California cities.

Notes

1. Looking at data from the U.S. Customs and Border Protection for January 12, 2006, for example, we find that the wait time for passenger vehicles at the California border was as long as that in Texas, even though the border and the number of entry points was smaller in California than in Texas—110 minutes total on the 54 lanes in the California border compared to 117 minutes and 99 lanes on the Texas border. In Arizona there were only 31 lanes for passenger noncommercial vehicles, and the wait was only about 51 minutes total.

2. We made an effort to look at all cities in these counties, but some data were not available for unincorporated places or for cities with less than 10,000 residents.

3. The remaining 2 million people were living in unincorporated places or in cities incorporated after 1980.

4. Although not shown on the map, these are also the regions where most of the new development has taken place since 1980. There are some new cities south of Lake Elsinore in Riverside down Highway 215, between Newport Beach and La Jolla on the Orange and San Diego coast, around Palm Springs in Riverside, and around Corona in the San Bernardino Mountains.

5. The median city in California in 2000 had 3,100 persons per square mile.

6. In the median California city the foreign-born population grew by 186% between 1980 and 2000.

7. Recent immigrants are defined as immigrants who entered the United States ten years prior to the survey year. In 2000, recent immigrants entered the United States in the 1990s.

8. We created three categories of cities: Traditional Destination, New Immigrant Destination, and Low/Stable Immigrant. In order to generate these categories, we looked at foreign-born residents in the state of California in 1980 and 2000. Traditional Destinations were cities at the top 25% quartile in terms of foreign-born residents in the state of California in 1980. New Immigrant Destinations were cities with above-average immigrant growth, large immigrant share in 2000, and low immigrant share in 1980. Low/stable Immigrant cities were those with low immigrant shares in 1980, 2000, and limited immigrant growth; or, they were cities with some growth but still low immigrant shares. Some Low/Stable Immigrant cities could soon become New Immigrant Destinations.

9. We combined Native Americans and Asians because they were combined in the 1980 Census file. Asians were the overwhelming majority of this group. Native Americans were only about 1% of the state's population.

10. If we include all incorporated cities in California, housing prices were even higher. The Census put the median in California at $211,500.

References

California Health Interview Survey. 2005. Collected by the UCLA Center for Health Policy Research. For additional information see http://www.chis.ucla.edu.

Loveless, Stephen C., Clifford P. McCue, Raymond B. Surette, and Dorothy Norris-Tirrell. 1996. *Immigration and Its Impact on American Cities.* Westport, CT: Praeger Press.

Myers, Dowell, and Seong Woo Lee. 1996. "Immigration Cohorts and Residential Overcrowding in Southern California." *Demography* 33(1): 51–56.

_____. 1999. "Immigrant Trajectories into Homeownership: A Temporal Analysis of Residential Assimilation." *International Migration Review* 32(3): 593–625.

Office of Human Relations Citizenship and Immigrant Services Program. 2000. "Bridging Borders in Silicon Valley: Summit on Immigrant Needs and Contributions." San Jose, CA. December 6.

Peralta, Paul C. 2001. "ATM-only Accounts an Alternative." *Atlanta Journal and Constitution,* Business, 1E. January 2.

U.S. Census Bureau. 1980 and 2000. http://www.census.gov.

———. 2000. "GCT-H9 Financial Housing Characteristics: 2000." Census 2000 Summary File (SF3) Sample Data. http://factfinder.census.gov (last accessed March 19, 2007).

CHAPTER FIVE

Maquiladora or Cross-Border Commute

The Employment of Members of Households in Five Mexican Border Cities

Marie-Laure Coubès

The purpose of this chapter is to analyze the employment patterns of household members in five Mexican border cities. I will focus on the job-family link in a context of urban cross-border interactions, economic integration, and increase in female labor-force participation. Mexico's northern border labor markets are closely integrated to the world economy, especially to the North American economic system, and thus present a high growth rate of employment that is remarkable relative to the rest of Mexico. This study offers new information about three important areas: families, female employment, and border specificity. Households in Mexico are constituted, in most cases, by relatives, which makes the analysis of households of great importance for the study of families (García and Rojas 2002). Likewise, the family-employment link is at the core of our understanding of the kinds and evolutions of female labor-force participation. Thus, it is fundamental to differentiate by family situation in any study of women's labor participation. A border study on household members' labor-force participation allows us to better grasp how the labor supply operates in those dynamic transnational labor markets.

Starting in the 1970s, the labor markets of Mexico's northern border region became important receptors of direct foreign investment (DFI), given the development of the *maquiladora* export industry and the proximity of U.S. cities. Since the middle of the 1990s the North American Free Trade Agreement (NAFTA) provided additional incentives for DFI primarily directed to the *maquiladoras* (CEPAL 2000); however, proximity to the United States also promotes a very dynamic service sector. In addition to the local demand, the border markets respond to the demand of U.S. border cities' residents, especially in regard to tourism, car repair, and personal and health care services.

In the context of these complex labor markets, and in response to diverse cross-border interactions, households develop a host of strategies for inserting their members into the labor market. Depending on their position within the household hierarchy, individuals draw on resources at the border in different ways. To address these issues, this chapter focuses on the following questions: What is the relative importance of each category of kinship in the labor market and in the different employment sectors? And which household members are most often found in typical border jobs?

The empirical analysis is based on the national urban employment survey (Encuesta Nacional de Empleo Urbano, ENEU) from 1998 to 2001.[1] This continuous quarterly survey allows us to observe the evolution of numerous employment indicators in the five largest Mexican border cities: Tijuana, Mexicali, Ciudad Juárez, Nuevo Laredo, and Matamoros. The first section presents the general context of employment in the border cities, followed by a brief discussion of the antecedents to the sociodemographic study of Mexican family employment. The second section discusses the methodology and the empirical results. It also includes a typology of household-member employment patterns in Mexican border cities.

Some Features of the Border Labor Markets

The first feature that distinguishes the border labor markets is the very high level of employment (Browning and Zenteno 1993; Coubès 2003;

Pedrero 1992). Numerous work opportunities, which are a consequence of the border's integration into international markets as well as of its location beside the United States, have generated high rates of urban growth. Throughout their history, the border cities have received important migratory flows. For the past twenty years, these flows have responded to their relatively good economic situation, which contrasts with the high rates of under- and unemployment in the rest of Mexico.

The second characteristic of border labor markets is the particularly high number of women in the industrial labor force required by the *maquila* export industry[2] (Carrillo and Hernández 1985; Fernández-Kelly 1983; Salzinger 2003). During the 1960s and 1970s (its first two decades), this industry was almost exclusively female, a notable exception in Mexico, where the manufacturing labor force was historically predominantly male. However, starting with the Mexican economic crisis of the 1980s, and more notably in the 1990s, and parallel to the introduction of new technology into assembly plants, there were changes in the employment policies of the *maquiladoras,* which have privileged or clearly increased their male labor to the point that the literature now discusses the "defeminization" of the assembly plants (De la O 2002).

The position of women in the labor market has become more vulnerable as a consequence of this evolution, as could be observed during the peso devaluation crisis of December 1994. Indeed, during the two years following the crisis, in 1995 and 1996, its negative effects on the labor market in the border cities were more significant for women than for men. During the postdevaluation period, unemployment increased for both sexes; furthermore, female employment rose in the informal sectors and microbusiness. In addition, there was a reduction in the percentage of female wage workers with social security (Coubès 2003). These results indicate that *maquiladora* demand did not protect women from the effects of the economic crisis. Rather, women appear to have been the classic victims of unemployment and informal employment (Coubès 2003). Today the labor situation of women in the border region is complex. Taking into account their position in the family and in the household will allow us to understand better the diversity of positions that women find in the border labor markets.

Yet the labor markets of the Mexican border cities are far from homogeneous (Browning and Zenteno 1993; Roberts 1993), which is due as much to their location and role within the Mexican economy as to the heterogeneity of their U.S. sister cities. On the one hand, the proximity to a prosperous urban center in the United States, such as San Diego, California, clearly has an impact different from that observed in cities contiguous to U.S. urban areas with high levels of unemployment and/or poverty, such as along the southern Texas border (Peach and Adkisson 2000). In this manner, it is possible to observe a significant differentiation in the labor market as well as in urban growth from east to west along the U.S.-Mexican border.

The recent evolution of employment in the NAFTA context evidences a notable polarization of the border cities. On the one hand, the role of Tijuana and Ciudad Juárez as industrial centers became more prominent; on the other hand, Matamoros and Nuevo Laredo, which were more sensitive to the national economic crisis and were less capable of taking advantage of their border situation and integration into the North American market, languished (Coubès 2003). I analyze the heterogeneity of border employment by studying each city separately.

Changes in the Economic Role of Women

During the last thirty years, Mexican families have undergone profound transformations that have engendered new patterns of organization in the economy of the family (Coubès et al. 2004). The sexual division of labor changed, and the traditional model of a single breadwinner—exclusively the male head of household—lost importance. On one side of the equation, the number of families with two providers (that is, families in which the wife participates in the labor market) has increased (García and Oliveira 1994). On the other side, we have witnessed an increase in the number of households headed by women (García and Rojas 2002).[3]

This evolution can be observed in the uninterrupted growth of female employment during the past thirty years. Numerous studies refer to both supply and demand factors to explain this growth as well as to the impact of short- and long-term factors (Ariza and Oliveira 2003; García and Oliveira 1994; Parrado and Zenteno 2001; Zenteno 1993, 1999). Several supply factors pushed women to enter the labor force in greater numbers. The transformation of Mexican society through increased educational attainment, a decreasing fertility rate, and urbanization had a considerable impact on women's circumstances. More educated and with fewer children, they now have greater expectations. Short-term factors were also important. Mexico experienced recurrent economic crises, beginning in the 1980s. The concurrent fall in real salaries and rising unemployment have pushed households to increase the number of workers. This change had the greatest impact on women from low-income families (Chant 1991; González de la Rocha 1994; Rendón and Salas 1993, 1996). The transformation of the Mexican economy also had a bearing on demand factors. The collapse of agriculture, which was traditionally male-dominated, and the parallel growth of the service sector and export industries resulted in an increased demand for female workers and actual increases in female employment (Ariza and Oliveira 2003; Fussell and Zenteno 1998). See Appendix, Table 5.3, for a breakdown of the economically active population in the five border cities in 2001.

While more women of all ages and family situations have entered the labor market in the last decades, married women within households have accounted for the most significant increases (García and Pacheco 2000; Cerrutti and Zenteno 2000). This alteration in the economic activity of married women cannot be understood without taking into consideration the conditions of life within the household. The new gender relations that define Mexican society have transformed the traditional concept of the woman as housewife (Cassique 2003; García and Oliveira 2003b), and increased labor participation by women has redefined the complex gender relationships within the household as well. Then again, the link between empowerment and labor activity is not always as linear as was initially thought.[4] In an original sociodemographic study of the labor participation of couples, Cerrutti and Zenteno (2000) concluded that a wife's propensity to work, as well as the type of work she will engage in and her relative level of income, depend on the nature and characteristics of her partner's work as much as on her personal and family characteristics.

Although it is true that the number of couples with two incomes increased significantly in Mexico during the last two decades, however, this rise has not been accompanied by a significant change in the relative contribution of women to the total income generated by the couple (Cerrutti and Zenteno 2000). This contribution continues to be well below the income generated by the male heads of household. This can be attributed to the fact that many women work fewer hours than their male counterparts. Indeed, among women over twenty years of age, part-time (under thirty-five hours per week) and marginal (under fifteen hours per week) work is more common than full-time (Rendón 2002). This finding nuances the vision claiming a dramatic increase in the rate of women's labor-force activity, particularly in regard to married women's contributions.

Contributions by Other Household Members

As for the rest of the household members, it has been demonstrated that the deterioration of the family's economic situation on account of the crisis has pushed families to mobilize potential workers (González de la Rocha 1994). In addition to married women, more male and female children and other female relatives have entered the labor force. Older women, who tend to have lower educational levels, have generally taken nonwage, seasonal, or other nonpermanent jobs (Cruz 1996). García and Pacheco (2000) have shown that, during the crisis year of 1995, the rise in labor participation of wives and other adult female relatives occurred not only in lower-income families, as a survival strategy, but also in the middle class, as a strategy to maintain a certain standard of living. All these factors have contributed to the widespread increase in female employment.

Previous studies have demonstrated that the model of a single, exclusively male breadwinner has lost importance; however, heads of household, especially if they are male, continue to be considered responsible for supporting the family. Thus, the other household members, traditionally defined as secondary labor, are expected to contribute only complementarily to the family income; and their primary role is still in the reproductive sphere (if adult women) and in rearing offspring.

In order to study the employment of the members of households in border cities, I specifically differentiate by gender and by type of labor force (principal or secondary). In addition, my analysis takes into account kinship relationships and the sex of the household members. (See Appendix, Table 5.5, for the percentage of workers in the five border cities and their type of employment and kinship.)

Employment of Border Household Members

Methodology

For the purposes of this study, I selected household members who are related by family links. Moreover, I define eight categories as a function of the variable "position in the structure of kinship of the household": male head of household, female head of household, female spouse, male spouse, son, daughter, other male relative, and other female relative (see Appendix, Table 5.3). The latter two categories include a diversity of kin, such as father, mother, father-in-law, mother-in-law, son-in-law, daughter-in-law, cousins, uncles, aunts, and so on, for the reason that, given their small frequencies, it would have been impossible to separate them. Each of these kinship categories will be analyzed as a function of three dimensions of border employment.[5]

The first dimension of analysis looks at the entry into the labor market measured by economic activity rates. The second dimension examines the specificity of the border labor market with two key categories: *maquiladora* employment, and cross-border employment. These two are specific to the border economy because they are the product of the social and economic interactions between the two neighboring countries. *Maquiladoras* are a consequence of macro-level interactions between U.S. capital and the Mexican labor force.[6] Cross-border workers, or commuters—that is, workers who live on the Mexican side and go to jobs "on the other side" in the United States—represent the economic interaction at a microlevel (Alegría 2002; Coubès 2003; Estrella 1994).

The third dimension of analysis allows us to compare Mexican border and non-border labor markets using cross-sectional indicators, such as unemployment, marginal employment, and informal employment. These indicators are generally found in studies of employment in Mexico. Indeed, types of labor in the Mexican labor markets are very heterogeneous; wage labor with legal benefits in large companies coexists with employment traditional to Latin American economies, such as self-employment and domestic and other nonremunerated work (Zenteno 1995). It is necessary to use diverse indicators to account for this heterogeneity. Thus, for the purposes of this study, I have selected two: marginal employment, and informal employment.

The rates of open unemployment do not accurately reflect the problem of insufficient labor absorption that Mexico suffers because in the absence of unemployment benefits, people who do not find an adequate job will "do anything" in order to earn something toward their survival, be it in a poorly paid position, a self-created job, or helping relatives or neighbors. In this context, working for a few hours (which is declared as employment in the ENEU) is generally disguised unemployment. Consequently, we have included the categories of unemployment and employment of less than fifteen hours per week under marginal employment (see Rendón 2002).

The low levels of labor absorption are not the only problem in the Mexican labor markets. It is also necessary to have an indicator for quality of employment. Although the concept of informality has been criticized, it does explain the realistic situation of the job market in Latin America and Mexico given the limitations of the unemployment indicator (Roubaud 1995). Following François Roubaud, I define the informal sector as those businesses that are not fiscally registered. This definition includes businesses that escape legal regulations, which is consistent with the definition of informal employment put forth by state regulations (Castells and Portes 1989).[7]

To analyze the different categories of employment with the variables of the database of the ENEU, I have used those found in Table 5.1.[8] With the quarterly ENEU data, I calculated the 1998–2001 period averages for each employment category. I used all the period data in order to strengthen the results because some categories, such as male spouse or other relative, are small and their distributions have an elevated standard deviation. By calculating the averages of sixteen quarters, I sought to protect the analysis from such variations.

Entry into the Labor Market

In this study, entry is defined as a worker's participation in the labor market measured by the economic activity rate (EAR) of each of the kinship categories. The data analysis shows that the EARs are similar among the five cities of this study—Ciudad Juárez, Tijuana, Matamoros, Nuevo Laredo, and Mexicali—and the case of Ciudad Juárez better exemplifies the three levels of labor market entry by kinship category (see Figure 5.1). Three categories of men, which include the

Table 5.1. Categories and Variables of Analysis, 1998–2001

Category	Variable
Entry into the labor market	Rate of economic activity
Maquiladora employment	Employment in the electrical, electronics, or automotive industries
Cross-Border employment	Persons who reside in Mexico and declare that they work in the United States
Marginal employment	Rate of open unemployment plus persons who work less than 15 hours per week
Informal employment	Employment in a nonregistered business

head of household, spouse, and other relative, indicate very high rates of economic participation, between 80% and 90%. Female heads of household and sons come next, with similar rates and levels between 50% and 60%. Finally, at a lower level of activity, are three female categories: daughter, wife, and other relative.

Rates of economic activity are particularly high for male heads, over 90%. This confirms the conventional wisdom, that the male head of household is the main provider responsible for supporting the household. In contrast, although it is true that female heads of household have the highest rates of economic activity of all female categories, they are well below their male counterparts, and, in all five cities, only a little over one-half of all female-led households are actually economically active.[9] This difference between sexes is explained in part by the age structure of each category. Indeed, economic activity is differentiated by ages, and female heads of household are older than male heads of household. In all five cities, the majority of male heads of household (54%) are between twenty-one and forty years old, but 66.2% of female heads of household are over forty. Furthermore, one-fourth of these women are over sixty years old (in contrast with only 11% of male heads of household), an age at which economic activity has often decreased (see Appendix, Table 5.4).

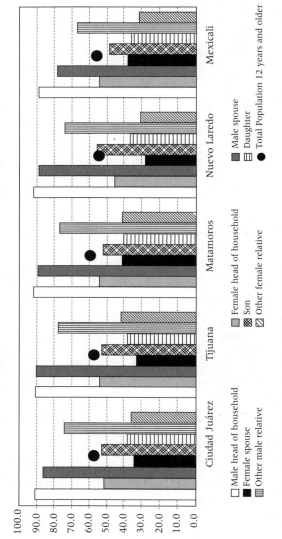

Figure 5.1. Economic Participation Rates by Kinship and City, 1998–2001

Male head of household □ Female head of household ■ Male spouse ▦
Female spouse ■ Son ▨ Daughter ▦
Other male relative ▦ Other female relative ▨ ● Total Population 12 years and older

Ciudad Juárez   Tijuana   Matamoros   Nuevo Laredo   Mexicali

100.0
90.0
80.0
70.0
60.0
50.0
40.0
30.0
20.0
10.0
0.0

Source: Author's estimations based on ENEU, 1998–2001.

These results underline the complexity of the female head of household category because not all these heads provide resources for the household. The literature about female heads distinguishes between declared head (the person who is recognized as such by the members of the household), economic head (the member of the household with the highest income), and labor head (the member who works the longest number of hours) (García and Rojas 2002). These three categories do not always concur in the female heads of households as they do in the case of male heads. Although wives are traditionally the least economically active women, their entry into the labor market is approaching that of other female categories because of the continued increase in their rates of labor participation since the 1980s (Garcia and Pacheco 2000). The clearest examples are in Matamoros, where their rate is upward of 40%, and in Mexicali, where it is higher than the rate of daughters. Nevertheless, although there is an increase in female employment, the substantial difference between sons' and daughters' rates (higher than 10% in every city) demonstrates the persistence of gender role disparity in the family.[10]

Other male relatives present high rates of activity, albeit lower than male head or spouse. This labor participation seems high if we take into account that this category, which has a very diverse composition, includes many young men (35% are between twelve and twenty years old). These young men, whether they be cousins, nephews, or grandchildren living in the homes of relatives, are more likely to be working than studying, or doing both concurrently. Other female relatives, in addition to young women, include older women. Whether they are mothers, mothers-in-law, or cousins, female relatives play an important role in household work and child care, which explains their lower rates of economic activity.

Male spouses have very high rates, only slightly below male heads (see Figure 5.1). This result is interesting because it means that, in the case of men, to be a spouse does not mean avoiding the role of provider of resources. We must remember, however, that this is an exceptional category; most female heads do not have a partner.

Maquiladora *Employment*

The current data demonstrate that activity in the *maquiladora* industry is differentiated by kinship categories and cities. Traditionally, *maquiladoras* offered employment to women and were reluctant to hire men.

Likewise, men only occasionally explored employment in these establishments (Carrillo and Hernández 1985; Salzinger 2003). We still find
this pattern in Matamoros, where the rates of employment in *maquiladoras* clearly portray a pattern of segregation by sex: women in all kinship positions have very high rates, around 35%, while men in all
kinship positions account for much lower rates, around 15% (see Figure 5.2). Browning and Zenteno characterized Matamoros as a city
with *"maquiladora* primacy without economic diversity"* (Browning
and Zenteno 1993: 17). This lack of diversity is associated with a rigid
segregation by sex. Although the masculinity index of *maquiladoras* in
Matamoros has increased, this index is the lowest among all border cities (INEGI 2001; De la O 2002).

Matamoros, however, appears to be the exception within the border
cities. In none of the other cities, where there is greater diversity in employment, do we find such segregation by sex. Rather, what is observed
is a differentiation between the secondary and principal labor force
(see also Figure 5.2). In these cities, *maquiladoras* flourish as an important venue for the secondary labor force of families: other relatives
(male and female), daughters and wives, and, to a lesser degree, sons
have the highest rates of participation. The participation of other male
relatives is particularly noteworthy (second highest rates in Ciudad
Juárez, third in Nuevo Laredo and Mexicali, fourth in Tijuana). In contrast, heads of household, male or female, present the lowest rates of
participation in this industry. Looking for the best income opportunities, heads of household turn to the other sectors of the economy. This
pattern can be observed plainly in Mexicali and Ciudad Juárez.

Also, while previously daughters were the predominate labor force
in the *maquiladoras* (see Carrillo and Hernández 1985), nowadays they
do not rate the highest in any of the cities. Instead, the other female
relative category now indicates the highest rate. Furthermore, we see
in Matamoros that female spouses have higher rates than daughters,
and in Ciudad Juárez other male relatives have higher rates than
daughters.

Cross-Border Employment

Over the course of the years, Tijuana and Mexicali have had a larger
proportion of cross-border employment relative to the other three cities (see Figure 5.3). This is due to their location alongside California,

Figure 5.2. Percentage of Workers Employed in *Maquiladoras* by Kinship and City, 1998–2001

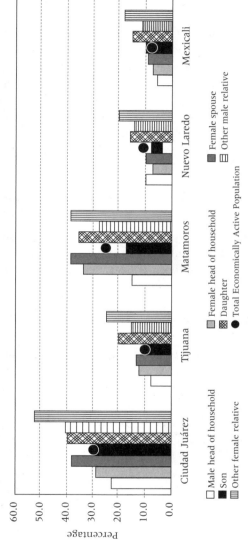

☐ Male head of household   ☐ Female head of household   ■ Female spouse
■ Son   ▨ Daughter   ▥ Other male relative
▤ Other female relative   ● Total Economically Active Population

Source: Author's estimations based on ENEU, 1998–2001.

whose dynamic economy attracts workers from the other side of the border. In contrast, on the eastern side of the border, the poorest counties of Texas do not offer many cross-border employment opportunities (Coubès 2003; Peach and Adkisson 2000).

Although it is true that the daily cross-border worker personifies an aspect of the sociocultural interaction between two populations (Estrella 1994), there is no actual binational labor market. Not every person has the option of cross-border work. In general, Mexicans must have documents to enter the United States legally,[11] speak a minimum of English, and especially have a social network to gain entrance into this market (Alegría 2002). These restrictions do not apply, however, in the same manner to the different members of the household. For example, the other relatives are underrepresented in this type of employment. In fact, it is possible to argue that this kinship category includes many relatives recently arrived in the city who have not yet acquired the skills or the documents to work on the other side. In contrast, we see in Tijuana and Mexicali that cross-border work affects primarily male heads of household. In these cities the number of male heads of household who commute is greater than the number of male heads of household in *maquiladoras*.

In addition, in Tijuana, the participation of female heads of household in cross-border employment is notable, thus indicating that the main strategy of a household provider is to seek higher income on the other side of the border. In Mexicali, the proportion of female heads of household is lower because in this area cross-border employment is essentially agricultural, which is generally male-dominated (Estrella 1994). The high rates of male spouses in this category might be because the male works on the U.S. side and perhaps does not return home every day (but rather every weekend or some other frequency), so the female declares herself head of household when she is interviewed for the ENEU. If this hypothesis is true, it would indicate the presence of a relationship between declared female headship and cross-border activity of the woman's partner that would be of special interest to the conceptualization of cross-border households.[12]

Marginal Employment

One would expect to encounter the highest rates of marginal employment (unemployment and employment under fifteen hours per week)

Figure 5.3. Percentage of Cross-Border Commuters by Kinship and City, 1998–2001

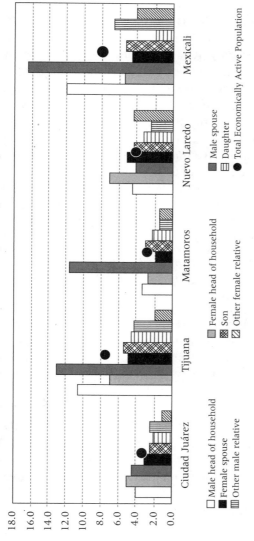

Source: Author's estimations based on ENEU, 1998–2001.

in the categories defined as the secondary labor force. Teresa Rendón (2002) contextualizes this point within a social structure that provides little support for child care. Therefore, the only option available for mothers within the labor market is to work reduced hours.[13] Moreover, we also know that unemployment is more common among women than men (Coubès 2003; Salas and Zepeda 2003).

The rates of marginal employment, which includes unemployment and employment for less than fifteen hours per week, clearly follow a polarization trend in the border economy. To illustrate this point, we can mention that in Ciudad Juárez and Tijuana, marginal employment is particularly low (in all categories below 5%) (see Figure 5.4), and thus neither unemployment nor reduced-hours employment is important in the job market of these two industrial centers. But in the other cities, less capable of taking advantage of their border situation and their possible integration into the North American market, marginal employment is more significant.[14] In Nuevo Laredo, unsurprisingly, female spouses present the highest rates of marginal employment. In Matamoros and Mexicali, however, it is sons and daughters.

Informal Employment

Most enterprises in the informal sector are small-scale ones, but not all of these are informal (or nonregistered).[15] Studies of the urban informal sector in Mexico and Latin America have shown that work in the informal sector may have different dimensions (Dombois 1992; Pries 1992; Tokman 1991; Zenteno 1993). At the one extreme, the person who is self-employed or manages a small informal business earns a higher income than a salaried employee, provided that he or she devotes many hours to work. For this reason, many heads of household opt for this type of employment (García and Oliveira 2003a).[16] At the other extreme, a dependent worker in an informal establishment encounters worse working conditions with generally very low wages and no social protection (Zenteno 1995). Many female spouses fall into this category, most often as an unpaid family worker in the husband's business (Cerrutti and Zenteno 2000). Young people (daughters or sons) can also be found in this category because they work in the family business (the father's), or, due to their lack of job experience, because they are unable to find employment in the formal economy.

Figure 5.4. Percentage of Marginal Employment by Kinship and City, 1998–2001

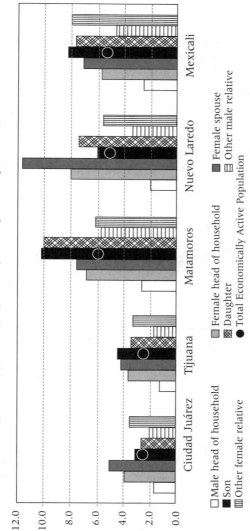

☐ Male head of household   ▨ Female head of household   ■ Female spouse
■ Son   ▩ Daughter   ▤ Other male relative
▤ Other female relative   ● Total Economically Active Population

Source: Author's estimations based on ENEU, 1998–2001.

In the five border cities these patterns, common elsewhere in Mexico, do not fully apply (see Figure 5.5). In the first place, informal employment as a haven for young people is not as strong along the northern border. Sons present rates similar to the sector average (except in Matamoros, where it is higher), but daughters are clearly underrepresented in informal employment. In the five cities, young female rates are well below all other kinship positions. On the one hand, one explanation is that young females have easy access to employment in *maquiladoras*. On the other hand, heads of household have the highest rate of informal employment, but it is interesting to note that women have higher rates than male heads of household in several cities and are highly overrepresented in Nuevo Laredo.

A Household Border Employment Matrix?

Using data on the type of employment for each household member category, the matrix in Table 5.2 shows the type of employment in which each category is significantly overrepresented and underrepresented.[17] The different modes of employment by kinship category describe the patterns of employment organization among the members of households. For each household member, we find at least one category of employment that is relatively overrepresented and another one that is underrepresented. Households, or domestic groups, adapt to the border reality, and their participation in the different sectors of the labor market is highly differentiated depending on the position of each member in the household.

The goal of the heads of household is to earn the highest income possible, and inasmuch as the best strategy at the border is working in the United States, the findings indicate that heads of household are overrepresented in cross-border employment relative to all other kinship categories. Nevertheless, within the heads of family category, this strategy is more male than female, since cross-border employment appears only as a third option for female heads of household. Two types of factors may explain this differentiation by sex. The first factor stems from historical processes. Many current commuters are persons who benefited from the IRCA legalization program, better known as the 1986 Simpson-Rodino law. Having obtained their residency card, many Mexicans decided to reside in Mexican border cities and commute. Now, because the legalization program was meant specifically for

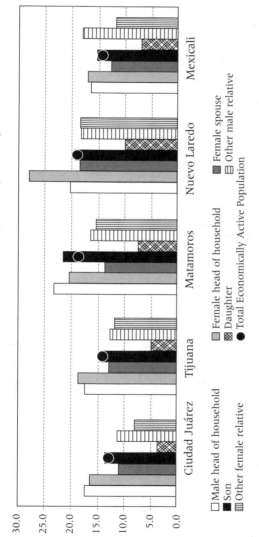

Figure 5.5. Percentage of Workers in Informal Business by Kinship and City, 1998–2001

Ciudad Juárez   Tijuana   Matamoros   Nuevo Laredo   Mexicali

☐ Male head of household   ☐ Female head of household   ■ Female spouse
■ Son   ▨ Daughter   ■ Other male relative
▥ Other female relative   ● Total Economically Active Population

Source: Author's estimations based on ENEU, 1998–2001.

Table 5.2. Type of Employment Matrix for Household Members in Five Border Cities

	Type of Employment	
Household Member	*Overrepresented*	*Underrepresented*
Male head	Cross-Border*	Marginal
	Informal[a]	*Maquiladora*
Female head	Informal	*Maquiladora*[b]
	Marginal	
	Cross-Border*	
Female spouse	Marginal	Cross-Border
	*Maquiladora**	
Son	Marginal	Cross-Border*
Daughter	*Maquiladora*	Informal
	Marginal	
Other male relative	*Maquiladora*	Cross-Border
Other female relative	*Maquiladora*	Cross-Border
	Marginal	

Note: Without (*) apply in more than two cities. With (*) apply in two.
[a] Apply only in Ciudad Juárez.
[b] Apply only in Nuevo Laredo.

agricultural workers—a predominantly male sector—more men than women were included in this program. As a result, this process promoted a concentration of men in the commuter category (Estrella 1994). The second factor that explains this point refers to the specificity of female employment. One may speculate that women seek employment in the United States with less frequency than men do (especially in the case of Tijuana) because the commute to work is longer, and, in these conditions, combining work and family becomes more difficult. Indeed, to add travel hours onto their already full days would additionally stress the daily lives of these very active women.[18] This difficulty can be clearly appreciated when we observe that marginal employment is the second type of overrepresented employment for female heads of household. Effectively, the difficulty of reconciling family life and work explains undeniably why even female heads of household, who by necessity should be breadwinners, work only a few hours per week.

Likewise, the effort to balance family and work might explain why female heads of household are more overrepresented in informal employment. To be self-employed allows these overburdened women to largely determine their own schedules and, up to a point, their place of work. For example, opening a business at home allows them to run the house and care for their children. This strategy is a relatively popular form of alternative female employment (López 2002), which does not exist in the formal sector, where work schedules are seldom negotiable. If we add the fact that self-employment, even if it is informal, offers the possibility of higher earnings than wage work (provided, as was mentioned above, that many hours of work are devoted to it), we can understand why female heads of household are overrepresented in this type of employment. For male heads of household, informal employment offers one of several opportunities for higher earnings, although they are overrepresented in this sector only in Ciudad Juárez (see Table 5.2). For their female counterparts the informal sector remains a more usual and viable alternative.

The other kinship categories, which represent the secondary family labor force, differentiate themselves markedly from heads of household with regard to their overrepresentation on types of employment.[19] These categories are overrepresented in two types: marginal and/or *maquiladora* employment (also see Table 5.2). Marginal work corresponds well to the concept of a secondary labor force that contributes only in a limited or sporadic manner to the family income. Female spouses and sons present the highest overrepresentation in this type of employment, which also includes the other categories of secondary work except for other male relatives.

The second type of overrepresented employment for the family labor force shows little resemblance to marginal employment. Jobs in *maquiladoras* are characterized by long workdays and rigid schedules (Fernández-Kelly 1983). The family, especially daughters and other male and female relatives, predominates in the *maquiladora* labor force. The latter (other male and female relatives) are most likely recently arrived migrants with less knowledge of the local market. Many of them are also young. This implies that *maquiladoras* do not block the entry of young workers without job experience or with experience outside manufacturing.[20] This characteristic of *maquiladoras* ties specifically to border labor market dynamics (Coubès 2001; Zenteno 1995). In the same way in which it is attractive to laborers with few other options, employment in *maquiladoras* is rejected by others, who actively try to avoid it. For example, men (except for the other relative category) avoid *maquiladoras*. Among women, heads of household do the same. Previous research on labor trajectories in Tijuana establishes that the strategy of laborers who know the market best, have been residents longer, and have more networks and education is to avoid working in *maquiladoras* (Coubès 2001). Research findings from this study indicate that heads of household too avoid work within the *maquiladora* industry.

Conclusion

The analysis of labor market participation is essential to understanding the reality of the border and, therefore, its specificity. In this chapter, I have examined the supply of labor in five border cities from the position of workers within the household structure. The great axes of differentiation are the classic ones between men and women, and between what has been called the primary and secondary labor forces.

The differentiation by sex is important with regard to entry into the labor market. The rates of labor participation of the different male kinship categories are similar and higher (except for sons), and the female category rates are generally similar and lower (with the female heads higher than the rest). Above all, for each kinship category, the economic activity rate is very different between males and females. This differentiation underlines the persistence of the traditional division of labor by gender in the household despite significant changes in Mexican families. The importance of marginal employment for all categories of women in the five cities discussed in this chapter validates this point.

The second axis of differentiation occurs between the primary and secondary labor forces when one analyzes types of overrepresented employment. It is relevant to note that the two types of employment that are specific to the border function in opposite ways for different members of the household. A given sector attracts and repels different kinship categories. *Maquiladoras* are the sector most overrepresented for the secondary labor force but the most underrepresented for the primary one. The opposite happens for cross-border employment. The way in which families are drawing on resources at the border is twofold: working in *maquiladoras* within the secondary family labor force, and commuting as part of the primary labor force.

Women heads of household, however, are the individuals who least meet these border characteristics. They try to avoid jobs in *maquiladoras*, but they do not take much advantage of cross-border employment. Thus, they are mostly found in the informal sector—a sector that is not really typical of the border—as it commonly functions throughout Mexico. The important differences in employment depending on kinship position confirm the relevance of considering the household as a unit that mediates the labor market as well as filters the demand and regulates the supply of labor (García et al. 1982). However, it is necessary to note that this body of research considers the members of a household as individuals, without introducing types of households. Future research should take into account the different socioeconomic levels of households. For example, according to Estrella (1994), cross-border employment corresponds more to a strategy of upward mobility for families rather than to one of survival of the domestic group, possibly explaining why it occurs more frequently in middle-class households than among the popular classes.

Appendix

Table 5.3.   Sample Size ENEU, 2001, Second Quarter

Kinship Categories	Ciudad Juárez	Tijuana	Matamoros	Nuevo Laredo	Mexicali
Male head of household	1,542	1,642	1,585	1,587	2,251
Female head of household	234	270	248	214	352
Female spouse	47	58	20	32	43
Male spouse	558	539	616	430	841
Son	532	572	537	590	700
Daughter	316	338	354	362	411
Other male relative	229	247	219	225	226
Other female relative	135	142	142	91	119
Total: Economically Active Population	3,593	3,808	3,721	3,531	4,943
Population 12 years old and more	6,496	6,840	6,488	6,626	9,290

Source: ENEU, 2001, second quarter. In each city sample, size is very similar for each quarter.

Table 5.4. Household Members (Percentage) by Kinship and Age Groups

Kinship Categories	Age Groups by Range of Years				
	12–24	*21–40*	*41–60*	*61 and more*	*Total*
Male head of household	1.4	54.0	33.3	11.2	100
Female head of household	1.8	32.0	40.1	26.1	100
Female spouse	3.1	51.2	35.1	10.6	100
Male spouse	3.6	60.4	30.1	5.9	100
Son	61.5	35.7	2.7	0.1	100
Daughter	63.5	33.5	2.9	0.1	100
Other male relative	34.9	52.1	7.7	5.3	100
Other female relative	32.6	40.3	11.5	15.6	100
Total	24.1	47.2	21.1	7.6	100
Sample size (people 12 years old and above)	6,496	6,840	6,488	6,626	9,290

Source: ENEU, 2001, Second Quarter

Table 5.5. Percentage of Workers by Type of Employment and Kinship

Kinship	City	Maquiladora	Cross-Border	Informal	Marginal
Male Head	Juárez	23.6	4.0	17.0	1.7
	Tijuana	7.2	10.6	16.8	1.3
	Matamoros	15.0	3.4	23.1	3.0
	Nuevo Laredo	10.0	4.5	20.3	2.1
	Mexicali	5.8	12.0	16.5	2.8
Female Head	Juárez	28.8	5.0	16.4	3.9
	Tijuana	13.5	7.2	18.1	3.7
	Matamoros	33.2	3.0	20.5	7.1
	Nuevo Laredo	7.1	7.0	28.0	8.0
	Mexicali	7.9	5.6	17.1	5.7
Male Spouse	Juárez	19.8	4.4	21.7	2.1
	Tijuana	5.9	13.1	17.7	1.9
	Matamoros	10.1	11.5	21.9	3.8
	Nuevo Laredo	4.6	4.2	28.7	2.5
	Mexicali	4.7	16.6	20.4	3.9

Table 5.5.   *(cont.)*

Kinship	City	Maquiladora	Cross-Border	Informal	Marginal
Female Spouse	Juárez	39.0	3.0	11.0	4.7
	Tijuana	15.7	5.2	12.8	4.3
	Matamoros	39.3	2.0	13.7	7.6
	Nuevo Laredo	10.2	5.0	18.0	11.4
	Mexicali	9.0	4.7	12.8	7.0
Son	Juárez	31.9	2.5	13.8	3.4
	Tijuana	13.4	5.5	14.3	4.5
	Matamoros	17.2	3.0	21.8	10.3
	Nuevo Laredo	11.5	4.3	19.7	6.2
	Mexicali	10.6	5.6	15.6	8.2
Daughter	Juárez	39.6	2.3	3.9	2.8
	Tijuana	19.5	4.7	5.1	3.4
	Matamoros	35.3	2.2	8.0	10.0
	Nuevo Laredo	15.9	3.3	10.0	7.5
	Mexicali	14.1	2.0	7.1	7.7
Other Male	Juárez	40.6	2.5	11.1	2.1
	Tijuana	14.6	4.4	13.7	1.8
	Matamoros	16.9	1.6	16.4	5.7
	Nuevo Laredo	14.5	2.9	17.8	3.3
	Mexicali	11.4	6.6	17.6	4.8
Other Female	Juárez	52.4	1.3	8.1	3.5
	Tijuana	25.1	2.1	13.1	3.4
	Matamoros	39.3	1.6	15.7	6.2
	Nuevo Laredo	19.5	4.1	17.8	5.7
	Mexicali	17.3	3.0	12.2	8.0
Total EAP (Economically Active Population)	Juárez	31.5	3.3	13.5	2.7
	Tijuana	12.2	7.5	14.4	2.7
	Matamoros	24.3	2.8	18.7	6.0
	Nuevo Laredo	11.3	4.4	19.0	5.0
	Mexicali	8.7	7.8	14.7	5.3

Source: Author's estimations based on ENEU, 1998–2001

Notes

Translated from the Spanish by Patricia Fernández de Castro. I would like to thank Eduardo Gonzalez and Lorena Aceves, research assistants at El Colegio de la Frontera Norte, for their important help in the preparation of the database and figures. I am very grateful for the precise review and accurate comments made by Las Fronterizas, in particular by Raquel Márquez, Catalina Palmer, and Belinda Reyes.

1. To obtain more information about the ENEU survey, see http://www. inegi.gob.mx/est/default.asp?c=4369.

2. *Maquila* is the name of the manufacturing industry that generally operates with foreign capital, assembles its output with parts or components sent from the United States, and directs the finished products to the United States without having to pay import or export taxes.

3. While the wife participates increasingly in the labor market, the male head of household shares only marginally in childrearing and even less actively in housework.

4. For in-depth sociodemographic studies of this issue, see Cassique 2003 and García and Oliveira 2003b. It was initially thought that female employment was a means of empowerment for women. However, the most recent studies suggest that this interpretation was naive and that employment does not, of itself, determine female empowerment. Other factors, such as control over earned income and the importance of the job in which a woman is employed outside the home, are more important.

5. In Mexico the working-age population is defined as the population over twelve years of age. It is this group that is considered when one calculates the Economically Active Population (EAP). In addition, the great majority of households in the border cities are nuclear. For this reason, the most frequent kinship categories among the population over twelve years old are male head and wife, followed by son and daughter. Then follow the categories of female head, other male relative, and other female relative (the latter two represent very similar proportions). The last is that of male spouse, which represents a tiny minority, less than 1% of the members of households. See Table 5.3 in the Appendix.

6. Some *maquiladoras* are funded by Asian or European countries, but the majority rely on U.S. capital (Carrillo and Gomis 2004).

7. A number of authors use microbusinesses as an approximation to the informal sector. The reason for doing so is the lack of indicators regarding the legal registry of such a business or the legal benefits offered to its workers, or in accordance to the point of view of the PREALC Regional Employment Program for Latin America and the Caribbean (1982–1997) OIT Program, which

defines the informal sector in terms of its low productivity and proposes the size of the business as an indicator of this low productivity. However, although it is true that in Mexico small businesses have a higher probability of not being fiscally registered and of not giving their workers legal benefits, some microbusinesses do not have these characteristics. The great variety of questions in the ENEU allows for a more precise definition of the informal sector than the size of the business, thus allowing also for a distinction between informal sector and microbusiness, which is pertinent to the five border cities.

8. I use the data of the ENEU, a quarterly survey of households that INEGI has continuously carried out in border cities since 1988, and between 1998 and 2001 for Mexicali. Note that ENEU breaks down manufacturing employment by categories and subcategories but does not specify whether *maquiladoras* are involved. It is necessary therefore to approximate. Following Browning and Zenteno (1993), I have chosen the categories presented in this table.

9. Except for Nuevo Laredo, where this rate is below 50%. In Tijuana, Matamoros, and Mexicali, female heads are more active and, at present, rate higher than their sons.

10. Some 80% of the economically active offspring are over eighteen years old. Thus, we can say that this category represents young adult offspring.

11. Although not all commuters have legal work permits, in general they have documents to cross the border (Alegría 2002).

12. For the conceptualization of border households, see Ojeda 1995.

13. Intermittent work has also been understood as a "solution" for mothers; the woman works for a few months when she is able to arrange for the care of her children, but when that arrangement breaks down, she must leave the labor market (Cerrutti 2000).

14. By studying a longer period of time, we can see that the rates of marginal employment activity also clearly follow the ups and downs of the economy. A year of crisis, 1995, presents the highest rates, and these decline between 1995 and 1998. The rates are then relatively stable until they pick up slightly in 2001 as a consequence of the deteriorating economic situation in that year (data not shown).

15. Generally, professionals' businesses are registered even when they are very small.

16. García and Oliveira's (2003a) results for Mexico City and Monterrey suggest that male heads of household are overrepresented in the self-employed category, which includes both registered and unregistered businesses.

17. The formula to calculate relative importance is: {Tpi / mTi}, where T = rate, mT = average rate of the members of the household, i = employment category, p = kinship category. Significant overrepresentation was defined as a relative importance equal or greater than 1.3, and significant underrepresentation as a relative importance equal or less than 0.7. The data that were used to build the matrix are available from the author on request.

18. Definitely the female head of household category is heterogeneous: older women with older children do not have such time pressures as do younger women with younger children. This heterogeneity has to be taken into account in further research.

19. Male spouses follow the employment pattern of male heads of household more closely than that of female spouses. However, this category is so small and exceptional that I have not taken it into consideration in this concluding section.

20. The opening of *maquiladoras* to the "external market," as understood in segmentation theory.

References

Alegría, Tito. 2002. "Demand and Supply among Mexican Cross-Border Workers." *Journal of Borderlands Studies* 17(1): 31–56.

Ariza, Marina, and Orlandina de Oliveira. 2003. "Tendencias y contratendencias de la feminización en México." In *La vulnerabilidad del modelo exportador en México,* ed. Fernando Pozos, 143–90. Guadalajara, Jalisco: Centro Universitario de Ciencias Sociales y Humanidades.

Browning, Harley, and René Zenteno. 1993. "The Diverse Nature of the Mexican Northern Border: The Case of Urban Employment." *Frontera Norte* 9(5): 11–31.

Carrillo, Jorge, and Redi Gomis. 2004. *La maquiladora en datos: Resultados de una encuesta sobre aprendizaje y tecnología.* Tijuana: El Colegio de la Frontera Norte (Northern Border Research Center).

Carrillo, Jorge, and Alberto Hernández. 1985. *Mujeres fronterizas en la industria maquiladora.* Tijuana B.C., México: SEP-CEFNOMEX.

Cassique, Irene. 2003. "Trabajo femenino, empoderamiento y bienestar de la familia." In *Nuevas formas de familia: Perspectivas nacionales e internacionales,* 271–99. UNICEF-UDELAR.

Castells, Manuel, and Alejandro Portes. 1989. "World Underneath: The Origins, Dynamic, and Effects of the Informal Economy." In *The Informal Economy: Studies in Advanced and Less Developed Countries,* ed. Alejandro Portes, Manuel Castells, and Lauren A. Benton, 11–37. Baltimore: Johns Hopkins University Press.

CEPAL. 2000. "La inversión extranjera en América Latina y el Caribe." *Informe 1999*. United Nations.

Cerrutti, Marcela. 2000. "Intermittent Employment among Married Women: A Comparative Study of Buenos Aires and Mexico City." *Journal of Comparative Family Studies* 31(1): 19–43.

Cerrutti, Marcela, and René Zenteno. 2000. "Cambios en el papel económico de las mujeres entre las parejas mexicanas." *Estudios Demográficos y Urbanos* 15(1)43: 65–95.

Chant, Sylvia. 1991. *Women and Survival in Mexican Cities: Perspectives on Gender, Labour Markets, and Low-Income Households*. Manchester, Eng.: Manchester University Press.

Coubès, Marie-Laure. 2001. "Trayectorias laborales en Tijuana: ¿Segmentación o continuidad entre sectores de empleos?" *Trabajo* 2(4): 189–220.

———. 2003. "Evolución del empleo fronterizo en los noventas: Efectos del TLCAN y de la devaluación sobre la estructura ocupacional." *Frontera Norte* 30(15): 33–64.

Coubès, Marie-Laure, Maria Eugenia Zavala Cosio, and René Zenteno, eds. 2004. *Cambio demográfico y social en México del siglo XX: Una perspectiva de historias de vida*. México: M.A. Porrua and El Colegio de la Frontera Norte (Northern Border Research Center).

Cruz, Rodolfo. 1996. "Growth, Instability, and Volatility: Female Employment in the Mexican Northern Border Cities." Ph.D. diss., University of Texas at Austin.

De la O, Maria Eugenia. 2002. "Trabajo femenino y dinámica regional: Desfeminización de la industria maquiladora de exportación." *Demos Carta demográfica sobre México* 15: 39–40.

Dombois, Rainer. 1992. "Trayectorias laborales y estructura del mercado de trabajo: El caso de los obreros en la industria Colombiana." In *Ajuste estructural, mercados laborales y TLC*, 33–57. México: COLMEX, Fundación Friedrich Ebert, COLEF.

Estrella, Gabriel. 1994. "Migración internacional y grupos domésticos en la frontera Norte de México." In *Familia y crisis económica*, 86–104. Monterrey, México: MacArthur Foundation and Mexican Population Association (AMEP).

Fernández-Kelly, María Patricia. 1983. *For We Are Sold, I and My People: Women and Industry in Mexico's Frontier*. Albany: State University of New York Press.

Fussell, Elizabeth, and René Zenteno. 1998. "Spatial Differences in Wage and Non-Wage Female Labor Force Participation in Mexico." Center for Demography and Ecology Working Paper Series, no. 97-11. Madison: University of Wisconsin-Madison.

García, Brígida, and Orlandina de Oliveira. 1994. *Trabajo femenino y vida familiar en México*. México: El Colegio de México.

———. 2001. "Cambios socioeconómicos y división del trabajo en las familias mexicanas." *Investigación Económica* 61(236): 137–62.

———. 2003a. "Trabajo e ingresos de los miembros de las familias en el México metropolitano." In *La situación del trabajo en México,* ed. Enrique De la Garza and Carlos Salas, 77–96. México: Plaza y Valdés Editores.

———. 2003b. "Trabajo extradoméstico y relaciones de género: Una nueva mirada." Paper presented at the annual meeting of the Latin American Studies Association (LASA), Dallas, Texas, March 27–29.

García, Brígida, and Edith Pacheco. 2000. "Esposas, hijos e hijas en el mercado de trabajo de la Ciudad de México en 1995." *Estudios Demográficos y Urbanos* 15(1)43: 35–63.

García, Brígida, and Olga Rojas. 2002. "Los hogares latinoamericanos durante la segunda mitad del siglo XX: Una perspectiva sociodemográfica." *Estudios Demográficos y Urbanos* 17(2)50: 363–79.

García, Brígida, Humberto Muñoz, and Orlandina de Oliveira. 1982. *Hogares y trabajadores en la Ciudad de México*. México: Universidad Nacional Autónoma de México (National University of Mexico).

González de la Rocha, Mercedes. 1994. *The Resources of Poverty: Women and Survival in a Mexican City*. Oxford: Blackwell.

INEGI, Instituto Nacional de Estadística, Geografía e Informática. 2000. "Sistema de cuentas nacionales de México: La producción, salarios, empleo y productividad de la industria maquiladora de exportación 1990–1999." México: Instituto Nacional de Estadística, Geografía e Informática.

———. 2001. "Estadísticas de la industria maquiladora de exportación 1995–2000." México: Instituto Nacional de Estadística, Geografía e Informática.

López, Silvia. 2002. "Work, Gender, and Space in a Dynamic Economy: Women's Home-Based Work in Tijuana, Mexico." *Journal of Developing Societies* 18(2–3): 169–95.

Ojeda de la Peña, Norma. 1995. "Familias transfronterizas y trayectorias de migración y trabajo." In *Mujeres migración y maquila en la frontera norte,* ed. Soledad González, Olivia Ruiz, Laura Velasco, and Ofelia Woo, 89–112. México: El Colegio de México.

Parrado, Emilio, and René Zenteno. 2001. "Economic Restructuring, Financial Crisis, and Women's Work in Mexico." *Social Problems* 48(4): 456–77.

Peach, James, and Richard Adkisson. 2000. "NAFTA and Economic Activity along the U.S.-Mexico Border." *Journal of Economic Issues* 34(2): 481–89.

Pedrero, Mercedes. 1992. "The Economically Active Population in the Northern Region of Mexico." In *Demographic Dynamics of the U.S.-Mexico Border,* ed. J. Weeks and R. Ham, 201–17. El Paso, TX: Western Press.

Pries, Ludger. 1992. "Del mercado de trabajo y del sector informal. Hacia una sociología del empleo: Trabajo asalariado y por cuenta propia en la ciudad de Puebla." In *Ajuste estructural, mercados laborales y TLC,* 129–55. México: El Colegio de México, Friedrich Ebert Foundation, El Colegio de la Frontera Norte.

Rendón, Teresa. 2002. "La división por sexo del trabajo en el México contemporáneo." In *Población y sociedad al inicio del siglo XXI,* ed. Brígida García, 319–74. México: El Colegio de México.

Rendón, Teresa, and Carlos Salas. 1993. "El empleo en México en los ochenta: Tendencias y cambios." *Comercio Exterior* 43(8): 717–30.

———. 1996. "Ajuste estructural y empleo: El caso México." *Revista Latino Americana en Estudios del Trabajo* 2(2): 77–103.

Roberts, Bryan. 1993 "Enterprise and Labor Markets: The Border and the Metropolitan Areas." *Frontera Norte* 5(9): 33–65.

Roubaud, François. 1995. *La economía informal en México: De la esfera doméstica a la dinámica macroeconómica.* México: Fondo de Cultura Económica, INEGI, ORSTOM.

Salas, Carlos, and Eduardo Zepeda. 2003. "Empleo y salarios en el México contemporáneo." In *La situación del trabajo en México,* ed. Enrique de la Garza and Carlos Salas, 55–75. México: Plaza y Valdes Editores.

Salzinger, Leslie. 2003. *Genders in Production: Making Workers in Mexico's Global Factories.* Berkeley: University of California Press.

Tokman, Victor, ed. 1991. *El sector informal en América Latina: Dos décadas de análisis.* México: CONACULTA.

Zenteno, René. 1993. "El uso del concepto de informalidad en el estudio de las condiciones del empleo urbano: Un ejercicio para la frontera norte y principales áreas metropolitanas de México." *Frontera Norte* 5(9): 67–95.

———. 1995. "Un marco analítico para el estudio de las condiciones del empleo urbano en la frontera norte de México." *Estudios Demográficos y Urbanos* 10(3)30: 491–522.

———. 1999. "Crisis económica y determinantes de la oferta de trabajo femenino en México: 1994–1995." *Estudios Demográficos y Urbanos* 14(2)41: 353–81.

CHAPTER SIX

Transborder Interactions and Transnational Processes in the Border Community of Laredo, Texas

Raquel R. Márquez

Laredo, Texas, represents one juncture on the extended continuum of the U.S. border with Mexico. The uniqueness and the complexity of the Laredo community, like other border cities, evolve from the meeting of two countries and cultures and the dynamics that result within this shared setting. Borderland residents have in common the region's natural resources, the Spanish language, transnational networks linking families across the boundary, and a rich Mexican cultural heritage.

Today, Laredo has transitioned from a small border town into a large city with high-paced growth. The city's economic basis relies on a winter vegetable-produce industry, ranching and hunting, and a thriving cross-border retail trade. Moreover, the economy is heavily tied to binational, cross-border commerce. As a result, Laredo has experienced a buildup of over twenty industrial parks where major warehouses support the heavy back-and-forth movement of goods between the United States and Mexico (City of Laredo 2005; Smith 2003). The Laredo area now plays a vital role in the flow of northward international supplies and commodities, thus significantly increasing the importance of this border juncture. This chapter addresses two questions about this border community. Are the families who live in the region prospering from this economic growth? And how does living in a cross-border environment impact these families' daily lives?

By identifying transborder interactions, also known as cross-border activities, and transnational processes that occur concurrently, the data in this analysis illustrate how these phenomena work to the benefit of families. The chapter provides a glimpse into the lives of twenty women and their families in Laredo, Texas, and in Nuevo Laredo, Tamaulipas, Mexico. The qualitative analysis is supported through interviews conducted on the U.S. side, but as the chapter indicates, the lives of all of the women extended across the formal divisions imposed by nation-state boundaries.

A Qualitative Approach

The data and findings for this chapter draw from in-depth interviews conducted in Laredo during May 2003. This research project leverages the broader work of Harriett D. Romo on San Antonio as a transnational community found in this volume (see chapter 3). An interview guide was adapted from the San Antonio study to address border dynamics. Overall, both studies seek to better understand the traditions, values, and strengths of Mexican families and their communities in regard to transnational processes.

Interviews were conducted with twenty Mexicanas living in Laredo at the time (see Table 6.1), although almost one-half of the respondents had previously lived or had been raised across the border in Nuevo Laredo. The women interviewed ranged in age from seventeen to eighty-two. Their work experience was varied: homemakers, two retired maids, university students, a restaurant cashier, and professionals. The women with professional careers were teachers, a librarian, a chef, a bank officer, an insurance agent, and a nonprofit organization administrator. Interviews were conducted in the respondent's

Table 6.1. Laredo Border Women Demographics

Pseudo	Age	Marital Status	Kids	Health Education	Occupation	2002 Income	Health Insurance	Health Care Services	Border Crossings
Rowena	82	widow	7	6th	retired	$3,600	no	Laredo	monthly
Felicia	79	widow	10	some college	retired	$6,000	no	Laredo	never
Helena	56	divorced, remarried	4	elementary, vocational	unemployed	0	no	Laredo	occasionally*
Rebeca	46	widow	3	commercial	domestic worker	$8,640	no	San Pedro, MX	2 times annually
Paloma	44	widowed, divorced	2	BA	grant writer	$37,000	yes	Monterrey, MX	weekly
Alicia	41	divorced	1	BA	teacher	$33,500	yes	Laredo, Nuevo Laredo, San Antonio	weekly
Serena	40	married	3	vocational	homemaker	0	yes	Laredo	1-2 times weekly*
Maria	39	single	1	secretarial	domestic worker	$8,640	no	Laredo, prefers San Pedro	2 times annually
Valeria	36	divorced	1	some college	insurance	$40,000	yes	Nuevo Laredo	2 times weekly*
Bettina	34	married	2	Associates	homemaker	$200	yes	Laredo & Nuevo Laredo	several monthly
Esther	34	single	0	BA	chef/caterer	$32,000	yes	Laredo	occasionally
Julia	32	single	0	2 Masters	university librarian	0	yes	Laredo	infrequently
Ronda	31	single	0	BFA	teacher	0	no	Nuevo Laredo	weekly
Carmela	28	married	5	GED	restaurant cashier	$24,000	yes	Nuevo Laredo	monthly
Mercedes	26	married	0	MA	budget officer	$39,000	yes	Laredo	occasionally
Monica	25	married	0	BA	teacher	$15,000	yes	Nuevo Laredo	weekly
Cristina	22	single	0	BA	work-study	$7,000	no	Piedras Negras, MX	regularly
Lorena	22	married	0	In college	student	0	no	Piedras Negras, MX	several monthly
Regina	21	single	0	BA	student orientation	$2,000	no	Laredo & Nuevo Laredo	weekly
Gloria	17	single	0	In college	work-study	$2,000	yes	Nuevo Laredo	daily

* Indicates that these women were regular daily crossers in the recent past.

language of preference—some in English, others in Spanish—while many interviews incorporated both languages. A database was developed using the qualitative software, Atlas Ti, to facilitate the coding and analysis of the interview data.

The Character of Transborder and Transnational Processes

Border towns are frequent destinations for Mexican migrants in search of work and a better quality of life for their families. Migration dynamics along the U.S.-Mexico border have long been the subject of scholarly research, but in the past the dominant theories viewed migration as a linear process in which one community sends and another receives (Bustamante 1973; Bach 1978; Cornelius 1976; Portes and Bach 1985). Today, migration scholars examining transnational processes agree that migration does not necessarily require renouncing allegiance to the sending community, and they acknowledge that individuals who lead transnational lives maintain intricate linkages across both communities (Massey 1987; Massey et al. 1994; Basch et al. 1994; Blanc et al. 1995; Levitt 2001; Levitt and Waters 2002).

In *The Transnational Villagers*, Peggy Levitt argues that a "transnational social field," or space, is created by the continuous interchanges between a person's sending and receiving communities, a space that enables the person to actively function in both places simultaneously (2001). While sociologist Alejandro Portes's research supports the addition of a transnational framework to existing immigration literature, Portes posits that early immigrants did not establish transnational linkages because of difficult communication and limited technology between countries during this time (Portes 1999: 223). Roberts, Frank, and Lozano-Asencio (1999) point out that while transnationalism offers a new way of examining migration linkages between sending and receiving communities, it is proximity that plays a key role for U.S.-Mexico transnational communities.

And while transnational discourse is gaining prominence within a wide range of disciplines, for those of us who have grown up and lived on the U.S.-Mexico border, transnational processes have long been part of our families' histories. As I began writing this paper, I reflected upon my own father's experience as a businessman in the 1960s. My father would travel to the interior of Mexico and purchase merchandise for his store located in Brownsville, Texas, a border town. He sought out goods that specifically met the tastes of his Mexican customers. Portes's point that limited technology and communication restricted transnational processes may apply to non-border immigrants, but many border residents would agree that their life experiences, both now and in the past, reflect daily, routine activities that frequently straddled both sides.

Transborder activities are distinct from transnationalism processes. Transborder transactions do not attempt to explain or analyze migration movements but simply define those transactions occurring specifically at the border that require direct proximity to it (Staudt and Coronado 2002). For example, the twenty women interviewed in this study shopped strategically in both locations and were keenly aware of which side of the border offered the better price for particular items.

Proximity to the border is not necessarily a prerequisite for transnationalism; however, this research indicates that transnationalism was integral to the lives of the women involved in this study. Applying a transnational framework at the exact border between two countries allows one to see more clearly those social, cultural, and family linkages that bridge two nations. The data in this paper demonstrate that transborder and transnational processes are an integral component of the everyday routines of this group of women. In effect, transborder activities and transnational processes actively shaped the lives of the women and their families.

Background to Border Dynamics

The richness and vibrancy of the borderlands stem from their role as a place where people from different countries and cultures meet. Countless daily transborder interactions give the region the appearance that it functions as one entity, yet border dynamics are as complex as they are intertwined and are often embedded with issues of power, race, nation, and class. Linkages between the two sides do exist, and very real bonds are supported through strong family networks, social affairs, and cultural commonalities. People at the border have a deep understanding of the other side's interests, and both sides recognize the acute, involved nature of border relationships (Márquez 1998; Bruhn and Brandon 1997).

An additional element of this complexity is expressed in the wide expanse of the Texas-Mexico border region that begins at the El Paso–Ciudad Juárez juncture and extends 1,254 miles to the most southern U.S. point, Brownsville. Fourteen Texas counties[1] are situated directly on the Texas-Mexico border in an area referred to by the Texas state comptroller as the Fourteen Actual Border Region counties (Strayhorn 2001, 2003a).

The Texas border region serves as a window onto the richness and vibrancy of the Mexican culture and highlights the character and strengths of Mexican families as they deal with crucial social processes that impact their participation in the United States. As illustrated by Vicki Ruiz in *Las Obreras: Chicana Politics of Work and Family,* Mexicanas have become skilled at negotiating community, family, and self and at accessing resources (Ruiz 2000). In this study, these determined processes accentuate the women's creative survival strategies as they negotiate life at the border (Hondagneu-Sotelo 1994).

Nonetheless, the Texas border region offers considerable economic challenges (Márquez 1998; Márquez and Padilla 2004; Robles, chapter 10 in this volume; Sharp 1998). A critical factor exists within the economic imbalance between northern Mexico and the southwestern U.S. border states. Economic resources often favor the Mexican side given the high level of economic activity exhibited there. The growth of the Mexican *maquiladora* industry has significantly contributed to this increased economic activity (Escobar-Lapati and Roberts 1998; Márquez 1998). The structure of the *maquiladora* industry primarily centers on assembly-line work, which requires an abundant and cheap labor force with relatively few skills (Marrujo and Ortiz 1995; Márquez 1998). Today's larger *maquiladoras* are primarily owned by foreign companies and are situated along sister-city points such as Laredo and Nuevo Laredo. Since its inception in 1967, the *maquiladora* industry has lured hundreds of thousands of Mexican workers to their country's northern border (Maril 1989; Ojeda and Morales 1992; Peña 1997).

Conversely, the Texas border economy is sometimes described as an economy that reflects "growth without prosperity" (Sharp 1998). Border Kids Count, a study sponsored by the Annie E. Casey Foundation, further identifies the area as one in which thirty-two border counties exhibit poverty rates higher than the national average (Border Kids Count 2005; Ready 2004). The argument can be made that the border's poverty, in part, is a by-product of a region that has historically been neglected by the social and political policymakers of Mexico and the United States. Cumulative negligence through the lack of state and federal monies directed to an area that has exhibited low levels of per capita income and high unemployment rates contributes significantly to the region's economic quandary (Maril 1989; Márquez 1998). The increased economic growth has not been enough thus far to help the area overcome the cumulative effects of social, political, and economic neglect that contribute to Laredo's persistent high levels of poverty. Moreover, the struggling U.S. border economy relates directly to the availability of a large labor pool with limited education and low-level job skills. The area has historically attracted labor-intensive industries, in particular manufacturers and *maquiladoras* that profit from a low-wage economy (Sharp 1998; Strayhorn 1998).

Table 6.2.   Overview of Border Counties along the Texas-Mexico Border

	Data	Laredo MSA[a]	The 14 Actual Border Region Counties	Texas
Population	2002	Total 193,117 Hispanic 182,296	2.1 million	21.8 million
Birth Rate	2001	29.9	23.7	17.2
Poverty Rate	2000 Census	31.0%	29.1%	14.5%
% of School Children in Poverty	2000 Census	39.0%	35.3%	18.6%
# and % of Children Under Age	2002	30%	16%	14%
19 Who Are Uninsured	Aggregate	21,853	113,430	886,000
Unemployment Rate	2002	7.0%	10.7%	6.3%
% of Population 25 Years and Older without a High-School Diploma	2000 Census	47.0%	43.2%	24.3%
Per Capita Personal Income	2001	$15,114	$16,493	$28,472
Death Rate from Diabetes	2001	75 deaths per 100,000 population	29.2 deaths per 100,000 population	25 deaths per 100,000 population
Infant Mortality Rate	2001	6.1 deaths of infants under 1 year old per 1,000 live births	4.6 deaths of infants under 1 year old per 1,000 live births	6 deaths of infants under 1 year old per 1,000 live births
Female-Headed Families (no husband present) as % of All Households	2000 Census	28.5%	17.0%	12.7%

Source: "Bordering the Future," 1998, Texas Comptroller of Public Accounts.
[a] According to the Texas Department of Health and the U.S. Census 2000, Laredo Metropolitan Statistical Area (MSA) shares the same demographic characteristics with Webb County.

A low-wage economy increases profits for companies, but a low economic base perpetuates a poverty-level per capita income. The Fourteen Actual Border Region counties that averaged a per capita income of $16,493 are recorded among the lowest in the United States (see Table 6.2). This rate compares dismally to the Texas average of $28,472 and to the national U.S. per capita income average of $28,546 (Strayhorn 2003b; Shapleigh 2003). Central to the region's task of improving its low economic base is the need to raise the educational base. The fourteen counties reported that 43.2% of the population over the age of twenty-five did not have a high-school education. The cumulative effects of such crippling educational factors resulted in one in every three school-age children living in poverty, and approximately 113,430 children under the age of nineteen are at risk for lack of health insurance coverage.

A Profile of the Laredo Community

Laredo, one community within the Fourteen Actual Border Region counties, is directly situated on the Texas-Mexico boundary. Originally settled by Spaniards in 1755, Laredo, with a population of nearly 200,000, is today the second fastest-growing city in Texas and one of the fastest-growing communities in the United States. As an early Spanish settlement, Laredo quickly became positioned along a north-south trade corridor between Mexico and the United States (Arreola 2002).

Like all Texas border communities, Laredo's population has a high concentration of Hispanics, 94%, with only 28% being foreign-born (U.S. Census Bureau 2000). Laredo represents the largest of twenty-five existing "continuous" Hispanic communities in the United States, meaning that Hispanics have maintained a majority presence during the city's entire existence. Interestingly, the extremely high Mexican concentration worked to spare Laredo residents from the discriminatory racial segregation that other mixed communities experienced throughout the American Southwest (Arreola 2002). Laredo residents are more likely to encounter segregation based on class differences due to the presence of *colonias* (Márquez 1998), which are small, unincorporated towns outside the city with limited public services and a lack of access to water, electricity, paved roads, and indoor plumbing (Texas

Department of Human Services 1998; Center for Housing and Urban Development, *"Colonias* Program" n.d. and *"Colonias* Program" 2000; Ward 1999).

The major Mexico border city of Nuevo Laredo, Tamaulipas, situated directly across the Rio Grande from Laredo, reports a population of over 500,000, thus increasing this metro area's total population three-fold to 693,000 (Laredo Development Foundation 2002). Laredo and Nuevo Laredo are also interconnected culturally. Historically, Laredo-ans have exhibited a high level of cross-border ties with Nuevo Laredo-ans (Arreola 2002). All twenty women interviewed in this study spoke of strong family ties and family responsibilities that extended across the border and rippled back and forth across the Rio Grande.

Laredo stands out as the largest U.S. inland port of entry. Equally important is its dominance as a port of entry for U.S. export trade with Mexico (Arreola 2002). Vital to the region is Laredo's status as a primary trade route connecting Canada, the United States, and Mexico, with an annual average of 17 million north and southbound vehicles and nearly 9 million north and southbound pedestrians crossing the Laredo border (Laredo Development Foundation 2002). The high traffic relates closely to the implementation of the North American Free Trade Agreement (NAFTA) in 1994. A major objective of NAFTA was to stimulate economic growth between the United States, Mexico, and Canada (NAFTA 1996). A latent effect from this increased activity is the transformation of Laredo from a sleepy border town. On any given day, trailer traffic at Laredo's five international bridges forms a long queue of cargo-laden trucks waiting to pass through Customs.

Laredo's low-level per capita income at $15,114 measures less than the per capita incomes of the other Fourteen Actual Border Region counties, which averaged $16,493. Not surprisingly, 39% of the city's schoolchildren are identified as living in poverty. Laredo's average poverty rate is higher than that of the Fourteen Actual Border Region counties, whose school-age children poverty rate averaged 35.3% (see Table 6.2).

The Border Family and Transborder Activities

The twenty interviewees in this study illustrate a relationship between family ties that extended across the border. The women used these cross-border connections to help make ends meet. Given the Laredo community's low per capita income and its high poverty rate, an important question to ask is, How do families in border communities such as Laredo meet their needs? The following highlights transborder activities used by individuals to negotiate the complexities of life in a poor border town. At times, the need to cross to the other side was tied to family responsibilities—visiting relatives, caring for elderly parents, or attending social events. At other times, work obligations dictated the circumstances. Across the interviews, the women discussed how the actual border crossing impacted their lives, and they also talked about the important role that a transborder setting played in terms of health care. They further explained how they were able to stretch their budgets by strategically making use of cross-border shopping practices.

The women interviewed discussed transborder activities as common, everyday occurrences. That transborder activities were the norm did not necessarily imply that these transactions were easy. For example, Valeria's job commute from Nuevo Laredo into Laredo became so time-consuming, costly, and stressful that she ultimately settled in Laredo. According to Valeria, "It took me three hours every day to come to work, to cross the bridge. I couldn't sit there for two or three hours [while waiting in the cars queue to cross] before I got into work. . . . Well, I noticed that the time I save, the money, the bridge money [toll fees] . . . I had to buy myself lunch. . . . Fourteen dollars, daily, just to come to work." Her everyday routine of negotiating the international bridge added stress to her life. Thus, any additional crossings were to be avoided.

A second pattern of transborder activities emerged in regard to the women's access to social services. For example, the women identified a lack of information to help them access health care in Laredo. They cited not knowing where to find physicians or how to obtain medicines, and they spoke about the difficulties of not having health insurance. The women's concerns aligned closely with the information presented in Table 6.3. In Laredo, two hospitals serve a population of approximately 193,117 persons, not including clients who may come from Nuevo Laredo. Some 59,413 people in Laredo, or close to one in every three persons below the age of sixty-five, lack health insurance. There are only 186 direct-care physicians in Laredo, a ratio of 1,038 patients per physician. Furthermore, a severe shortage of dentists leaves only eighteen in Laredo, a ratio of 10,729 patients for every dentist.[2]

Table 6.3.   Laredo MSA /Webb County Health Statistics

Population	193,117
Total Persons less than 65 without Health Insurance	59,413
Less than 19 Years	21,853
19 to 64 Years	37,560
Tuberculosis	43 cases
Death Rate from Diabetes	75 deaths per 100,000
Total Unduplicated Count of Medicaid Eligible	57,632
Total Direct Care Physicians	186
Ratio of Population per Direct Care Physician	1,038
Ratio of Population per General/Family Practice	5,852
Ratio of Population Females (15–44) per Ob/Gyn	2,871
Total Dentists	18
Ratio of Population per Dentist	10,729
Total Acute Care Hospitals	2

Source: Texas Department of Health, Selected Facts for Webb County, 2000.

As a result of limited health-care providers in Laredo, the high cost of U.S. medical services, and the difficulty in securing medical coverage, adaptive strategies emerged among the women. Nine of the twenty women lacked medical insurance, two were students and obtained their health insurance through school policies, and the remaining nine had bought their own insurance policies. As an international student, Gloria's coverage was mandatory: "I have health insurance because the university requires it. Since I am an international student, I need to have it." However, Gloria was the anomaly within her family: "My parents don't have [insurance] and my grandmother doesn't either."

The group described accessing health care on the American side as cumbersome, but the women commonly consulted doctors on both sides of the border. Paloma explained, "It takes forever here [Laredo], but [I use] mostly my dentist [in Nuevo Laredo], the pediatrician in

Monterrey [150 miles inland into Mexico]." Similarly, Cristina attended to her medical needs when she returned to her small Mexican hometown, one hundred miles from Nuevo Laredo. She told us, "I wait to go home. I call my mom and my grandma. If I get sick . . . just a cold or if it's something that I know what they would give me . . . I do that. I cross [into Nuevo Laredo] maybe if it's pills that I know. . . . No, I usually wait. . . . If I'm that sick, though, my mom would have to drive here [to Laredo] and pick me up and take me over there."

The high cost of medical care on the U.S. side was another concern. Helena, a mother of four, spoke frankly about how she managed without either money or insurance: "If you have an emergency . . . and you don't have money, you're going to the hospital, and you know that they're going to charge you a lot, then you go running for Nuevo Laredo. Because you know that you can be attended to." With five children to support, Carmen's salary as a cashier leaves little money to assist with her mother's medical care. Instead, the more affordable care in Nuevo Laredo became her financial safety net. She explained, "My mom doesn't have insurance so I take her to the clinic over there [Nuevo Laredo]. She was sick a month ago, so I took her over there because it's cheaper." Carmen's statement supports the notion that, without insurance, access to medical care is limited and expensive. For many, the solution lies in crossing to Nuevo Laredo.

Monica was fortunate to have medical insurance policies on both sides of the border. Nevertheless, the cost of care on the U.S. side pushed her to use the Mexican health-care system: "I have two insurances. Under my dad's employment he insured me [in Mexico]. Over there you don't have to pay anything. No co-payment. I'd rather go over there because it's free. Over here [Laredo] it's like $25 per consultation plus I don't know how much for outrageous, expensive drugs. On that side [Nuevo Laredo] you get the drugs free." As a schoolteacher with a low income, Monica took the extra, expensive step of paying for U.S. health insurance. Nonetheless, she recognized that the Mexican health-care system offered her an affordable alternative.

Along with crossing the border for health-care needs, shopping for material goods and food was another pattern. For Alicia, shopping in Nuevo Laredo can be cost-effective despite the hassle of crossing back and forth: "Well, it is a lot less expensive [in Nuevo Laredo] than here [in Laredo]. Yes, the problem is going and coming. Sometimes I do go buy groceries. The fruits and vegetables you can't cross [bring legally into the United States], but I do like the taste over there. Sometimes I go and eat the mangoes over there because you can't cross them so I eat them over there. When I have the time to go to the supermarkets, I'll go there and shop for everything, medicines, whatever I need. It's less expensive."

Esther similarly exhibited preferences for certain Mexican goods. Plus, a trip to Nuevo Laredo gave her the opportunity to eat foods that she particularly likes from Mexico. She stated, "We buy jewelry sometimes. Go out to eat. I buy a few Mexican ingredients for cooking. The vanilla, and the produce over there is really nice. . . . I shop casually, go hang out. Maybe pick up a few gifts here and there at the *mercado* [outdoor market]." And Alicia also felt the same way about the food she bought and ate in Nuevo Laredo: "My *chile bufalo,* and *bolillos,* or breads. The good *bolillos* . . . the cheese. Even though they sell *panela* here [Laredo], I love the taste of the cheese over there [Nuevo Laredo]. Even the garbage [junk food], the *chacharritos,* soda drinks, and the *papitas,* potato chips, have a different taste. I love to go eat tacos; I love to eat *gorditas* that you don't find here. . . . I love it."

Transborder shopping was not restricted to Americans crossing into Mexico. In Valeria's case, her brother, a restaurateur in Nuevo Laredo, preferred to use American ingredients in his restaurant. Her parents crossed daily into Laredo to purchase supplies. She explained, "They help out my brother with stuff for the restaurant. If you want to buy American products in Mexico, it's twice as much. They go to Sam's Club and they go to Sysco's [wholesalers]. . . . Everyday they take merchandise for the restaurant, so my brother can make more money. That's what they do." For Valeria's family, proximity to the border allowed for cross-border purchases that contributed to the profitability of her brother's business.

The Border Family and Transnational Processes

In a contiguous border setting, one frequently looks across from one country's back yard into the neighboring country's front yard. Border dynamics are commonly viewed through this transborder lens, which helps explain the back-and-forth movement. However, a transborder vision sometimes fails to identify underlying transnational connections at a deeper personal level for border residents. Family relationships accentuate those processes that allow border residents to maintain intricate networks in both communities without relinquishing allegiance to either country. The transnational linkages identified in this study often appeared in the women's family relationships but were additionally expressed in terms of identity.

Serena conceptualized family ties as a "transborder family," but she further identified them as a "family that transcends a divisive border." She stated, "My parents still live in Nuevo Laredo as well as one sister, and I have my two brothers who live on the American side. Here in Laredo, they are all within a mile or two. I have a lot of cousins and relatives that live in Laredo as well as in Nuevo Laredo. . . . I had friends from this side, so going back and forth is no big deal. We're one big community. We are just separated by the river. . . . But life was always on both sides." Indeed, the distances are real, but the connections created a firm family unit. According to Serena, "I have family in Monterrey and in Mexico City, and I don't see them as often as I would like to. But maybe on the average of twice a year, they come to Laredo to visit the family. My mother's sister lives in Monterrey, and they come shopping to Laredo. She will come to see her sisters. My aunt in Mexico City has children living here in Laredo, and she comes a lot."

Similarly, distance did not weaken Helena's family ties. On the contrary, her family relationships flowed easily between the border and Monterrey, particularly for holidays. She noted, "My cousins in Monterrey, they can't wait until Thanksgiving. They are always here. For my son's birthday, my cousin from Monterrey was here and we had a *carne asada* [barbeque]. . . . New Year's is when we get together with them, or they come here to celebrate." Serena's and Helena's extended families remain intact despite their diffusion across different places in Mexico and the United States.

In addition to discussing transnational family units, the twenty women described themselves in a very transnational sense. At times they experienced conflicts, and at other times they described the shifting nature of their identity. Their Mexican heritage was central to their identity, of which cultural expressions of pride and loyalties not necessarily tied to birthright were also a part.

Valeria was born in the United States and had previously lived away from the border, yet she considered herself Mexican. When asked if she felt more or less Mexican now, she replied: "I guess my more personal side is Mexican. I like being over there. I like the food and I like the people. I like the houses, but I guess I have to make a living, so I play the part. I mean, I'm here. But, probably, it is very conflicting for me. . . . I don't even know how to answer this question. It's weird. I don't think I can define my ties to Mexico. . . . I mean, not with words. . . . We have, like, double identities. I mean, half of my papers are Mexican, half of the other ones are American. And there's two different addresses and two different everything."

Paloma was born in Mexico, lives in Laredo, and has dual citizenship. She views herself as Mexican but felt fewer personal conflicts than those expressed by Valeria. She stated, "I think I feel more of a Mexican. I stand more for the things that I brought with me. For some reason, they become stronger in you once you are here, even though you have to deal with other ways of being, beliefs, and values. I believe I kept my tradition and culture pretty much." Paloma's weekly crossing into Mexico served to reinforce her Mexican-ness. She vividly described a strong consciousness of her Mexican identity, and how that identity took on a new importance once she no longer lived in her country of origin.

The experiences of Lorena distinguish in her thoughts between her ethnic identity and her birthright status as an American. She explained, "I feel that I am Mexican, but I'm not really from there because I was born in the United States. But then I don't completely belong here [the United States] because I don't speak English. . . . Sometimes I feel that I don't belong nowhere."

Alicia, on the other hand, a longtime resident of Laredo, continued to identify strongly with her Mexican heritage: "I don't feel that I have ties in the United States, to tell you the truth. I take advantage of the things you have here, the opportunities. But I think that my mind and everything is over there [in Mexico]. But I don't know, it has been such a long time [since I lived in Mexico] that I don't know if it's only my memories and how I feel about it, and then growing and feeling completely different from here." Alicia's transnational background is complex in that she identifies herself as a *chilanga* (a Mexico City native) who lives on the border with dual citizenship, and as a Jewish woman who is fluent in Yiddish, Hebrew, Spanish, and English.

Place and Space

Place and space played a role in the women's lives as they negotiated ties between two countries. In Regina's account, transnationalism serves as a way of life for her family. Regina, at twenty-one, has U.S. alien-resident status and lives in Laredo with her grandmother during the week. Every weekend, however, she and her older siblings travel to the family home, an hour and a half away in the interior of Mexico. What makes Regina's family unique is that all of her cousins who migrated internally within Mexico also return home regularly to the same community. She explained, "We go almost every weekend, or every other weekend. We go to relax. All my family has a house there, but we all go during the weekends, and we have good conversations and relax."

Place and space were equally important for Helena, who was born in Laredo and has lived on both sides of the border. She currently resides in Laredo, and Helena's family ties extensively weave back and forth to Nuevo Laredo. Her sense of place acutely reflects her strong ties to both cities: "I love Mexico a lot, but I also love this country, because in this country I have been taught to work more. This is where my children have grown up. . . . No, definitely, if something happens in Laredo, it affects me in some way. And if something happens in Nuevo Laredo, it affects me even more. I don't know what's going to happen to me when I die. Hopefully they are going to throw the ashes into the middle of the river from the bridge, so that half of it goes to one side and the other half stays on this side."

Regina moved to the border region from a small town that offered little in terms of an education and work opportunities. She now lives in Laredo and attends the university there but maintains ties to her hometown. "Economically, we're a lot better than when we go back and if we would have stayed there. So, I have the best of both of them [both places]. I'm not there [Mexico] during the whole week, but I do go back and visit during the weekend." For her, transnationalism kept her from the need to forgo allegiance to either place.

When asked what "home" meant to her, Valeria stated, "I suppose I'm very 'American' in that going home is where I am. It is very individualized in that. The 'Mexican,' I guess, would be where the whole family is. But going home is where I am." Even in distinguishing her own space, Valeria wove family and Mexican identity into her personal sense of home. She also shed light on how border life and transborder activities create a transnational space for other residents. Valeria described how this process works for some of her car insurance clients: "A lot of clients have houses here [Laredo] and over there [Nuevo Laredo]. They have two offices because either they are custom brokers, or are in transportation. And so, I do my work. I'm not supposed to sell American insurance in Mexico, but nobody says anything. I mean, I go over there and see them, maybe at the Mexican office, but it isn't legal for me to do that, yet I do it. It's a different space [here on the border]." Valeria points to a duplicity that sometimes comes with living at the border which further serves to strengthen and maintain the transnational ties of many families.

Transborder Activities and Transnational Processes

The most fundamental transborder activity is the actual border crossing process. Its daily form and extent are endless, but crossing the border often poses major challenges for Laredo residents (Ortiz-Gonzalez 2004). As indicated by the twenty women in this study, long traffic lines and toll fees, for example, are very real obstacles. Yet, crossing into Mexico served important purposes for these women. It is only reasonable to assume that these difficulties will continue to worsen in the current heightened security status of the United States.

Despite new growth and with some wealthy families living in the area, Laredo remains an impoverished border community. For the Laredo poor, the high cost of social services is compounded by a limited availability of health-care providers, inadequate access to doctors and dentists, and the lack of medical insurance and affordable medical care and prescriptions. These are critical factors that affect many border families and the quality of their children's lives. The border has a long history of being a disadvantaged territory (Arreola 2002; Bruhn 1997; Maril 1989; Márquez 1998; Márquez and Padilla 2004), and past research has identified transborder health-care practices as survival mechanisms for those individuals whom the U.S. health-care system fails (Warner 1999; Warner and Reed 1993; Benavides-Vaello and Setzler 1998; Brandon et al. 1997). Other research has pointed out that "crossing into another country to obtain affordable medical services" is a phenomenon that occurs only at the U.S.-Mexico border and nowhere else in the world (Brandon et al. 1997). The data in this study indicate that Laredo women employ transborder activities as a calculated strategy to meet their families' needs. For example, in Laredo, when the cost of medical care was too expensive, or when access to care became cumbersome or nonexistent, the women tapped into Mexico's health-care system. Moreover, as Victor Ortiz-Gonzalez pointed out in his El Paso–Cuidad Juárez research, informal cross-border networks are a sign of resourcefulness and play a vital role in poor border residents being able to make ends meet (Ortiz-Gonzalez 2004). Three-fourths of the Laredo sample crossed on a regular basis into Nuevo Laredo.

Equally important to the women in the Laredo border setting are the transnational processes that support familial linkages. The bonds enabled the women's family ties to extend and remain intact across the boundary. Peggy Levitt (2001) has found similar intensive transnational ties between Dominicans living in Boston and their families in the Dominican Republic. Interestingly, in his El Paso research, Ortiz-Gonzalez (2004) argues that family ties have weakened at this border juncture due in part to the many obstacles faced in crossing. The Laredo sample, in contrast, expressed their continued ties to Mexico in a very transnational sense. Their networks were not solely dependent on crossing to the other side. These women described ties that were intact despite living in two different countries. In the same manner, the transnational space facilitated the creation of a far-reaching social system that can transcend a divisive border (Levitt and Waters 2002). Moreover, in the Laredo setting, the women indicated that their families remained intact within a transnational corridor extending far beyond the contiguous border.

Finally, in this transnational context the twenty Laredo women demonstrated a continual negotiation of identity. A transnational identity "overrides identities grounded in a fixed, bounded location" (Levitt and Waters 2002). The shifting nature of self-identification of women in the Laredo-Nuevo Laredo area was complex, at times empowering and at times conflicted. The women's reality embraced a combination of transborder activities directly linked to living in a contiguous border setting with transnational processes that transcend an unsympathetic border. The high rate of poverty in Laredo suggests that many families are not prospering from the city's increased economic growth. The women in this study, however, are active agents who combine adaptive transborder strategies with transnational processes for the benefit of their families.

Notes

I am most grateful to the women who graciously shared their life stories for this body of research. My deepest gratitude goes to Ana Marie Argilagos and the Annie E. Casey Foundation for their continued support and for their willingness to address border concerns. I also offer my heartfelt thanks to Tamara Casso, who used her contacts to access our respondents, and Crissy Rivas; I was blessed to have such smart, sharp, dependable, motivated, and caring research assistants.

1. The Texas Comptroller of Accounts identifies the Fourteen Texas Actual Border Region counties that share an adjoining boundary with Mexico as Brewster, Cameron, El Paso, Hidalgo, Hudspeth, Jeff Davis, Kinney, Maverick, Presidio, Starr, Terrell, Val Verde, Webb, and Zapata.

2. The alarmingly low number of health-care providers is due in part to the lack of medical training facilities farther south than San Antonio (Strayhorn 1998).

References

Arreola, Daniel D. 2002. *Tejano South Texas: A Mexican American Cultural Province*. Austin: University of Texas Press.

Bach, Robert L. 1978. "Mexican Immigration and the American State." *International Migration Review* 12 (Winter): 536–58.

Basch, Linda G., Nina Glick Schiller, and Cristina Blanc-Szanton. 1994. *Nations Unbound: Transnational Projects, Postcolonial Predicaments. and Deterritorialized Nation-States*. Langhorne, PA: Gordon and Breach.

Benavides-Vaello, Sandra, and Heather Setzler. 1998. "Migrant and Seasonal Farmworkers: Health Care Issues." In *U.S.-Mexico Border Health: Issues for Regional and Migrant Populations*, ed. J. Gerard Power and Theresa Byrd, 224–57. Thousand Oaks, CA: Sage Publications.

Blanc-Szanton, Cristina, Linda G. Basch, and Nina Glick Schiller. 1995. "Transnationalism, Nation-States, and Culture." *Current Anthropology* 36(4): 683–86.

Border Kids Count. 2005. Annie E. Casey Foundation, Baltimore. http://www.aecf.org/kidscount.

Brandon, Jeffrey E., Frank Crespin, Celinda Levy, and Daniel M. Reyna. 1997. "Border Health Care Issues." In *Border Health: Challenges for the United States and Mexico,* ed. John G. Bruhn and Jeffrey E. Brandon, 37–72. New York: Garland.

Bruhn, John G. 1997. "Border Culture." In *Border Health: Challenges for the United States and Mexico,* ed. John G. Bruhn and Jeffrey E. Brandon, 3–12. New York: Garland.

Bruhn, John G., and Jeffrey E. Brandon, eds. 1997. *Border Health: Challenges for the United States and Mexico.* New York: Garland.

Bustamante, Jorge A. 1973. "The Historical Context of Undocumented Mexican Immigration to the United States." *Aztlan* 3: 257–81.

Center for Housing and Urban Development. 2000. "*Colonias* Program: *Colonias* in Texas." Bryan: Texas A&M University.

Center for Housing and Urban Development. n.d. "*Colonias* Program." Bryan: Texas A&M University. Available at http://chud.tamu.edu/ (last accessed October 25, 2002).

City of Laredo. 2005. http://www.cityoflaredo.com.

Cornelius, Wayne. 1976. "Mexican Migration to the United States: The View from Rural Sending Communities." Working Paper, Center for International Studies, M.I.T.

Escobar-Lapati, A., and B. Roberts. 1998. *Migration and Economic Development along the U.S.-Mexico Border.* Austin, TX: Population Research Center.

Hondagneu-Sotelo, Pierrette. 1994. *Gendered Transitions.* Berkeley: University of California Press.

Laredo Development Foundation. 2002. *Location and Population.*

Levitt, Peggy. 2001. *The Transnational Villagers.* Berkeley: University of California Press.

Levitt, Peggy, and Mary C. Waters, eds. 2002. *The Changing Face of Home: The Transnational Lives of the Second Generation.* New York: Russell Sage Foundation.

Maril, Robert Lee. 1989. *Poorest of Americans: The Mexican Americans of the Lower Rio Grande Valley of Texas.* Notre Dame, IN: University of Notre Dame Press.

Márquez, Raquel. 1998. *Migration Processes: Impoverished Women Immigrants along the Texas-Mexico Border.* Ph.D. diss., University of Texas at Austin.

Márquez, Raquel R., and Yolanda C. Padilla. 2004. "Immigration in the Life Histories of Women Living in the United States-Mexico Border Region." *Journal of Social Work Practice with Immigrants and Refugees* 2: 1–2.

Marrujo, Olivia Ruiz, and Laura Velasco Ortiz. 1995. "Mujeres en la frontera norte: Su presencia en la migración y la industria maquiladora." In *Mujeres, migración y maquila en la frontera norte*, ed. Soledad Gonzalez, Olivia Ruiz, Laura Velasco and Ofelia Woo, 13–33. Tijuana, B.C., México: El Colegio de la Frontera Norte.

Massey, Douglas S. 1987. *Return to Aztlán: The Social Process of International Migration from Western Mexico*. Berkeley: University of California Press.

Massey, Douglas S., Luin Goldring, and Jorge Durand. 1994. "Continuities in Transnational Migration: An Analysis of Nineteen Mexican Communities." *American Journal of Sociology* 99(6): 1492–1533.

North American Free Trade Agreement (NAFTA). 1996. Available at http://www-tech.mit.edu/Bulletins/nafta.html.

Ojeda, Raul A. Hinojosa, and Rebecca Morales. 1992. "International Restructuring and Labor Market Interdependence: The Automobile Industry in Mexico and the United States." In *U.S.-Mexico Relations: Labor Market Interdependence*, ed. Jorge A. Bustamante, Clark W. Reynolds, and Raul A. Hinojosa Ojeda, 397–428. Stanford, CA: Stanford University Press.

Ortiz-Gonzalez, Victor. 2004. *El Paso: Local Frontiers at a Global Crossroads*. Minneapolis: University of Minnesota Press.

Peña, Devon G. 1997. *The Terror of the Machine: Technology, Work, Gender, and Ecology on the U.S.-Mexico Border*. Austin: Center for Mexican American Studies Books, University of Texas at Austin.

Portes, Alejandro, and Robert L. Bach. 1985. *Latin Journey: Cuban and Mexican Immigrants in the United States*. Berkeley: University of California Press.

Portes, Alejandro, Luis E. Guarnizo, and Patricia Landolt. 1999. "The Study of Transnationalism: Pitfalls and Promise of an Emergent Research Field." *Ethnic and Racial Studies* 22(2): 217–37.

Ready, Tim. 2004. "Border Counties and Border States." Presentation to the Annie E. Casey Consultative Border Kids Count Session. Baltimore.

Roberts, Bryan R., Reanne Frank, and Fernando Lozano-Asencio. 1999. "Transnational Migrant Communities and Mexican Migration to the United States." *Ethnic and Racial Studies* 22(2): 238–66.

Ruiz, Vicki. 2000. "Claiming Public Space at Work, Church, and Neighborhood." In *Las Obreras: Chicana Politics of Work and Family*, ed. Vicki Ruiz, 13–39. Los Angeles: UCLA Chicano Studies Research Center Publications.

Shapleigh, Senator Eliot. 2003. "Texas Borderlands: Frontier of the Americans." El Paso, TX.

Sharp, John. 1998. "Bordering the Future: Challenge and Opportunity in the Texas Border Region." Austin: Texas Comptroller of Public Accounts.

Smith, Wilbur, and Associates. 2003. "U.S. 83 Texas Corridor Initiative." Available at http://www.fhwa.dot.gov/planning/econdev/us83texas.htm.

Staudt, Kathleen, and Irasema Coronado. 2002. *Fronteras No Mas: Toward Social Justice at the U.S.-Mexico Border*. New York: Palgrave Macmillan.

Strayhorn, Carole Keeton. 1998. "Bordering the Future." Austin: Texas Comptroller of Public Accounts.

———. 2001. "The Border Where We Stand." Austin: Texas Comptroller of Public Accounts.

———. 2003a. "Strayhorn Report: Border, Center of the Americas." Austin: Texas Comptroller of Public Accounts.

———. 2003b. "The Border Snapshot." Austin: Texas Comptroller of Public Accounts.

Texas Department of Health, Selected Facts for Webb County, 2000.

Texas Department of Human Services. 1998. "*Colonias* Factbook." Austin.

U.S. Census Bureau. 2000. http://www.census.gov.

Ward, Peter. 1999. *Colonias and Public Policy in Texas and Mexico: Urbanization by Stealth*. Austin: University of Texas Press.

Warner, David C. 1999. "The Medical Care Systems in Mexico and the United States: Convergence or Deterioration? The View from the Border." In *Life, Death, and In Between on the U.S.-Mexico Border: Asi Es la Vida*, ed. Martha Oehmke Loustaunau and Mary Sanchez-Bane, 177–90. Westport, CT: Bergin and Garvey.

Warner, David C., and Kevin Reed. 1993. *Health Care across the Border: The Experience of U.S. Citizens in Mexico*. Austin: LBJ School of Public Affairs, University of Texas at Austin.

CHAPTER SEVEN

Coming of Age across Borders

Family, Gender, and Place in the Lives of
Second-Generation Transnational Mexicanas

Patricia Sánchez

Living in both worlds means that I learn to say, *Buenos días y buenas tardes* [Good morning and good afternoon], or *saludo* [greet] people around me—which is not usually practiced here [the United States]—and show great respect to all of my elders. But it also means I have to learn to respect customs that I don't necessarily agree with. For example, in Mexico, the woman's role is very defined and limited, and coming from the United States where women are theoretically equal to men, it's hard for me to be able to fully accept those ideas and conform to the roles that I am expected to.[1]

These opening words are those of Genobeba Duarte, one of the three young women in this study who reside in northern California and maintain close ties to a rural community in western Mexico. While much of the research in this volume addresses life in border towns along the physical *línea* (line) of the United States and Mexico, this chapter highlights the transnational practices of second-generation Mexicanas living in urban centers five hundred miles north of the *línea*. Based on a larger three-year qualitative study, I outline the border landscape of three transnational urban youth who regularly visit their parents' natal ranchos or pueblos in Jalisco.[2] Using ethnography and participatory research in multiple field sites, I examine what it means to come of age as a second-generation Mexicana engaged in transnationalism—with a particular emphasis on the role of family, gender, and place. The findings demonstrate how familial, social, and religious practices intersect with both gender and the transnational social space, shaping parenting strategies as well as the negotiations made by the young women in their respective communities and daily lives. In the following sections, I outline the literature on immigrant children and transnationalism and the methods utilized in this study as well as the context of the young women's lives in two places, followed by the findings and implications of experiencing such an upbringing.

Immigrant Children and Transnationalism

In the United States today, children of immigrants comprise the fastest-growing segment of the under-eighteen population—one out of every five children is the son or daughter of immigrants (Levitt and Waters 2002). Additionally, the fastest-growing group of children in U.S. public schools is Latino (Suárez-Orozco and Páez 2002). Over 60% of these Latino children are of immigrant stock, meaning that either they or one (or both) of their parents were born in another country (Rumbaut 2002). In California, in fact, Latinos already comprise the largest ethnic group in state schools.[3] And by the year 2006, Latinos will constitute the majority of children entering California kindergartens (Richardson and Fields 2003).

Presently, Latino school-age children are transforming school calendars in California because of their strong transnational ties. For example, in Williams, a small town of 3,700 residents and sixty miles north of the state capital, schools have altered their yearly start dates, moving the beginning of classes to early August (Gazzar 2001). They have done so since the 2000–2001 academic year, according to an elementary/middle school principal: "Because many students have families in Mexico whom they like to visit during Christmas vacation, it was decided [in 2000] that school would start a week earlier and Christmas would last three weeks instead of two" (ibid). These changes took place because 85% of the 520 students at the school are Latino (ibid). The transnational practices of Mexican immigrant families demanded a response from the school district.

Carr Intermediate School in Santa Ana, a city in southern California, did the same by starting classes early in August and giving students one month off for the winter break (Yi 2001). In this district, close to 1,100 students return to Mexico each holiday season. This annual pilgrimage depletes classrooms and affects attendance at many southern California schools with large Mexican immigrant populations. Officials at the 22,000-student Anaheim City School District, for example, said that attendance dips by about 5% in December and January, and that affects the funds received from the state (ibid.) While not all school districts or officials in California (or elsewhere) are responsive to the exodus produced by transnational families,[4] there is a mounting recognition of the strength of these ties abroad—as measured by the students' absences and by the loss of state funds for local schools.

Even though schools have begun to recognize transnational movement among their students and even though the numbers indicate that many children and youth in the United States lead transnational lives, there is still a dearth of literature on the young people who engage in this transnational movement.[5] Childhood experiences in particular have not been fully addressed in recent works on Latino transnationals (Georges 1992; Goldring 1998, 2001; Hondagneu-Sotelo and Avila 1997; Levitt 2001; Menjívar 2000; Rouse 1992; Smith 1998). Instead, what is often examined are the transnational practices of adult male actors in the public sphere, especially those involving entrepreneurship, political participation, and community infrastructure projects (Escala-Rabadán 2002; Guarnizo 1998, 1999; Guarnizo et al. 2002, 2003; Smith 1998). In the meantime, the private sphere, including the family and the socialization of children, has remained less of a focus by scholars examining issues of transnationalism.[6] When we take into account that the next generation of young adults in California will include a Latino majority,[7] and when this majority has strong ties to an immigrant and transnational experience, it becomes exceedingly important to understand the dynamics of this life experience. Without insight into this complex picture, we lose a valuable opportunity to appreciate and understand children who carry out their lives in two very different worlds.

The Context of Transnational Mexicana Youth

For over three years (2000–2003), I worked with three young women—Genobeba Duarte, Carlota Duarte, and María Topete—on an organic participatory research project in Oakland, California.[8] Each week, the four of us (who had all grown up as transnationals in immigrant Mexican homes) would meet at a local nonprofit organization to design and carry out our own study on transnationalism and Latino families. Over the course of our collaborative research project, we traveled to Mexico together to our families' natal communities to conduct fieldwork, interviewed each other and family members in both the United States and Mexico, and co-presented our findings at local, state, and national research conferences.[9] In addition, we used this research to inform, author, and illustrate a bilingual children's book on transnationalism.[10]

This chapter, however, comes from the ethnographic portion of this collaborative project. Employing "global ethnography," as Michael Buroway (2000) describes it, I captured the "multi-sited" (Marcus 1995, 1998) experiences of these three second-generation Mexicanas throughout the time we worked together. Because either they, family members, goods, money, messages, or affection were constantly slipping across the border in both directions, I had to follow these flows to capture every side of their transnational experience. George Marcus (1995) offers methodological approaches in conducting multisited ethnography, whereby researchers "follow the people," "follow the thing," "follow the metaphor," "follow the plot/story/allegory," "follow the life/biography," and "follow the conflict" because "the object of study is ultimately mobile and multiply situated" (pp. 102–10). In addition to extensive field notes and participant observation, I conducted fourteen formal and sixteen informal interviews with transnational community members as well as five focus groups with the young women themselves.

Transnational Social Space in Northern California

All three of the young women in this study were born in northern California to parents from rural and semirural Jalisco, Mexico (except for María Topete's mother, who is from Guanajuato). Each of the fathers first came to the United States in their mid- to late-teen years through the Bracero Program or via a male-immigrant social network originally established through this guest-worker program. Though they all started their work careers in *el norte* in either crop harvesting or light manufacturing, today they are each well-positioned contractors or supervisors in commercial construction, working long, physical hours six days per week. All three mothers have been homemakers at some point in their married lives, but, currently, Mrs. Alejandra Topete works in a clothing factory and Mrs. Rosaura Duarte (Carlota's mother) has a job in a local school district's library department; Mrs. Azucena Duarte (Genobeba's mother) has never been employed outside her home. All three of the Duarte and Topete families are homeowners. The eldest child of each family has enrolled in or graduated from a four-year university.

Genobeba Duarte and Carlota Duarte reside in the Fruitvale district of Oakland, which has close to 56,000 residents.[11] (Oakland itself has a population of nearly 400,000.)[12] Fruitvale has experienced rapid ethnic transformation in the last fourteen years with Latinos comprising 46% of the district's population (up 43% from 1990). In addition, other well-represented immigrant groups include Asian and Pacific Islanders (21%) and a substantial population of African Americans (21%). The distribution of household income for families in Fruitvale is skewed toward the lower economic end, with 42% earning less than $32,000 per year. In addition, the most common languages spoken in Fruitvale are Spanish, Chinese, Tagalog, and Vietnamese.

Genobeba lives with two younger sisters in a two-bedroom house and works in Fruitvale at an urban Latino community center. Through scholarships, she was able to attend a private all-girls' Catholic high school. Today, she is a sophomore in college studying political science and Spanish while working full-time during the summers at the same construction company where her father is employed. Her life is consumed by her studies, her job, family obligations, and social engagements made readily available by Cimarrón Chico, Jalisco's strong and

well-connected immigrant enclave in Oakland. Members of this enclave hold many formal and informal social events together and regularly raise funds for community improvement projects back in Jalisco.

Carlota is Genobeba's first cousin and is the youngest of four children. When the study began, she attended an urban public high school
in Oakland, hoping to go to a local state university and to study nurs-
ing. Carlota has worked with Genobeba in the Fruitvale Latino community center and presently has a part-time job in a shoe store while
she attends college. She and Genobeba are often inseparable and go together to as many of their transnational community's social events as
possible.

María resides in San Pablo, California, which has a little over 30,000
residents. This community, too, has experienced dramatic ethnic transformations in the last ten years; presently, it is comprised of Latinos
(45%), Asian and Pacific Islanders (18%), African Americans (18%),
and whites (16%).[13] Some 41% of the people in San Pablo are foreign-
born, and the median household income is just over $37,000. María is
a junior in high school and has an older half-brother and two younger
sisters with whom she loves to spend time. She is involved in the Raza
Club at school and active in her church, but her social world is made
up of an ethnic enclave comprised primarily of her mother's extended
family from Guanajuato.

Transnational Social Space in México

The two cousins, Genobeba and Carlota Duarte, visit family in Cimarrón Chico, a small agricultural community within the *municipio*, or municipality, of Mascota, Jalisco.[14] This is a rancho of approximately 250
residents located along a mountainside in the Sierra Occidental, with a
four-room elementary school, a church, a plaza, two one-room mini-
general food stores, and one phone line for the entire community. The
closest city to Cimarrón Chico is a thirty-minute truck drive along a
steep and rocky, unpaved seven-mile road. The community is close
knit yet isolated; along this mountainside, transportation is limited to
horses, mules, a few trucks, and an old but brightly painted American
school bus that makes its way to each of the ranchos once per day on
its way to the closest city of 7,909 residents.[15] Populations have been
steadily declining in this region for the last thirty years.[16] Most families

who remain in Cimarrón Chico live off their land through subsistence farming, microenterprises such as the sale of *tamales de atole,* or of gold jewelry and remittances sent by relatives in the United States.

María goes every year to her father's natal community of San Miguel el Alto, Jalisco, which is one of the many small towns (27,000 residents) in the semirural region referred to as Los Altos.[17] Like other areas of Jalisco, San Miguel has had a long tradition of out- and return-migration to *el norte* for the last one hundred years. One of the community's most celebrated local events is *la serenata,* the weekly promenade around the plaza on Sunday evenings. Here, all the young women walk around the edge of the plaza, counterclockwise, while the young men stand in a line along their path and toss confetti and flowers at the girls whom they hope to court. San Miguel has a bustling plaza and small business area, banks, a *mercado,* churches, beauty salons, schools (K–12), *salones de baile* (places where dances are held), bakeries, cyber cafés, a *tortillería,* and even a modest mall (*La Plaza del Vestido*) on its outskirts.

While in Mexico, all three of the girls integrate into the place they call "home" by staying with the same relatives each year: at the house of a *tía* (aunt) or *abuela* (grandmother), usually where their cousins live. A typical day for Genobeba and Carlota in Cimarrón Chico includes washing their clothes on a cement washboard, doing other household chores, visiting several relatives, and spending time at the plaza during the evening. For María, days at Tía Caridad's home in San Miguel include joining the seven-sibling household and participating in daily chores, going to classes with her same-age cousin if school is still in session, helping the family run its *papelería* (a mini paper products and school supplies store), and amusing themselves in the plaza each evening. These daily routines in both Cimarrón Chico and San Miguel are complemented by weekly or biweekly celebrations in the plaza or *salones de baile.*

Transnationalism Bounded by Family

For the girls and families in this research project, transnational processes are inscribed by familial and religious practices. Trips to countries of origin are taken not for tourism but for specific family celebrations and maintenance of kinship ties as well as for attendance at religious holidays and festivals. Often, travel to Mexico revolves around a wedding, a *quinceañera*,[18] or a community's Catholic patron saint's day. During the three-year period of this study, cousins Genobeba and Carlota participated as *damas*[19] in the *quinceañera* of another cousin, a transnational relative who chose to hold this event in Mexico. Both María and her younger sister celebrated their *quince años* in San Miguel el Alto in consecutive summers.

While it is fair to argue that families who observe their daughters' coming of age in the parents' natal communities in Mexico are exercising strategies of social mobility,[20] it also holds true that these immigrant families are choosing to reinforce a cultural practice that includes more of the transnational community by enacting the event in rural and semirural Mexico. The same Mexican family members who attend these celebrations south of the border often cannot make the trip to *el norte* because of legal and financial constraints. Indeed, the mobility of the transnational community that resides in the United States—whose members have both means and *papeles* (legal documents)—plays a decided role in how certain family and community practices are enacted across the transnational social space. One of the major goals of these familial-social-religious events is to ensure maximum attendance by the extended family.

Another telling point regarding family participation in the transnational social space is how social practices deviate from tourist practices. Many transnationals return to Mexico to be with family and do not necessarily "vacation" in the mainstream sense. For example, it was rare for the young women to visit popular tourist spots while in Mexico. Genobeba describes getting picked up at the Guadalajara airport and staying with an aunt in this metroplex until she makes the last four-hour leg to Cimarrón Chico:

> my aunt that picks me up, she's my dad's sister and lives in Guadalajara. So it's, like, because she has picked me up, I can't be, like, "Thanks, I'm leaving." I stay—the most I've stayed with her is two weeks. . . . I don't stay there much because there's nothing to do . . . all of my aunt's children are married. They are either married, or here [in the States], or working all of the time so they are never home. My uncle is always working and so he's never home, and it's usually my aunt that's home. And I don't think she even knows

how to drive, so she never takes me anywhere. So because I'm under her care, I can never go anywhere unless one of my cousins is kind enough to take me out. . . .That's why I dread going there, going to Guadalajara. And that kind of sucks 'cause I want to do some sightseeing, 'cause I know there's some pretty places, and I just never get to go, or been able to see them, despite the fact that I've gone so many times.

Guadalajara, the capital of Jalisco, is the second largest city in Mexico with nearly 3.5 million inhabitants in its metropolitan area,[21] and a favorite tourist destination for both Mexicans and foreigners. Even so, for Genobeba it was more important to "be like family" when "with family," as she asserts that she could not readily leave her aunt. Perceived family expectations and obligations outweighed her own desires to continue on to Cimarrón Chico. For the three young women, transnational engagement is intricately circumscribed by the greater practice of "being family."

Parenting in a Transnational Context

If the young women and their families are "being family" across a transnational social space, then what does parenting look like in this context? Indeed, the parenting strategies in this Mexico-U.S. sphere are similar to the findings in Orellana et al. (2001). Trips to Mexico for the three young people are part of a disciplinary strategy that parents engage in, as they were for the Mexicano, Central American, and Yemeni children whom Orellana et al. researched. However, the young women's parents in this study use travel to family hometowns as rewards for good grades and conduct during the academic year, not as punishment for misbehavior. This also differs from the structural "punishment" in the case of the Salvadoran gang members (Wallace 2000; Cruz 1998) deported from California to their home countries, and Matthei and Smith's (1998) findings of Garifuna families in Los Angeles who send youth back to Belize after they have been caught in drug or gang activity.

María, for example, promised to pull up her English grades during the 2000–2001 academic year in return for a summer trip to Jalisco.

She relates how this "bargain" works with her father: "Uh, yeah, if I keep on getting good grades. . . . Well, I have to get at least a B or an A to be able to go. If I get a C, well, I probably won't be able to go because my dad wants us to get good grades. See, that's the kind of reward we get. If we get good grades throughout the whole year, we get to go to Mexico, and if we don't, we have to stay in California and go to summer school and be sad the whole time. . . . He's been telling us this since I was in third grade."

In another instance, Genobeba recalls striking a deal with her parents after her younger sister, Alicia, declined to go to the family's rancho one summer: "Yeah, like Alicia, when I went last [summer], they actually told her to go, and I was, like, 'Since she doesn't want to go, I'll take her plane ticket. I'll just bring in the grades and you pay for the plane ticket, and I'll pay for all of my clothes.' And they [my parents] would try to get her to go because they didn't want me to go. They told me that once I turned fifteen, I wouldn't be able to go [to Mexico], and I was like, 'No I have to go,' and so they let me." Here, the Duarte parents are encouraging Alicia to travel to their rancho at Cimarrón Chico because she is only twelve years old. The parents know that because she is not yet fifteen, she will not be allowed to dance with a male partner at any of the local social events. They also know that other family members will readily report any "transgressions" on Alicia's part back to them in the United States.[22]

However, because Alicia's older sister, Genobeba, is already fifteen, and—according to the cultural traditions of their family, the transnational community, and Mexican society in general—she would be able to meet and dance with her male counterparts at any celebrations she attended. Genobeba explains in more detail her parents' hesitation in allowing her to return to Mexico: "[If I returned], I would be able to dance y ellos no querían. Well, at least that was always my theory— they never gave me a straight reason. It was more like they did it innuendoly [sic]. I was, like, 'I'm still going, one way or another.' And once I heard that Carlota was going, . . . I was, like, 'Okay, I need to go.' And so finally, we made a deal that if I brought good grades, I would be able to go. . . . I told them, 'You don't need to pay for anything other than my plane ticket.' And that was our little deal." The Duarte parents in this context are using the transnational space to regulate their daughter's behavior by controlling or selecting the environment in which she can participate as a young woman. They are denying Genobeba an opportunity to socialize among the many other same-age transnationals who will be returning to Mexico as well as the local Jaliscienses who will attend the same familial-social-religious events. Mr. and Mrs. Duarte realize that curtailing their daughter's trip can also serve as a tool to regulate her student or "academic" behavior in the United States because Genobeba is motivated to do well in school to be able to return to Cimarrón Chico once more.

This strategy of encouraging good academic deportment in their daughter is again different from the families studied by Orellana et al. (2001) and Matthei and Smith (1998). In those studies, Yemeni and Belizean children were sent back to their families' homelands as a parenting strategy to "correct" American behavior deemed problematic. This method is effective for such transnational families because the children were either 1.5 generation immigrants—migrating to the United States after age six—or were raised in their home countries until their emigrated parents sent for them. Genobeba, Carlota, and María, however, were all born in the United States and their parents emigrated here at younger ages, which helped them integrate more fully into American society than if they had been born in Mexico. Thus, sending these teen Mexicanas "back" to (semirural) Mexico means something completely different because the girls themselves have never permanently lived in their parents' natal communities. Understanding the complexity of transnational families as well as the intricacies of each family within a particular transnational immigrant/ethnic community is critical in seeing *la profundidad,* or the depth, of how transnationalism works in the daily practices of youth and families—in particular, those practices related to raising children (or alternatively, constructing childhoods).

Negotiating Gender across Borders: Constraints and Freedoms

While some studies have detailed gendered forms of transnationalism (Mahler 1998, 2001; Mahler and Pessar 2001; Fouron and Glick Schiller 2001; Goldring 2001; Sôrensen 1998), few or none have considered gender as it is practiced by female youth in transnational settings. Pierette Hondagneu-Sotelo's (1994) work with Mexicana immigrants focuses on gendered transitions upon emigrating to the United States. However, the youth in this study are continually moving across borders and negotiating their gender roles.

Genobeba, Carlota, and María transition in and out of different gendered practices depending on their locality. As they traverse various physical and social terrains, they play distinct roles in different community settings. Understanding the patterns of these transnational practices helps us to see how the young women negotiate these different social spheres where gender roles and participation have different expectations and meanings.

The findings suggest that the youth's gendered roles, for example, affect their social interactions in both translocalities. One main difference is with which types of boys the young women can visibly interact in Mexico: boys who are not relatives are generally off-limits, and even the companionship of male cousins can be problematic unless this contact is controlled or regulated. María, the youngest participant in this study, describes the difference for a boy or for a girl in returning to semirural Jalisco each year:

> I don't think it's different [if you are a girl or boy in Mexico] . . . Well, maybe a little. Well, . . . it's like, we really don't hang out with my guy cousins. We hang out more with our girl cousins because it's like my mom—well, not my mom, but like my aunt has always had this theory that guys should hang out with guys, and girls should always hang out with girls. But I don't think it's right because, it's like, you're cousins. You should all hang out together, you know—not be separated, guys with guys, girls with girls. So I really don't believe in that, so I just hang out with all my cousins. I don't care if they're girls or guys.

María defies adhering to the proscribed gender roles in Mexico enforced by her aunt. She also maintains that even though there are certain restraints in her social interactions with males, she is still allowed many more privileges and greater physical movement while in Jalisco: "We [she and her sisters] get to do anything we want, go anywhere we want, whenever we want. Yeah, with anyone, you know, like, cousins—not strangers, even though I don't think they're strangers. The whole town knows us . . . they know my dad."

Genobeba's aunt who lives in Cimarrón Chico acknowledges this freer movement when transnational children return to the rancho because of the safety afforded by the close-knit community: "For the children, I think it's really good for them to return because here there is more freedom. Here they are free, they aren't closed up inside, and they—I see that they feel really good here, too" [translation]. Genobeba concurs: "When I go by myself [to Jalisco], I go to get away from my parents, which is a big thing for me because I am under their eye 24/7. Every little thing that I want to do, I have to ask them for permission—always, always, always." For the three young women in this study, growing up in urban centers such as Oakland, many constraints are imposed by parents who aim to protect them from the real (and perceived) dangers of the inner city.[23]

This protective stance on the part of parents translates into close monitoring of the young women while they are in the United States, thus explaining part of Genobeba's exasperation. María agrees:

It's very different [in Mexico] because my dad doesn't give us that much liberty here [in the States]. He doesn't really let us go out anywhere, you know, like to stores, or hang out with friends, go to a movie. He does, but it has to be with an adult. And over there [in Mexico], I don't even have to be with an adult. I can go with my cousins who are like at least four years younger than me—like, five-year-old cousins—and he'll let me go. But here, they won't let me do that. They say it's dangerous here. Hello! I really don't think that, but, well, I do think that, but then I don't think it's that dangerous, but then at the same time I do because I hear too much—things on TV and in the news . . . like, on Sunday, when was it that it came on the news? That they raped a girl at Willard [Middle School]? Like, on Monday? Friday? . . . She was an ESL student and she got raped by eleven different guys . . . I think it was at school. . . . She got raped by guys her age.

María refers to a real and horrible case of sexual assault that occurred in the progressive school district she attends, but it was directed not toward an ESL student but toward a "12-year-old developmentally disabled girl."[24] The urban environments in which the Topete and Duarte families reside in the United States are a direct contrast to the type of communities to which they return each year in Mexico.

Carlota, for example, relates how the only telephone operator in the 250-member community knew where she was on the particular day that her American boyfriend called:

> Like, here [in the States], you know, I don't even know the person that lives across the street! But over there, everybody's like related to each other. . . . They know who you are for sure. . . . Like one time my boyfriend called from here to over there, and he asked to talk to Carlota, and they asked him, "*¿Cual Carlota? ¿La de Gerardo, la de Daniel o la de Los Mazos?*" [Which Carlota? Gerardo's daughter, Daniel's daughter or the one who lives in Los Mazos?] He said, "Uh, *la de Gerardo.*" And they said, "*No, no está. Está en el otro rancho.*" [No, she's not here. She's visiting the other rancho.] They know who you are.

The one or two workers in this small phone business, which was run out of a local home, knew Carlota's whereabouts without her ever giving them her day's agenda.

Genobeba shares more insight on the ways this close-knit community in Mexico keeps tabs on both its local and transnational members. Again, the telephone operator is the primary aide in this endeavor:

> I don't know how they do it, that from one day to another, people know what we've done here [in Mexico]. So I knew that if I wanted to do something, I would have to do it in a way that nobody would think I was doing something bad and then it gets back to my parents. I don't think I did anything bad. So, *si les llegaban chismes* [if my parents got wind of certain rumors], I could just be, like, be, "Well, that's not true 'cause my cousins were always with me and they always knew what I did, and they know I didn't do anything bad." So they were my witnesses and my backup. But I don't know how people do it, that one day *llaman acá* [they call over here] and they know everything. God! *¡La gente es bien chismosa!* [The people there are such busybodies!]

While Genobeba dismisses the community's surveillance, she has her own ways of dispelling half-truths linked to her own behavior. Her female cousins' words helped to reduce her parents' anxiety when they heard about questionable incidents during their daughter's yearly visits.

This same community surveillance has, at times, worked to María's advantage. For example, while in San Miguel, upon turning fifteen, she was allowed to sit on the front steps of her aunt's house and socialize with teenaged *pretendientes,* or suitors. This type of interaction, however, is unheard of in the United States. María explains her frustration: "In San Miguel, *puedo estar con él* [I can be with him], you know, there in front of my Tía Caridad's house. But here, with Manuel in front of my house—he's right there—no way! They [my parents] trip. They don't get it. It drives me crazy."

From a different perspective, what the young women have mentioned as "freedoms" or "liberties" in Mexico may come off to others as excessive permissiveness. Tía Caridad has her own perceptions of the Mexican immigrant families who frequently visit San Miguel:

> Well, since I can remember, since my first recollection, they have always gone to the United States. The poor to improve themselves, and others for their perdition, you could say . . . they leave, they take their family. And because over there they confuse liberty with a lack of moral restraint, they think that they can already be free in their adolescence, and that's not true. All of the adolescents are mistaken. That's why I say that some do go to improve themselves and others for their perdition. . . . *Libertinaje* to me means that they can make and unmake [*hacer y deshacer*]. That is, they can go wherever they want, or it doesn't matter to them if they sleep in their own house or in another's, and, well, for my upbringing, that—that does not sit well with me. [Translation]

For Caridad Pérez, her nieces are given too much freedom in their literal and physical movement throughout San Miguel as well as in their comportment. This liberalness, or *libertinaje,* in some ways reflects a loss of groundedness in the community's traditional past. It is important to note, too, that the label of *libertinaje* only applies to young women. Second-generation Mexican males residing in California who visit San Miguel are not described in this way.

Coming of Age as a Young Female Transnational

For the three young women coming of age in this study, family plays a definitive role in their participation in transnationalism. If their parents did not have such ties to their homeland communities, then the young women would not by any means "inherit" this interest in Mexico or take part in such an engaged manner. Genobeba, Carlota, and María contribute to their families' continued transnationalism by wanting to return to Jalisco on their own or wanting to hold their *quinceañera* there.

The young women's parents' disciplinary strategies within this space differ in comparison to other immigrant groups. Moreover, the "generation" of when the children emigrated to the United States affects this style of discipline. While I discussed gender in a separate section in this chapter, it permeated the entire analysis because gender intersects with other social categories and is intertwined with everyday practices. As other academics have found, gender is an ongoing, fluid process experienced through many social institutions such as family and the state (Mahler and Pessar 2001; Hondagneu-Sotelo 1990; Ortner 1996). However, to highlight other aspects of the young women's lives as transnationals, the focus centered on family and parenting to show the impact of these social institutions on the daughters' participation in the transnational social space.

The young women in this study feel freer when they return to Mexico, and they relish this spatial mobility; however, some of their relatives may perceive this mobility as an example of too-permissive behavior. In a somewhat paradoxical sense, while the youth feel freer in Mexico, this freedom is made possible only because of the close-knit rural community in which everyone knows everyone else, and everyone else's doings. Parents can feel at ease because this close-knittedness, which is a deterrent to crime in small Mexican communities and also serves as surveillance over their daughters while they are outside the United States. This is not to say, however, that the young women do not resist this surveillance. They do, in fact, find ways to get around it.[25] Essentially, Genobeba, Carlota, and María trade one type of strict monitoring for another that will allow them at least some greater physical mobility.

Transnational and female, these young women are also inscribed in their experiences by age as younger members of their community, where they are supposed to follow a particular normed behavior. In addition, this identity is layered by the traditional view of family as well as by their own respect for the women relatives with whom they interact in female-centered spaces in Mexico. Genobeba, Carlota, and María possess an appreciation for the often arduous labor their relatives perform on a daily basis and have come to see the household division of labor as a place where other feminisms can and do surface. They do not impose a Western feminist framework on women of color or on Third World women's realities (Mohanty 1986, 2003a, 2003b; Ong 2003), as do many white feminists. Though the young women do contend with many negotiations, they are careful not to pass judgment on their female counterparts. Instead, they share in the gendered division of labor while in Mexico, in solidarity with their relatives, and enjoy the many social events in these small rural communities that would be off-limits in their U.S. environments.

Coming of age in this borderscape means that there are constant symbols and real enactments of community, family, home, and womanhood. Negotiating through these images and realities is a constant process that requires distinct *modos de ser* (ways of being), as one participant called it.[26] There is no doubt that the young women embrace particular notions of gender. These they have picked up in the United States either at school, through the media, or within their own families. But, nonetheless, the three youth still adhere to certain gendered practices based on the traditional cultural views of the Mexicano family. More and more second-generation youth, such as Genobeba, Carlota, and María, are coming to experience this family trope (and reality) transnationally and across borders.

Notes

I sincerely thank the young transnational Latinas in this study who opened their homes and shared their lives with me. In addition, I would like to thank Soo Ah Kwon for insightful comments on an earlier draft of this chapter. Also, I am grateful to the Paul and Daisy Soros Fellowships for New Americans, the University of California-Berkeley Graduate School of Education's Spencer Research Training Fellowships, the UC-Berkeley's Center for Latin

American Studies Summer Research Grant, and the Mini-Grant Program sponsored by the Center for Latino Policy Research as well as the Chancellor's Opportunity Pre-Doctoral Fellowship, and Deans Mary Ann Mason and Elaine Kim for their generous support.

1. Genobeba Duarte made this statement at a national research conference. The three young women and I co-presented findings from our participatory research project at several conferences.

2. While all participants have selected or have been given pseudonyms, the names of places (neighborhoods, schools, cities) have remained unchanged. This chapter is part of a larger ethnography grounded in the realities and real places of two transnational communities whose members experience many different "border crossings" (gender, citizenship, legal boundaries, age) each day. Because the study of transnationalism has a fairly recent history in traditional sociological immigration literature, I purposefully hope to continue the documentation of the real places in which transnational communities are forged. It is important for other academics to do the same so that we can compose a broader and more comprehensive picture of a particular community over time. "Snapshots" such as these can, in effect, serve as a longitudinal portrait of the same community if we document it with its real name.

3. The ethnic breakdown of California students in public schools is 42% Latino, 37% white, 11% Asian/Pacific Islander, 9% African American, 1% Native American. (Retrieved on January 15, 2003, from www.cde.ca.gov.)

4. In the same article by Daniel Yi (2001), a Los Angeles Unified School District spokeswoman stated, "Our calendar is not changed to accommodate students' vacation plans."

5. A notable exception is Peggy Levitt and Mary C. Waters's *The Changing Face of Home* (2002). See also Brittain (2002), Orellana et al. (2001), Zhou (1998).

6. Again, *The Changing Face of Home* (2002) looks at the transnational participation of various immigrant groups.

7. In data from 2003–2004, Latinos comprised 44% of the student state population in Texas, while whites followed with 39%, and African Americans and Asian/Pacific Islanders made up 14% and 3% of the population, respectively. (Retrieved on April 1, 2004, from http://www.tea.state.tx.us/adhocrpt/adste04.html.) This means that two of the nation's five largest immigrant-receiving states are undergoing Latinoization.

8. Participatory research is considered a more democratic way of conducting investigations where "subjects" are not just participants but are also co-researchers who ideally initiate, design, and carry out the research as well as analyze the findings (see Hall 1992 and Maguire 1987). By "organic," I

mean those who share the same life experiences as those being studied; I have borrowed the term from Antonio Gramsci (1971), who proposed that organic intellectuals—the working class and marginalized who have theorized their own positions—come forward to undo the oppression and harm that the disenfranchised classes undergo at the hands of those in power, the elites. Traditional research could be seen as a form of elitism that has often produced misguided or inaccurate portrayals of many communities of color (Valencia and Solorzano 1997). Including members of these communities in the research process becomes one way to avoid this pitfall.

9. Some of these conferences include the California Association for Bilingual Education (CABE), the National Association for Bilingual Education (NABE), the National Association for Chicana and Chicano Studies (NACCS), and the American Educational Studies Association (AESA).

10. The children's picture book, *Recuerdo mis raíces y vivo mis tradiciones / Remembering My Roots and Living My Traditions*, was published by Scholastic and made available in their nationwide book clubs in 2004. It has also been used in their *Lee y Serás* Latino literacy campaign.

11. All data on Fruitvale are from the *Fruitvale Community Information Book 2001*, Alameda County Public Health Department.

12. The data source is the 2000 U.S. Census. Oakland is also 36% African American, 24% white, 22% Latino, and 16% Asian/Pacific Islander.

13. All data on San Pablo are from the 2000 U.S. Census.

14. A *municipio*, or municipality, in Mexico is that nation's smallest political entity with a government of its own; it is an administrative subdivision similar to a county in the United States.

15. Mascota is the municipality head and largest city in this region. The data source is Centro Estatal de Estudios Municipales de Jalisco, February 2000, as cited on the following Website, retrieved on January 7, 2004: http://www.e-local.gob.mx/enciclo/jalisco/.

16. Ibid.

17. Ibid.

18. A *quinceañera* is the elaborate celebration of a Latina girl's fifteenth birthday. See Sánchez (2002) for a more detailed description.

19. A *dama* is a female escort in a *quinceañera* celebration. There are usually fourteen *damas* and fourteen *chambelanes* (male escorts).

20. In several interviews with Mexico-based members of the transnational community, I learned that the *quinceañera* in these small ranchos or towns has been greatly transformed by those who live in the United States and return to hold a daughter's celebration in Jalisco. These celebrations have been both materially and culturally transformed and no doubt include new meanings of social status.

21. Guadalajara's metropolitan area includes Guadalajara, Zapopan, Tlaquepaque, and Tonalá. These figures are from the 2000 population census conducted by Mexico's Geography and Statistic National Institute (INEGI), downloaded January 7, 2004, from the Website http://www.guadalajara.gob.mx.

22. See the next section for a more detailed discussion of this type of community surveillance.

23. From 2001 to 2003, Oakland has incurred a steady increase (up 30%) in yearly homicides: 87 murders in 2001, 113 in 2002, and 114 in 2003 (Harris 2004). In 2004 there were already seventeen murders in the first six weeks of the year (Reynolds 2004).

24. Nine boys repeatedly raped the girl after school for five hours in eleven different locations throughout the middle-school neighborhood. Seven of the boys were between the ages of eleven and fourteen, while two were between fifteen and sixteen. Two newspapers, the *Daily Californian* and *San Francisco Chronicle*, covered the story: http://www.dailycal.org/article.php?id=3859 and http://www.sfgate.com/cgi-bin/article.cgi?file=/news/archive/2000/11/09/national1117EST0553.DTL.

25. See Sánchez 2004 for a more detailed discussion.

26. Ibid.

References

Brittain, Carmina. 2002. *Transnational Messages: Experiences of Chinese and Mexican Immigrants in American Schools*. New York: LFB Scholarly Printing.

Burawoy, Michael. 2000. "Introduction: Reaching for the Global." In *Global Ethnography: Forces, Connections, and Imaginations in a Postmodern World*, ed. Michael Buroway, 1–40. Berkeley: University of California Press.

California Department of Education. 2000. http://www.cde.ca.gov (accessed January 15, 2003).

Centro Estatal de Estudios Municipales de Jalisco. 2000. http://www.e-local.gob.mx/enciclo/jalisco/ (accessed January 7, 2004).

Community Assessment, Planning, and Education Unit. 2001. *Fruitvale Community Information Book 2001*. Public Health Department. Alameda County Health Services Agency.

Cruz, José Miguel. 1998. *Solidaridad y violencia en las pandillas del gran San Salvador: Mas alla de la vida loca*. San Salvador, El Salvador: Universidad de Centro América.

Dueñas, Tomasa, Patricia Sánchez, and Montserrat López. 2004. *Recuerdo mis raíces y vivo mis tradiciones / Remembering My Roots and Living My Traditions*. New York: Scholastic.

Escala-Rabadán, Luis. 2002. "Old and New Horizons for Transnational Migrants' Associations: The Quest for Political Empowerment among Hometown Associations in Los Angeles, California." Paper presented at the Colloquium on International Migration: Mexico-California, March 2002, at the University of California-Berkeley.

Evans, Will. "City's Police Investigate Alleged Group Rape: Suspects to be Charged and Suspended." *Daily Californian*, November 8, 2000. http://www.dailycal.org/article.php?id=3859.

Figueroa, Julie, and Patricia Sánchez. (forthcoming). "Technique, Art, or Cultural Practice? Ethnic Epistemology in Latino Qualitative Studies." In *Handbook of Research Methods in Ethnic Studies*, ed. Tim Fong. Walnut Creek, CA: AltaMira Press.

Fouron, Georges, and Nina Glick Schiller. 2001. "All in the Family: Gender, Transnational Migration, and the Nation-State." *Identities: Global Studies in Culture and Power* 7(4): 539–82.

Gazzar, Brenda. "Early Return Gives Students an Extended Christmas." *Appeal-Democrat*, August 14, 2001.

Georges, Eugenia. 1992. "Gender, Class, and Migration in the Dominican Republic: Women's Experiences in a Transnational Community." In *Towards a Transnational Perspective on Migration*, ed. Nina Glick Schiller, Linda Basch, and Cristina Blanc-Szanton, 81–99. New York: New York Academy of Sciences.

Goldring, Luin. 1998. "The Power of Status in Transnational Social Fields." In *Transnationalism from Below*, ed. Michael P. Smith and Luis E. Guarnizo, 165–95. New Brunswick, NJ: Transaction Publishers.

———. 2001. "The Gender and Geography of Citizenship in Mexico-U.S. Transnational Social Spaces." *Identities: Global Studies in Culture and Power* 7(4): 501–37.

Gramsci, Antonio. 1971. *Selections from the Prison Notebooks*. London: Lawrence and Wishart.

Guarnizo, Luis E. 1998. "The Rise of Transnational Social Formations: Mexican and Dominican State Responses to Transnational Migration." *Political Power and Social Theory* 12: 45–94.

———. 1999. "On the Political Participation of Transnational Migrants: Old Practices and New Trends." In *Immigrants, Civic Culture, and Modes of Political Incorporation*, ed. John Mollenkopf and Gary Gerstle, 213–63. New York: Sage and Social Science Research Council.

Guarnizo, Luis E., Alejandro Portes, and William Haller. 2002. "Transnational Entrepreneurs: The Emergence and Determinants of an Alternative Form of Immigrant Economic Adaptation." *American Sociological Review* 67: 278–98.

————. 2003. "Assimilation and Transnationalism: Determinants of Trans-national Political Action among Contemporary Migrants." *American Journal of Sociology* 108(6): 1211–48.

Hall, Budd L. 1992. "From Margins to Center? Development and Purpose of Participatory Research." *American Sociologist* 23(4): 15–28.

Harris, Harry. "Police: Selfish Mind-Set Culprit in High Crime Rate." *Oakland Tribune,* February 11, 2004.

Hondagneu-Sotelo, Pierette. 1990. "Introduction: Gender and Contemporary U.S. Immigration." *American Behavioral Scientist* 42(4): 565–76.

————. 1994. *Gendered Transitions: Mexican Experiences of Immigration.* Berkeley: University of California Press.

Hondagneu-Sotelo, Pierrette, and Ernestine Avila. 1997. "'I'm Here, But I'm There': The Meanings of Transnational Latina Motherhood." *Gender and Society* 2(5): 548–71.

INEGI. 2000. Instituto Nacional de Estadística, Geografia e Informática. http://guadalajara.gob.mx. (accessed January 7, 2004).

Levitt, Peggy. 2001. *The Transnational Villagers.* Berkeley: University of California Press.

Levitt, Peggy, and Mary C. Waters, eds. 2002. *The Changing Face of Home: The Transnational Lives of the Second Generation.* New York: Russell Sage Foundation.

Maguire, Patricia. 1987. *Doing Participatory Research: A Feminist Approach.* Amherst, MA: Center for International Education.

Mahler, Sarah J. 1998. "Theoretical and Empirical Contributions toward a Research Agenda for Transnationalism." In *Transnationalism from Below,* ed. Michael P. Smith and Luis E. Guarnizo, 64–100. New Brunswick, NJ: Transaction Publishers.

————. 2001. "Transnational Relationships: The Struggle to Communicate across Borders." *Identities: Global Studies in Culture and Power* 7(4): 583–619.

Mahler, Sarah J., and Patricia R. Pessar. 2001. "Gendered Geographies of Power: Analyzing Gender across Transnational Spaces." *Identities: Global Studies in Culture and Power* 7(4): 441–59.

Marcus, George. 1995. "Ethnography in/of the World System: The Emergence of Multi-Sited Ethnography." *Annual Review of Anthropology* 24: 95–117.

————. 1998. *Ethnography through Thick and Thin.* Princeton: Princeton University Press.

Matthei, Linda M., and David A. Smith. 1998. "Belizean 'Boyz 'n the 'Hood'? Garifuna Labor Migration and Transnational Identity." In *Transnationalism from Below,* ed. Michael P. Smith and Luis E. Guarnizo, 270–90. New Brunswick, NJ: Transaction Publishers.

Menjívar, Cecilia. 2000. *Fragmented Ties: Salvadoran Immigrant Networks in America.* Berkeley: University of California Press.

Mohanty, Chandra Talpade. 1986. "Under Western Eyes: Feminist Scholarship and Colonial Discourses." *Boundary 2* 12(3): 333–58.

———. 2003a. " 'Under Western Eyes' Revisited: Feminist Solidarity through Anticapitalist Struggles." *Signs: Journal of Women in Culture and Society* 28(2): 499–536.

———. 2003b. *Feminism without Borders: Decolonizing Theory, Practicing Solidarity.* Durham and London: Duke University Press.

Ong, Aihwa. 2003. *Buddha Is Hiding: Refugees, Citizenship, the New America.* Berkeley: University of California Press.

Orellana, Marjorie F., Barrie Thorne, Anna Chee, and Wam Shun Eva Lam. 2001. "Transnational Childhoods: The Participation of Children in Processes of Family Migration." *Social Problems* 48(4): 573–92.

Ortner, Sherry B. 1996. *Making Gender: The Politics and Erotics of Culture.* Boston: Beacon Press.

Reynolds, Martin G. "Oakland Murders: Enough Is Enough." *Oakland Tribune,* February 11, 2004.

Richardson, Lisa, and Robin Fields. "Latino Majority Arrives—Among State's Babies." *Los Angeles Times,* February 6, 2003.

Rouse, Roger. 1992. "Making Sense of Settlement: Class Transformation, Cultural Struggle, and Transnationalism among Mexican Migrants in the United States." In *Towards a Transnational Perspective on Migration,* ed. Nina Glick Schiller, Linda Basch, and Cristina Blanc-Szanton, 25–52. New York: New York Academy of Sciences.

Rumbaut, Rubén G. 2002. "Severed or Sustained Attachments? Language, Identity, and Imagined Communities in the Post-Immigrant Generation." In *The Changing Face of Home: The Transnational Lives of the Second Generation,* ed. Peggy Levitt and Mary C. Waters, 43–95. New York: Russell Sage Foundation.

Sánchez, Patricia. 2001. "Adopting Transnationalism Theory and Discourse: Making Space for a Transnational Chicana." *Discourse: Studies in the Cultural Politics of Education* 22(3): 375–81.

———. 2002. "*Quinceañera.*" In *Mexico and the United States,* ed. Lee Stacy Leney and Gordon Leney, 684–85. Tarrytown, NY: Marshall Cavendish.

———. 2004. "At Home in Two Places: Second-Generation *Mexicanas* and Their Lives as Engaged Transnationals." Ph.D. diss., University of California, Berkeley.

San Francisco Chronicle. 2000. "Twelve-year-old Girl Allegedly Sexually Assaulted by Nine Boys." November 9. http://www.sfgate.com/cgi-bin/article.cgi?file=/news/archive/2000/11/09/national1117EST0553.DTL.

Smith, Robert C. 1998. "Transnational Localities: Community, Technology, and the Politics of Membership within the Context of Mexico and U.S. Migration." In *Transnationalism from Below,* ed. Michael P. Smith and Luis E. Guarnizo, 196–240. New Brunswick, NJ: Transaction Publishers.

Sôrensen, Ninna Nyberg. 1998. "Narrating Identity across Dominican Worlds." In *Transnationalism from Below,* ed. Michael P. Smith and Luis E. Guarnizo, 241–69. New Brunswick, NJ: Transaction Publishers.

Suárez-Orozco, Marcelo M., and Mariela M. Páez, eds. 2002. *Latinos: Remaking America.* Berkeley: University of California Press.

Texas Education Agency. 2004. "2003–2004 Student Enrollment Reports." http://www.tea.state.tx.us/adhocrpt/adste04.html. (accessed April 1, 2004).

U.S. Census. 2000. http://www.census.gov.

Valencia, Richard, and Daniel Solorzano. 1997. "Contemporary Deficit Thinking." In *The Evolution of Deficit Thinking in Educational Thought and Practice,* ed. R. Valencia, 160–210. The Stanford Series on Education and Public Policy. New York: Falmer Press.

Wallace, Scott. 2000. "You Must Go Home Again: Deported Gangbangers Take Over El Salvador." *Harpers Magazine* (August): 47–56.

Yi, Daniel. 2001. "Many Skip School to Spend Holiday in Mexico." *Los Angeles Times,* December 26.

Zhou, Min. 1998. "'Parachute Kids' in Southern California: The Educational Experience of Chinese Children in Transnational Families." *Educational Policy* 12: 682–704.

CHAPTER EIGHT

"I'm *Bien Pocha*"

Borderlands Epistemologies and the
Teaching of English in Mexico

Mary A. Petrón

I'm just me, I'm *bien pocha* . . . I guess I am not from here or there,
I'm both from here and there. That doesn't sound too good, but it
is. It really is. I like being in both places. And I think it is good to
be from both places. Like I see the world or life bigger than just
Americans or Mexicans see it. And really I can live here or I can
live there. It doesn't really matter that much. But I can't live there
without coming here *de vez en cuando* [sometimes], and I can't live
here without going there sometimes.

Lidia, one of the participants in this study, suggests above that
transnational individuals who inhabit the borderlands have unique
ways of viewing and understanding the world that are nurtured on
both sides of the border. These ways of knowing and understanding, or
"borderlands epistemologies" (Villenas and Foley 2002), are a key part
of the transnational experience.

Transnationalism and borderlands epistemologies are inseparably linked. "Transnationalism" has usually been defined in terms of various social, economic, and cultural practices designed to allow transnational individuals to carve out a "third space" between (and within) national spaces (Earle 1999). "Borderlands epistemologies" refers to the entire complex of beliefs, attitudes, and ideologies that result from these transnational practices. The relationship between transnationalism and borderland epistemologies is dialectical; each is forever shaping and being shaped by the other. Together, borderland epistemologies and transnationalism constitute borderland individuals' "ways of being" in the world (Villenas and Foley 2002). The following sections briefly review the literature on transnationalism and borderlands epistemologies, followed by the research context, and some of the findings of an ethnographic study conducted in 2001–2003 with transnational teachers of English in rural Nuevo León, Mexico.

Transnationalism

Scholars have recently begun to formulate a more accurate picture of immigration issues past and present. This newer portrayal includes attention to "transmigrants" who live within a "transnational social space" (Pries 2001). Arriving at a single, comprehensive definition of the term "transnationalism" is difficult in that the field of transnational studies is in its infancy, and different scholars in a variety of disciplines have used the term to signify different phenomena (Levitt and Waters 2002). Frequent, regular contact between transnationals and the ancestral country is at the heart of what Portes, Guarnizo, and Landolt (1999) have defined as "core transnationalism." This core transnationalism exists when interaction occurs on a regular, patterned basis and thus forms an integral part of participants' lives. The core transnationalism of Portes et al. can be contrasted to the "broad transnational practices" described by Itzigsohn et al. (1999). Broad transnational practices are those that occur only sporadically, involve somewhat limited levels of participation, and are not well institutionalized. A further contrast can be made with "narrow transnational practices" (Itzigsohn et al. 1999), in which interaction is highly institutionalized, rigidly structured, and constant.

Much literature on transnationalism has arisen from the context of the United States, with a focus on the ways in which transnational ties and practices are maintained *from* the United States *with* the country of origin by immigrants and their children (Levitt and Waters 2002). In contrast, this study involved the second generation, children of immigrants to *el norte,* who now live and work as teachers of English in Mexico. Research on immigrant parents and their children who return to live and/or work in Mexico is relatively scant. Ludger Pries (2001) conducted primarily quantitative fieldwork with transnationals in Mexico and New York City. He argued that "transmigrants"—or those who settle in the United States for several years, return to Mexico for several years, and so on—have created transnational social spaces. Patrick Smith (2006) highlighted linguistic issues in Mexico related to the teaching of bilingual children of returning immigrants. Enrique Trueba (1999) noted that research centers in Mexico, such as those at the University of Colima and the Tamaulipas Research Center in Ciudad Victoria, are beginning to collect data on the "binational experience and lives of the increasing number of repatriated workers in Mexico."

As a whole, Mexican statistics are problematic with respect to the classification of transnationals for a variety of reasons. Both undocumented and documented residents of the United States are still Mexican citizens and are categorized as such in the Mexican census data. Therefore, they do not show up as anything other than Mexican citizens. Children of Mexican immigrants may indeed be U.S. citizens by birth. However, the official number of U.S. citizens living in Mexico appears to be small. Mexican census information (Consejo Nacional de Población 2001) indicated that in the year 2000, approximately half a million persons residing in Mexico were foreign-born. Of this number, 69% of the total were born in the United States.[1] The data do not distinguish between U.S.-born individuals with a family history in Mexico and those who do not have family ties across the border. For example, 6.9% of the total number of U.S.-born individuals residing in Mexico were age sixty or older, which would include American retirees with family connections in Mexico and those retirees without any family history in Mexico. These numbers tell us little about the transnational population, as discovered through this research. All of the participants in this study and their family members who had been born in the United States also possess Mexican birth certificates.[2] Even those who had become naturalized U.S. citizens and later returned to their homeland live as citizens of Mexico with that country's birth certificates and voter registration cards.

Borderlands Epistemologies

Gloria Anzaldúa, in the preface to the first edition of her seminal work, *Borderlands/La Frontera: The New Mestiza,* defined the borderlands as follows: "[T]he Borderlands are physically present whenever two or more cultures edge each other, where people of different races occupy the same territory, where under, lower, middle, and upper classes touch, where the space between two individuals shrinks with intimacy" (1987). Borderlands, therefore, represent more than the area surrounding the physical dividing line between two nation-states. They also represent the juxtaposition, interaction, and melding of cultures, social classes, sexes, and races (Ernst-Slavit 2000; Rosaldo 1993).

Borderlands theory, whether as a discourse or in reference to the ways of knowing of people who live between different worlds, was taken up by some Chicana/o scholars in the 1980s and 1990s in a wide range of fields, from literary criticism to critical ethnography (Elenes 1997; González 2001; Murillo 1999; Vásquez, Pease-Álvarez, and Shannon 1994). Such scholars themselves are a people in-between U.S. and Mexican cultures "with identities that are in constant flux" (Elenes 1997). As Villenas and Foley (2002) state, "The border, borderlands, and border crossing are a shared and collective naming of the cultural and bodily experiences under Spanish and U.S. colonialism, and U.S. and México nationalisms. . . . It is the present and future way of being in the world—the juggling [of] cultures and of embracing ambiguity, struggle, and solidarities across heterogeneities, while rejecting modernist nationalisms even as we live under modernist oppressions."

A borderlands perspective is not just rooted in unearthing practices of subordinate communities and contrasting such practices with those of the dominant cultures. Those with such a perspective seek to capture "the rich and creative borderland of interchanging identities of *mexicano,* Latino, immigrant, Mexican American, Chicano and American" (Vásquez, Pease-Álvarez, and Shannon 1994). A borderlands perspective is uniquely capable of illuminating the creative, dynamic, and ever-changing world of those persons who inhabit transnational spaces.

The Research Context

Participants

Five women who live in their parents' area of origin in rural Nuevo León, Mexico, and teach English were selected to participate. All of the participants taught English for the Programa de Inglés en Primaria (English in Primary School Program) at the time of this study. Some also had positions teaching English in *preparatorias* (high schools)[3] and in private schools. All five have siblings and/or parents living in the United States in what is essentially a second home base. In fact, out of the five sets of parents and twenty-five children total, all but one live in the home base in rural Nuevo León, or the home base in the United States. Their parents are from the marginalized working class in rural Nuevo León and consequently had little or no access to formal education. All were driven by economic circumstances to emigrate to the United States. Consequently, all of the participants acquired their English as children in the United States. Although their parents have little formal education,[4] all of the participants have at least one diploma, either from a high school in the United States or a *preparatoria* in Mexico. The participants share similar backgrounds; however, each has a unique life history worth examining in some depth.

Nora was born in the United States and attended school in California from kindergarten through the eighth grade. Her parents were migrant agricultural workers who then later secured a relatively permanent position on a large strawberry farm in California. Because Nora was unable to get her U.S. elementary- and middle-school transcripts validated when the family returned to Mexico, she completed primary, middle, and high school in Mexico through adult education programs there, and she then completed a three-year degree at a private secretarial school. At age nineteen, she returned to the United States to work for two years as a clerk at K-Mart. Then, she went back to Nuevo León, where she has been living full-time for approximately seventeen years. She has three brothers and one sister living in the United States; she visits them several times per year. She is currently completing a degree in education in Mexico and hopes to teach bilingual education for at least a few years in Texas so that her daughter will be able to attend school there.

Carely was born in Illinois but returned to rural Nuevo León as an infant and lived there until age six. Her mother works in Texas as a bartender; she has never had much contact with her father, although he was also born in the United States. Carely attended school from first through fifth grade in Texas and sixth grade through *preparatoria* in Mexico. She has been living in Mexico for the past ten years and visits her mother and two sisters in Texas several times per year. She is currently completing a degree in education in Mexico. Like Nora, Carely wants to teach bilingual education in Texas for a few years so that her two children will be able to attend elementary school there.

Elvira is the youngest of nine with a ten-year gap between her and her closest sibling. Her father worked as a carpenter in the United States for over forty years while her mother cleaned houses. Elvira's mother returned to Mexico for the birth of each of her nine children and left them in the care of their maternal grandparents because she feared that they would be drafted into the U.S. military. Elvira spent extended periods of time in *el norte* beginning at age five, when her parents were granted *la amnestía*.[5] She completed first grade through middle school in Mexico and then attended three years of high school in Texas. She had just returned to Mexico after graduating from high school when this study began. Six of her eight siblings currently live in Texas; her parents, who are now retired, spend time in both places.

Lidia was born in the United States, as were her parents, although her parents had been raised in Mexico. Her father is a mechanic and her mother is a hospital worker in Chicago. Lidia attended Head Start and kindergarten in Chicago, first and second grade in Mexico, third through sixth grade in Chicago, two years of middle school in Mexico, and finally ninth through twelfth grade and one year of community college in Chicago. Lidia had been living in Mexico for approximately two years at the time of my study. Her parents and four of her siblings live in Chicago; two more siblings live in Mexico. Lidia goes back to Chicago at least twice a year.

Laura moved with her parents to the United States at age two, attended kindergarten through fourth grade in Colorado, and fifth grade through *preparatoria* in Mexico. Her father is employed as a mechanic and her mother is a housewife. Both now live in Texas, as does one of Laura's brothers. Another brother goes back and forth because he works primarily in Texas, but his wife and child are still in Mexico. Laura has lived and worked in Texas off and on for the past ten years. She had been living in Mexico for approximately one year at the time of the study. She had not wanted to return to Mexico until her son completed elementary school in Texas, but her husband insisted that the family go back. She visits her family in Texas several times per year.

It is important to note that while this account briefly describes the participants' continuing visits to the United States, information has not been provided regarding the number of visits to Mexico made by their relatives in the United States. In the fourteen months of the study, different family members came to visit from the United States every one to two months. During these visits, Spanish, English, and a mixture of Spanish and English were spoken in the home.

Setting

Nuevo León, Mexico, is officially a U.S.-Mexico border state, although the physical border is only about ten miles wide. It is known as an industrial powerhouse with strong economic ties to the United States. Monterrey is the capital of Nuevo León and the third-largest city in Mexico, with 83% of the population of the entire state of Nuevo León residing in the Monterrey metropolitan area (Instituto Nacional de Administración Pública 1997). The five participants in this study all lived and worked in their parents' place of origin in rural Nuevo León, three to five hours from the U.S.-Mexico border.

English Language Instruction in Nuevo León

In the Mexican state of Nuevo León, the importance of English has increased exponentially in recent years. Overall, there is a general sense that English is no longer a luxury, but rather a necessity in today's world. English is a required subject at the *secundaria* (middle school) and *preparatoria* levels. Major universities such as El Instituto Tecnólogico y de Estudios Superiores de Monterrey and La Universidad de Monterrey have an institutional version of the TOEFL exam, which all students must take regardless of their field of study. Course texts are often in English because the ability to read in English is taken as a given at the university level. Thus, English is now both the hallmark of an educated man or woman in Nuevo León, and a gateway to employment. With the strong economic ties between Nuevo León and the United States and the back-and-forth movement of goods across the border, mechanics and factory workers are also confronted with demands for spoken and/or written English.

Official discourse illustrates the need for English in relation to the Tratado de Libre Comercio (North American Free Trade Agreement, or NAFTA) or in rather generic terms of *globalización* (globalization), as is evident in this excerpt from a training manual for English teachers: "The English in Primary School Project was created in 1993 in response to the social, cultural, and economic process of globalization that requires the knowledge of a foreign language" (Secretaría de Educación Pública de Nuevo León 2002) [translation]. Even in rural areas, the demand for English has increased as *maquiladoras* (foreign-owned assembly plants) have sprouted in such places to take advantage of labor cheaper than that available in border cities. As one *maquila* manager told me, "We have to learn English because they (referring to his American bosses) aren't going to learn Spanish" [translation].

The availability of English instruction in the private sector has skyrocketed with the proliferation of bilingual and immersion institutes (Grimaldo 2001). Although once limited to Monterrey, there are now private bilingual and immersion institutes in smaller cities in Nuevo León. Access to extensive English instruction within Nuevo León, like the rest of Mexico, still tends to be strongly related to social class, with more affluent parents paying dearly in an attempt to ensure that their children acquire the English language. One English immersion school in Montemorelos, Nuevo León, charged over one thousand dollars per child per month in 2004–2005 (Maestra Evangelina Arroyo, personal communication, July 14, 2005), a fee far beyond the means of working-class and many middle-class Mexicans. What is unique about the transnational individuals in this study is that these children of manual laborers already possess the English skills that everyone seems to want these days. One participant, Carely, is clearly aware of this contradiction: "It's strange, but those from above want the English that we, those from below, already have" [translation].

In acknowledgment of the growing importance of English in Mexico and in an effort to provide greater access to English instruction in the public sector, the Secretariat of Public Education of Nuevo León established the Programa de Inglés en Primaria (English in Primary School Program) first in Monterrey and later in rural areas (Secretaría de Educación Pública de Nuevo León 2002). The program provides two hours of English-language instruction per week to sixth graders enrolled in public elementary schools, provided that there is someone available to teach the language (Maestra Lupita Martínez, personal communication, August 20, 2001). At present, there is a lack of trained teachers who know English. Consequently, at the time of this study, the majority of the teachers working for the Programa de Inglés en Primaria were not trained educators but rather individuals who had passed a written and oral exam in English. Although the long-term goal is to prepare *normalistas,* or women graduates of teacher-training schools, to teach English, currently it seems that without transnationals, there would be no Programa de Inglés en Primaria in rural areas. While no official statistics exist, authorities of the Secretariat of Public Education in Nuevo León estimated that over 90% of the English teachers working in rural public elementary schools in Nuevo León acquired their English as children in the United States (Maestra Lupita Martínez, personal communication, May 11, 2002). This figure is not surprising considering that, historically, immigration to the United States was primarily a rural phenomenon, although this has changed somewhat in recent years.

The Transmission of English and Borderlands Epistemologies to the Next Generation

A primary concern for all of the participants is transmitting their borderlands understandings to their own children. While passing on the English language is an important part of this process, the participants in this analysis also value passing on cultural knowledge, and they place a great deal of emphasis on raising the next generation of border crossers.

The idea of English as a heritage language in Mexico may seem odd. However, for these participants, English is certainly not a foreign language. In most cases, they acquired English and Spanish simultaneously. It is part of their families' past, present, and future. It is one of the languages spoken by their cousins, their aunts and uncles, their nieces and nephews, and their own brothers and sisters. English was acquired, learned, and is continually renewed as a result of their transnational heritage. Within the context of Mexico, English is very much a heritage language for these participants, much as Spanish would be their heritage language in the United States.

Like their counterparts on the other side of the border, the participants display many of the same linguistic strengths and weaknesses in English that speakers of Spanish as a heritage language often display in the U.S. For example, they have high degrees of oral/aural proficiency in nonacademic contexts but less developed literacy skills. None speak what would be considered a prestigious or standard variety of English. Instead, they speak either Chicano English (Fought 2003) or regional variations of working-class American English. However, in contrast to many Spanish-as-a-heritage-language speakers in the United States, who are often viewed as deficient in Spanish as measured against an educated monolingual Spanish speaker (Potowski et al. 2002; Valdés and Geoffrion-Vinci 1998; Villa 1996, 2000, 2001, 2002; Villa and Villa 1998), these individuals are viewed as English-language experts within the context of Mexico. Indeed, they are not measured against an educated, monolingual English speaker but rather against the average English-as-a-foreign-language individual in Mexico. Their high degree of oral/aural conversational English is respected rather than deemed deficient. Furthermore, they are extremely proud of their proficiency; there is no trace of what Stephen Krashen (1998) terms "language shyness." They view themselves and are viewed by others as native speakers of the English language. Indeed, it is quite telling that education officials refer to these individuals as *maestras mexicana-americanas* (Mexican American teachers).

Like many bilinguals on the U.S. side of the border, moreover, these participants engaged in a high degree of code-switching between English and Spanish, or what they referred to as Tex-Mex, Spanglish, or *espanglés*. Code-switching is defined as the alternation of two different languages at the word, phrase, clause, or sentence level (Valdés-Fallis 1981). Code-switching is a common phenomenon among bilinguals the world over, although it is stigmatized in both Mexico and the United

States (Titone 1988). Spanish monolinguals, or English as-a-foreign-language individuals in Mexico, refer to code-switching as *hablar mocho* or *hablar pocho*, both of which would best be translated, "to speak Americanized Spanish." In the United States, the mixing of English and Spanish, whether in the form of code-switching or of borrowing English words and phrases and transforming them into Spanish, is generally referred to as Spanglish or Tex-Mex (at least in Texas). The term "Spanglish" has derogatory connotations (Stavans 2003), although in recent years both the term and Spanglish itself have gained some acceptance in the United States, as is evidenced by a popular Website, pocho.com, which proudly proclaims "Spanglish is my language," or the use of Spanglish in the popular mainstream cartoon, "Mucha Lucha," which airs on the Kids WB and the Cartoon Network.

Raising the Next Generation of Transnationals

All of the participants acknowledge the value of English in Mexico and want to pass this cultural capital on to their own children. The fact that they are earning a living in rural Nuevo León based on this cultural capital makes its value very salient. However, they mention the importance of English in Mexico only in passing, usually with a quick phrase about globalization and/or NAFTA. In contrast to their brief comments concerning the importance of English in the age of globalization, they spend considerably more time talking about the need to pass on their English and transcultural, borderlands understandings to the next generation for reasons other than those related to the global economy. For most, it is a matter of identity, much like their self-identification as *pochas*. As Nora stated, "English is a part of who I am. . . . I want my daughter to know me, and that means she has to know English." As English and the United States are a part of their family's history, they also see both as part of their children's future. However, their desire for wanting to pass on English to their children springs directly from their transnational understandings—that is, they realize that their children, like themselves and their parents, are likely to spend a great deal of their lives living and working in the United States (Kandel and Massey 2002).

The transmission of English and transcultural knowledge to the next generation is viewed by these participants as part of a contingency plan in case their economic situation changes in Mexico. It must be remembered that these transnationals are the children of yesterday's rural poor, who were forced by economic circumstances to emigrate. For family members, living and working in the United States is still a necessity. For example, most of Elvira's siblings are in the United States because there are no employment opportunities in rural Nuevo León. Although these participants now live comfortably in Mexico, they do not view their economic situation as being necessarily stable. Indeed, they see returning to the United States to live and work as a distinct possibility. When they ponder their own children's future, they consider the realities of both sides of the border. Laura, her husband, and her son have had to relocate to the United States twice for economic reasons. In the following excerpt, she draws attention to the importance of transmitting both her English and transcultural knowledge to her son as she compares her husband to her son: "I mean, Eddie, my husband, he's only from here [Mexico]. He doesn't know English and, worse, he doesn't know what to do over there [the States]. . . . It was better the second time we lived there, but still he hates it over there and that's hard. I don't hate it. Maybe because I know what to say and I know what to do. And I want my son to know what to say and what to do over there. . . . Who knows when we will go back next?"

The possibility of returning to the United States becomes apparent in the great effort put forth by these women in maintaining their own legal status in *el norte* and in making sure that their children also have legal U.S. status. Both Nora and Carely, who are American citizens, are involved in the lengthy and costly process of obtaining citizenship for their children born in Mexico. Carely, who was pregnant with her second child at the beginning of the study, went north to have her baby. Laura had her son in the United States so he would never have any trouble crossing back and forth. Furthermore, the events of September 11, 2001 in the United States aroused fear among those participants and/or their family members who are not citizens that their permanent resident status would be revoked. Elvira sums up the general feeling about the relative instability of Mexico and the worry that a post-September 11 policy would put their legal status in jeopardy. Elvira states: "Another part of the reason I am becoming a citizen now is *todo eso del once de septiembre* [all this about September 11]. I have a *mica* [resident card] and all, but who knows what *la migra* [the INS] will do? We're all changing our citizenship. I'm still Mexican in my heart, but I need that passport *por si acaso* [just in case], because you never know what's going to happen in Mexico either."

Legal status in the United States is important to these individuals because they see their future in Mexico as uncertain. They live comfortably now but believe that economic conditions in Mexico could deteriorate overnight. They and their parents have benefited from immigration and from having legal status in the United States, and they want the same benefits for their children. Their contingency plans involve more than just legal maneuvering, however; they are very concerned about providing their children with the skills necessary to survive in the United States *por si acaso* (just in case). All of the participants, whether they have children yet or not, have a plan to ensure that their offspring develop these skills. A key part of this plan is to have their children attend elementary school in the United States for several years. Laura, Nora, and Carely already had children at the time of this study; all three women speak English to their children. However, Laura is the only participant with a school-age child. She did carry out this plan, although not for the length of time that she, her parents, and siblings living in the United States thought was necessary. Laura explains, "I always talk to Eddie [her son] in English, but I kept telling my husband that wasn't enough. I wanted him to be in school over there like I was at least till fourth or fifth grade. My mom and dad said the same thing to him [her husband], but he didn't want to stay. So we came back. And I told him that now Eddie was going to have an accent in English, like my youngest brother does, and that's not good."

Like Laura, all of the participants see elementary school as the key to mastering English because it is crucial for their children to develop native-like pronunciation. As with the case of Laura's brother, their obsession with pronunciation is tied to their own families' transnational experiences. All of the participants, except Nora, state that their parents eventually did learn English and that their English is intelligible but heavily accented. They believe that Americans in general have a low tolerance for accented English and that their own children need to excel at native-like English in order to be treated well in the United States.

None of the new private immersion or bilingual schools would do for their children because these parents believed that no school in Mexico could provide their children with native-like English proficiency, nor would these schools provide them with the appropriate cultural tools. They want their children to know what to say and what to do in the United States, to be able to negotiate with the same skill and ease that they themselves possess. From their perspective, this cannot be taught in Mexico. Their contingency plans include living in the United States for several years regardless of whether they are doing well financially in Mexico. In this way, their children will experience life across the border while attending elementary school there.

Inside the Transnational Classroom

All of the participants teach English to working-class students at the primary-school level in rural Nuevo León, Mexico; Nora and Laura also teach advanced classes of English to working- and lower-middle-class students at the secondary level in the same area. These transnational individuals bring their borderlands understanding to the teaching of English. Their classrooms are centers of language and cultural lessons informed by their own experiences in the United States as well as by their understanding of social class structure in Mexico. In contrast to the rhetoric used by Nuevo León's Secretariat of Public Education, which focuses on the value of English within Mexico, they teach English to their working-class students with an eye toward their eventual emigration north. They constantly substitute and/or add to textbook vocabulary with what they believe are more widely used terms. For example, "store" is substituted for "shop," while "children" and "kids" are interchanged freely. These teachers speak in contractions and require their students to do the same because, as Elvira stated, "If you can't hear the difference between *should* and *shouldn't* and you don't say them right, you're going to have problems over there (referring to the States), 'cause nobody says the whole thing."

Nonstop Language and Cultural Lessons

As teachers in Mexico, these participants are constantly providing cultural "translations" of English textbook pictures that typically depict the U.S. school setting. Such pictures are often incomprehensible to children in rural Nuevo León, and no explanations are given in the text. The following example illustrates a typical language and culture lesson given by these transnational teachers. Lidia is interpreting an illustration that shows a schoolboy carrying a lunch tray:

> *Mira el dibujito del* boy. *Tiene una bandeja con su* food *porque allá te dan de comer en la escuela al mediodía. Allá los* kids *están en la* school *desde las* eight in the morning *hasta las three* in the afternoon *y por eso,* they eat at school *en vez de la casa. Y ¿Y ves el cartoncito ahí?* It's milk. *Porque todos los* children *tienen que tomar* milk in school. Ramón, do you like milk? [Look at the picture of the boy. He has a tray with his food because over there they feed you in school at noon. Over there, kids are in school from eight in the morning until three in the afternoon and that's why they eat at school instead of at home. And see the little carton there? It's milk. Because all the children have to drink milk in school. Ramón, do you like milk?]

In this cultural lesson, Lidia code-switches to English those words and phrases that the children already know or are learning. She explains to her students that the American children eat lunch at school because the children in Nuevo León generally go home for the midday meal.[6] Most children attend classes either in the morning or in the afternoon, thus allowing many public schools to function essentially as two schools.[7] Furthermore, milk is typically not a staple of Mexican children's diets past infancy. Finally, she uses the words "kids" and "children" interchangeably. Although the textbook vocabulary does not include the word "kids," she has taught this term to her students because she knows of its common use in the United States.

In contrast to the methods employed by these transnational teachers, I never observed a non-transnational teacher[8] who had learned English as a foreign language in Mexico deviate from the textbook. Instead, they tended to follow the textbook as if it were a bible of sorts. They translated from one language to the other rather than code-switch. They did not use contractions when speaking English and tended not to teach them with any degree of emphasis. They provided no additional vocabulary or cultural mini lessons.

Culture per se does not appear in the Programa de Inglés en Primaria curriculum supplied by the Coordinación del Programa de Idiomas.

Instead, learning objectives center on particular grammatical structures. Certainly, the curriculum itself is very heavy considering the
number of contact hours. Yet, the data from this study point to transnational teachers' need to add what they believe to be important vocabulary and cultural mini lessons. When asked why they felt obliged
to add to an already crowded curriculum, all drew a distinction between "book English" and "real English," as did Laura: "I think it is
important for the kids to know real English. *Al otro lado* [on the other
side] nobody talks like the book. They need real English to be able to
make it."

Pedagogical Code-Switching

As is also evident in Lidia's excerpt, these transnational teachers engaged in a high degree of code-switching between English and Spanish.
Yet the type of code-switching illustrated above is not the same as that
engaged in by these transnational teachers with their transnational family members. In pedagogical code-switching, they slow their rate of
speech as well as stress and carefully enunciate the English words and
phrases. Furthermore, they are very conscious of which words they
will use in English, thus demonstrating a keen awareness of the realities of their classrooms. Here, Lidia is responding to a request made
by an education official calling on English teachers to use only English
in the classroom: "Use all English, yeah, right, like that will work. I
mean, come on, these kids only have English for two hours a week,
and that is if they don't have to practice for *Día de la Bandera* [Flag Day]
or some other thing. So I always use the English words they are learning, or already should know, and Spanish so they will be able to figure
out what the hell is going on."

Lidia clearly articulated the pedagogical need for code-switching,
which is very much based in the realities of the classroom. Although
education officials in Mexico express a desire that teachers in this particular statewide primary-school English program use only English in
the classroom, that strategy is very difficult to implement when the
children have little exposure to English each week and the teachers
work at several schools. In reality, both transnational and non-
transnational teachers used a lot of Spanish in the classroom. However,
there is a clear difference between the way that transnational and non-

transnational teachers used Spanish and English. The non-transnational teachers whom I observed never code-switched as the transnationals did. Instead, they translated on a sentence-by-sentence basis: first a sentence in English, followed by the same sentence in Spanish, or vice versa. Their students caught on quickly so that it was not necessary to listen to the English at all. In contrast, the students in the classrooms of the transnational teachers had to pay attention to the English in order to follow the conversation.

Pronunciation, Pronunciation, and More Pronunciation

These transnational teachers spend an inordinate amount of time imparting their particular variety of American English pronunciation to their students. This is seen as one of the benefits of having transnational teachers in the classroom. An official of the Secretariat of Public Education stated, "The students of Mexican American teachers speak better, that is, they pronounce the words better" [translation]. However, the emphasis that these transnational teachers place upon pronunciation is directly related to their own experiences in the United States, specifically to the treatment that their parents received as nonnative speakers of English in the United States. Laura stated: "My parents know English now. They didn't when we first lived there, but they learned it. I mean, they lived there for thirty years. Of course, they know English. But I feel so sorry for them sometimes. Like my mom, people just don't want to talk to her because she has an accent." In their minds, accurate pronunciation is an integral part of being able to survive in the United States and is a key to not experiencing discrimination. Consequently, the participants in this study spend a great deal of time attempting to teach their students native-like pronunciation. This attention to pronunciation directly relates to their views of where their students will use their English.

English for Use Outside Mexico

The official discourse in Mexico surrounding the need for English relates to increasing foreign investment and global economic ties. English is seen for use within the borders of Mexico itself. However, the transnational teachers project their own family history onto their students. They think that economic conditions in these rural areas will force many of their charges to seek employment in the United States, much like their own parents did. Lidia stated concretely what the participants tended to believe: "I know lots of these kids *van a ir para el otro lado* [are going to the other side]. It's bad for them, and I think it's getting worse. So what choice do they have?"

In this way, these transnational teachers view English as necessary for survival in the United States rather than for use in Mexico. Fluency in native-like English within the borders of Mexico is not essential; a basic grasp of the language would do, since an English-speaking businessman or tourist would be in a dependent position. However, native-like English is required to be treated well in the United States. These transnational teachers are attempting to prepare their students for the language and culture they will encounter *al otro lado*. The following example is from one of Nora's classes:

Nora: Okay, now, *el libro dice yes, pero les voy a enseñar otra palabra más importante que significa lo mismo* [the book says yes, but I'm going to teach you a more important word which means the same thing.] Yeah. Now, everybody: Yeah.

Student: *Ticher, ¿Cómo se escribe* yeah? [Teacher, How do you write yeah?]

Nora: *No importa como se escribe. Lo más importante es que lo digas bien.* [It doesn't matter how it's written. What is important is that you say it well.] Yeah.

Student: Yeah.

Nora: *Porque si te para la migra al otro lado y te pregunta,* "Are you a U.S. citizen?" *Eres ciudadano? Y tú le dices,* "yes," . . . *pues, la migra va a saber de inmediato que no eres de allá porque los de allá dicen,* "yeah." [Because if the INS (Immigration and Naturalization Service) stops you on the other side and asks you, "Are you a U.S. citizen?" and you tell them, "yes," . . . well, the INS is going to know right away that you are not from there (the States) because everyone from there says "yeah."]

Shifting Identities, Transnational Education

The literature on transnationalism tends to focus on how immigrants and their children living in the host country maintain ties with the country of origin (Goldin 1999; Levitt and Waters 2002). In the case of Mexican immigrant families, the emphasis is often on the maintenance (or loss) of the Spanish language and Mexican cultural practices (Portes and Rumbaut 2001; Rumbaut 2002). This study fills a gap in the research literature by viewing the phenomenon from the Mexican side of the border. Exploring both sides is critical for a deeper understanding of transnationalism because, contrary to the stereotype in the United States, the migratory flow of people across the U.S.-Mexico border is bidirectional. In the case of these participants, the boundaries of host country and country of origin blur, as do the dichotomous identities inspired by the respective nation-states. When the participants of this study returned to live in Mexico, they did not revert to some essentialized notion of Mexican-ness, but instead were influenced by their experiences on both sides of the border. They now identify themselves (*pocha*) and are often named by others (*maestras mexicana-americanas*) as a product of both.

Trueba (1999) posited that Latinos in the United States have multiple, shifting identities. As is evident in this study, these participants did not leave their multiple, shifting identities behind when crossing the border into Mexico. This ability to shift, to feel at home on both sides of the border, is part of their cultural heritage. It is this heritage that they, as parents, seek to pass on to the next generation so that their children will be able to participate fully in familial networks that transcend the border (Kandel and Massey 2002; Massey 1987; Massey, Goldring, and Durand 1994). This transnational heritage is manifested linguistically through their use of English, Spanish, and Spanglish. Researchers have documented the linguistic practices of Mexican immigrants and their offspring in the United States (González 2001; Guerra 1998; Vásquez, Pease-Álvarez, and Shannon 1994). To date, I have found no studies documenting the linguistic practices of immigrants and their bilingual children who return to Mexico. However, as is evident in this study, such individuals do not revert to historical, pre-immigration language patterns. Nora's daughter sings "The Itsy

Bitsy Spider" and "Un elefante"[9] with equal enthusiasm because Nora has taught her both. Spanish, English, and Spanglish represent the linguistic heritage of these transnational families.

While much has been written about the effects of Mexican immigration on the school system in the United States, very little exists regarding the same phenomenon in Mexico. Certainly, Mexican scholars have begun to investigate transnational educational issues (Smith 2006; Tuirán 2001; Weller Ford 1999, 1995; Zuniga 2001), but these scholars are rarely read in the United States. Much work needs to be done in this area as increasing numbers of families return to their homeland with extensive experiences in the United States. It is necessary to understand the migration to *el norte* as a cultural norm or rite of passage in many areas of Mexico and the effects of this migration on the educational system both north and south of the border (Kandel and Massey 2002).

This study represents an attempt to explore transnational education issues from the Mexican side. Transnational teachers in Mexico are playing a critical role in the Americanization of Mexican youth both linguistically and culturally. They are a valuable source of pre-immigration information (Brittain 2002). The *maestras mexicana-americanas* are influencing the way that English is taught in rural Nuevo León. In contrast to the official discourse, which emphasizes English for use *within* Mexico, these transnational teachers stress English for use *outside* Mexico. The participants in this study understand the economic realities that their working-class students face because they relate them to their own parents' experience. They believe that immigration to the United States is a likely future path for many of the rural, working-class children whom they teach. Thus, they stress the importance of providing the children with the language and skills necessary to survive in the United States. These transnational teachers transmit their borderlands understandings to their students, thus preparing them for future journeys through the physical and cultural borderlands.

Notes

Many heartfelt thanks to the participants, their families, *y todos en México* who made this study possible. I would also like to thank the Fulbright Program and the Comisión México-Estados Unidos para el Intercambio Educativo y

Cultural as well as the University of Texas at Austin for their financial support. A special thanks to Patricia Sánchez and to all Las Fronterizas for their help and support.

1. There are substantial U.S. expatriate communities of Anglo Americans in various parts of Mexico, such as at San Miguel de Allende, Guanajuato, and Lake Chapala, Jalisco.

2. It is common practice for transnational families to have relatives in Mexico obtain Mexican birth certificates for any children born in the United States. Although the practice is technically illegal, it is much easier than registering the birth at a Mexican consulate in the States.

3. A *preparatoria* is similar to a U.S. high school; however, students may study a trade rather than college preparatory work.

4. Out of the five sets of parents of the participants, only one parent had completed elementary school. The rest had been forced by economic necessity to leave school after a couple of years or had never attended at all.

5. The Immigration Reform and Control Act (IRCA) of 1986 included two related programs that were designed to identify and legalize undocumented immigrants. These became popularly known as La Amnestía, or Amnesty.

6. The midday meal is the main meal of the day in Mexico. Pilot programs have begun in some public elementary schools in Nuevo León in which the children attend classes all day; however, generally there is a two-hour break so that they may return home for the main meal of the day. Private schools have extended hours of attendance by beginning earlier in the morning and ending an hour or two later, but the school day ends around 1:00 or 2:00 when the children go home to eat.

7. Two schools often share the same physical plant at different times of the day. For example, in the morning session, or *turno matutino*, a school has one name and one set of teachers and administrators. During the afternoon session, or *turno vespertino*, the same building takes on a different name and a different set of teachers and administrators.

8. Non-transnational teachers of English are common in Monterrey. I had the opportunity to observe three such teachers in Monterrey on several occasions during the course of this study.

9. "Un elefante" is a common children's song in Mexico. It is sung with gestures, like "The Itsy Bitsy Spider."

References

Anzaldúa, Gloria. 1987. *Borderlands/La Frontera: The New Mestiza*. San Francisco: Spinsters/Aunt Lute Books.

Bogdan, Robert C., and Sari Knopp Biklen. 1998. *Qualitative Research for Education: An Introduction to Theory and Methods*. 3d ed. Boston: Allyn and Bacon.

Brittain, Carmina. 2002. *Transnational Messages: Experiences of Chinese and Mexican Immigrants in American Schools*. New York: LFB Scholarly Publishing.

Consejo Nacional de Población. 2001. *La población de México en el nuevo siglo*. México, D.F.: Consejo Nacional de Población.

Earle, Duncan. 1999. "The Borderless Borderlands: Texas Colonias as Displaced Settlements." In *Identities on the Move: Transnational Processes in North America and the Caribbean Basin*, ed. L. R. Goldin, 169–83. Albany, NY: Institute for Mesoamerican Studies and the University at Albany.

Elenes, C. Alejandra. 1997. "Reclaiming the Borderlands: Chicana/o Identity, Difference, and Critical Pedagogy." *Educational Theory* 47: 359–75.

Ernst-Slavit, Gisela. 2000. "Confronting the Walls: Border Crossing, Gender Differences, and Language Learning in Academe." In *Immigrant Voices: In Search of Educational Equity*, ed. E. Trueba and L. I. Bartolomé, 247–60. Lanham, MD: Rowman and Littlefield.

Fought, Carmen. 2003. *Chicano English in Context*. New York: Palgrave Macmillan.

Goldin, Liliana R., ed. 1999. *Identities on the Move: Transnational Processes in North America and the Caribbean Basin*. Albany, NY: Institute for Mesoamerican Studies and the University at Albany.

González, Norma. 2001. *I Am My Language: Discourses of Women and Children in the Borderlands*. Tucson: University of Arizona Press.

Grimaldo, Andrea. 2001, November. "ESL in the Private Sector in Monterrey, Mexico." Paper presented at the TexTESOL State Conference: An ESL Odyssey, Austin, Texas.

Guerra, Juan C. 1998. *Close to Home: Oral and Literate Practices in a Transnational Mexicano Community*. New York: Teachers College Press.

Instituto Nacional de Administración Pública. 1997. *La administración local en México*, vol. 2. México, D.F.: Instituto Nacional de Administración Pública.

Itzigsohn, José, Carlos Dore Cabral, Esther Hernández Medina, and Obed Vázquez. 1999. "Mapping Dominican Transnationalism: Narrow and Broad Transnational Practices." *Ethnic and Racial Studies* 22(2): 316–39.

Kandel, William, and Douglas S. Massey. 2002. "The Culture of Mexican Migration: A Theoretical and Empirical Analysis." *Social Forces* 80(3): 981–1004.

Krashen, Stephen D. 1998. "Language Shyness and Heritage Language Development." In *Heritage Language Development*, ed. S. Krashen, L. Tse, and J. McQuillan, 41–49. Culver City, CA: Language Education Associates.

Levitt, Peggy, and Mary C. Waters. 2002. "Introduction." In *The Changing Face of Home: The Transnational Lives of the Second Generation*, ed. Peggy Levitt and Mary C. Waters, 1–30. New York: Russell Sage Foundation.

Massey, Douglas S. 1987. *Return to Aztlán: The Social Process of International Migration from Western Mexico*. Berkeley: University of California Press.

Massey, Douglas S., Luin Goldring, and Jorge Durand. 1994. "Continuities in Transnational Migration: An Analysis of Nineteen Mexican Communities." *American Journal of Sociology* 99: 1492–1533.

Murillo, Enrique G., Jr. 1999. "Mojado Crossings along Neoliberal Borderlands." *Educational Foundations* 13: 7–30.

Portes, Alejandro, and Rubén G. Rumbaut. 2001. *Legacies: The Story of the Immigrant Second Generation*. Berkeley and New York: University of California Press and Russell Sage Foundation.

Portes, Alejandro, Luis Guarnizo, and Patricia Landolt. 1999. "Introduction: Pitfalls and Promise of an Emergent Research Field." *Ethnic and Racial Studies* 22(2): 217–37.

Potowski, Kim, Maria Hernández, and Mariela Cordero. 2002. "Placement of Heritage Spanish Speakers." Paper presented in November at the Convention of the American Council on the Teaching of Foreign Languages: Beyond Our Customary Borders, Salt Lake City, Utah.

Pries, Ludger. 2001. "The Disruption of Social and Geographic Space." Available at http://www.ruhr-uni-bochum.de/soaps/download/publi-2001_lp_thedisruption.pdf (last accessed May 16, 2003).

Rosaldo, Renato. 1993. *Culture and Truth: The Remaking of Social Analysis*. Boston: Beacon Press.

Rumbaut, Rubén G. 2002. "Severed or Sustained Attachments? Language, Identity, and Imagined Communities in the Post-Immigrant Generation." In *The Changing Face of Home: The Transnational Lives of the Second Generation*, ed. Peggy Levitt and Mary C. Waters, 43–95. New York: Russell Sage Foundation.

Secretaría de Educación Pública de Nuevo León. 2002. *Coordinación del programa de idiomas en Nuevo León: Manual de inducción*. Monterrey, México: Secretaría de Educación Pública de Nuevo León.

Smith, Patrick. 2006. "Transnacionalismo, bilingüismo y la planeación lingüística en contextos educativos mexicanos." In *Los retos de la política del lenguaje en el siglo XXI*, 2:419–41. México, D.F.: Universidad Nacional Autónoma de México.

Stavans, Ilan. 2003. *Spanglish: The Making of a New American Language*. New York: HarperCollins.

Titone, Renzo. 1988. "From Bilingual to Mixtilingual Speech: Codeswitching Revisited." *Rassegna Italiana de Linguistica Applicata* 20(2): 15–21.

Trueba, Enrique T. 1999. *Latinos Unidos: From Cultural Diversity to the Politics of Solidarity*. Lanham, MD: Rowman and Littlefield.

Tuirán, Rodolfo. 2001. "Migración México-Estados Unidos: Hacía una nueva agenda bilateral." In *Migración México-Estados Unidos: Opciones de política*, ed. R. Huirán, 11–30. México: Consejo Nacional de Población.

Valdés, Guadalupe, and Michelle Geoffrion-Vinci. 1998. "Chicano Spanish: The Problem of the 'Underdeveloped' Code in Bilingual Repertoires." *Modern Language Journal* 82(4): 473–501.

Valdés-Fallis, Guadalupe. 1981. "Codeswitching as Deliberate Verbal Strategy: A Microanalysis of Direct and Indirect Requests among Bilingual Chicano Speakers." in *Latino Language and Communicative Behavior,* ed. R. P. Durán, 95–108. Norwood, NJ: ABLEX.

Vásquez, Olga A., Lucinda Pease-Álvarez, and Sheila M. Shannon. 1994. *Pushing Boundaries: Language and Culture in a Mexicano Community.* Cambridge, Eng.: Cambridge University Press.

Villa, Daniel J. 1996. "Choosing a 'Standard' Variety of Spanish for the Instruction of Native Spanish Speakers in the U.S." *Foreign Language Annals* 29(2): 191–200.

———. 2000. "Languages Have Armies, and Economies, Too: The Presence of U.S. Spanish in the Spanish-Speaking World." *Southwest Journal of Linguistics* 19(2): 143–54.

———. 2001. "A Millennial Reflection Sobre la Nueva Reconquista." *Southwest Journal of Linguistics* 20(1): 1–13.

———. 2002. "The Sanitizing of U.S. Spanish in Academia." *Foreign Language Annals* 35(2): 222–30.

Villa, Daniel J., and Jennifer Villa. 1998. "Identity Labels and Self-Reported Language Use: Implications for Spanish Language Programs." *Foreign Language Annals* 31(4): 505–16.

Villenas, Sofia, and Douglas Foley. 2002. "Chicano/Latino Critical Ethnography of Education: Cultural Productions from La Frontera." In *Chicano School Failure and Success: Past, Present, and Future,* 2nd ed., ed. R. Valencia, 195–225. London and New York: Routledge Falmer.

Weller Ford, Georganne. 1995. *Un nuevo desafío para la planificación lingüística en México y en los Estados Unidos: La presencia de indígenas mexicanos en zonas fronterizas.* México: Informe Final Fideicomiso para la Cultura México/USA.

———. 1999. *Diseño de un modelo de atención educativa de nivel primaria para niños y niñas jornaleros agrícolas migrantes.* México: Dirección General de Investigación Educativa.

Zuniga, Victor. 2001. "Migrantes internacionales de México a Estados Unidos: Hacía la creación de políticas educativas binacionales." In *Migración México-Estados Unidos: Opciones de política,* ed. R. Huirán, 299–327. México: Consejo Nacional de Población.

CHAPTER NINE

The Real and the Symbolic

Visualizing Border Spaces

Amelia Malagamba-Ansótegui

It is very difficult in these times to think of, or to imagine, a world without borders. Some are being redrawn, some have disappeared, and some are contested on military, religious, or cultural grounds. Paradoxically, at a time when the concept of globalization seems to address not only the economies of the world but also its many cultural practices, the U.S.-Mexico border, as a concept and as the reality of a very localized place, seems more relevant than ever. The accumulated experiences of pain, loss, and opportunities found at the border between Mexico and the United States are the bases from which the border artists create signifying systems that articulate place and space. The new practices of representation inspired by this emerging aesthetic language seem to find a fertile ground on the world's art scene, thus globalizing the border spaces they represent.

This chapter deals with some of the multiple articulations of place and space in the visual language of artists working at, and about, the border between Mexico and the United States. Some of these articulations involve the everyday cultural and social practices of the region and the geopolitical line that divides it. Many articulations explored by border artists, both Mexican and Chicana/o, have contributed to changing, or challenging, the existent signifying systems; that is to say, artists have produced new meanings and new positions from which one imagines and lives the border. These signifying systems, or practices of representation, have underlined the place—being on one side or the other of the line—and the asymmetries, contradictions, and negotiations that occur by this placement. They have also stressed the differences in naming and writing the history of the border.

Naming the Border

El norte, la frontera, la línea, el otro lado, the north, the frontier, the line, the other side—the border between Mexico and the United States has long been the source of wars, disputes, tension, and social and political change.[1] It has been the site of much conflict.[2] The mass media have both glamorized and badmouthed the border, and it has been both the subject and the central protagonist for novelists, storytellers, and essayists.[3] At the end of the twentieth century, social scientists have come to recognize the border as an increasingly important field of study,[4] and it now is often considered a spatial geographical area.[5] In Mexico the border is called *la línea;* we can even refer to the border as "her," since *la línea* in Spanish is feminine.[6] Mexicans also call "her" *la frontera,* the physical limit of something that has a determined center; in other words, the border designates the margin or the periphery. The people residing along it, *los fronterizos,* imply the border itself when positioning themselves geographically. We also refer to it as *el otro lado* to convey the idea of a whole, which has at least two sides.

In the Mexican collective imagination, *la frontera* has a layered meaning of something mysterious or unknown. Although this connotation was established in past centuries, a layer of mystery and strangeness is possible to "see" and "hear" today.[7] Mexicans call the border region *el norte,* a term that harbors references to the "barbaric" land, the place of *la carne asada,* of the Chichimeca tribes and the desert. Particularly for the Mexican migrant population from the center and south of the country, *la frontera* brings to mind the geographical proximity to the United States, "the land of opportunity." However, it is also associated in the collective imagination with drugs, prostitution, and death.[8] Films produced in Mexico and Hollywood, which have given rise to an entire cinematic genre about *la frontera*, constantly reinforce these associations.[9]

From the U.S. perspective, and in the English language, the border region is known as "the Far West" in written history. For many scholars, novelists, and producers of the "western" movie genre, the Far West refers not only to a specific geographical area and time period but also to an indiscriminate Anglo desire for colonization and expansion from the seventeenth into the twentieth century. The term *border* is used with a meaning similar to that in Mexico, connoting a center and its margin. Since the Prohibition era of the 1920s, the term *border* has carried another meaning: that of a symbolic zone of tolerance in which the illegitimate is legitimized. It is imagined simultaneously as a zone of transgression and tolerance.

The notion of "the frontier" generally implies the right to colonize savage peoples and indomitable lands, which, historically, translated into Anglo annexation dreams of the territories of California, Arizona, New Mexico, Nevada, Texas, and parts of Colorado. We find this term in various treaties and official requests made by Anglo colonizers to the U.S. government prior to the Treaty of Guadalupe Hidalgo (1848). With regard to popular culture, the term *frontier* brings to mind cowboy movies with a cast of Anglo heroes who are defined by their whiteness. Their powerful bodies and stern visages suggest their strength of character and their conviction that reason is on their side. These Anglo heroes were, and are, always the good guys.[10] (Today, Hollywood continues to reproduce these themes as the United States continues to explore and conquer space, the last frontier.)

As a counterpart to the heroes in movies about the "frontier," we find the savage Indian, who needs to be eliminated to make a better world. Another member of the cast of Hollywood characters is the lazy, tricky, and sleepy Mexican. This usually male character does not display a conscience of his own and thus has no knowledge of good and evil. Mexican females are generally portrayed as *mansas, humildes y cariñosas* (docile, humble, and loving). If they do not follow this profile, they are usually seen as prostitutes, traitors, or *vendidas* (sellouts).

If one moves from the representations, stereotypes, and labels created or supported by the media to historical shifts beginning in the

1960s, concepts of the border have undergone profound changes brought about by an accelerated development of the region in both countries. This development reflected northern Mexico's age-old desire for political decentralization of the region; challenging Mexican centralism, the expansion of transnational corporations (*maquilas*) has resulted in a distinct economy that has contributed to changes in the political landscape. Although the peoples on both sides of *la línea* have shared the historical experience of the border, these experiences have not been equal.

The asymmetry of the economic, political, cultural, and labor relations, together with the enforced sharing of natural resources between the two countries, have created new border paradigms that reflect globalization. As the concepts of "cultural" and "national" identities apparently have begun to lose their political power and symbolic meaning, related concepts, such as sovereignty and a country's "destiny," are increasingly questioned when economies are becoming deeply interdependent. Like these monolithic concepts, the globalization of the concept of "borders" has begun to be reevaluated. How does one think about borders when there is such interdependency at the global level? What, then, are borders? What do, or can, they mean in this era of globalization?

The globalization of the concept of the border has not caused a loss of the various meanings described in the above paragraphs. Rather, other associations have recently been added to those well-documented notions, thus influencing in powerful ways theories of language, material culture, and the visual arts. When we think of *la frontera* today, we tend to think more of processes of fragmentation, dislocation, translation, and cultural negotiations. The Chicana/o and Latina/o communities in the United States have played key roles in the development of these new meanings of *la frontera*.

A View into Border Art: The Power of Place and Remembered Geographies

Chicana/o and border artists have tapped into the many problematic, rich, and complex currents that come to meet, confront, struggle, and negotiate a line drawn in a landscape. This line, enforced with barbed wire, not only has divided Mexico from the United States but also has provided artists with a fertile symbolic field.

Rupert García and Malaquías Montoya, for example, began their careers as part of the Chicano Movement in the 1960s. Both artists were original members of the influential early collective, Mexican American Liberation Art Front (MALAF), first organized in 1969 (Maciel 1990: 116). Both also created seminal, powerful works that explore the icon of the barbed wire. For instance, in García's serigraph, or silkscreen, *¡Cesen Deportación!* (Stop Deportation!) from 1975, three horizontal lines of black barbed wire cross the vibrant red ink that covers the whole composition from end to end. In the right top corner is the title of the work in yellow letters. For someone who knows the border, the message, which criticizes the tactics of the Immigration and Naturalization Service (INS) in combating migration from Mexico to the United States, is instantly clear. The image clamors to stop deportations of Mexicans. Yet, other meanings may be found. Black and red also represent syndicalism. The artist conveys the need for unified actions to stop the politics of harassment at the border. Moreover, the red background seems to suggest an ocean of blood, and the three lines of barbed wire resemble scars from an unnamed wound. Anticipating the imagery of subsequent generations of Chicana/o artists, García creates a relationship between the iconographies and meanings of the Mesoamerican and Catholic religions with references to bloodletting, sacrifice, crucifixion, and offerings as well as to migration, civil rights, and cultural citizenship.

Malaquías Montoya is one of the most prolific *veteranos* from the Chicano art movement. Barbed wire is one of his most recurrent icons. In murals, serigraphs, and paintings, Montoya introduces barbed wire as a reminder of border conflict. In his serigraph *Undocumented,* from 1981 (see Figure 9.1), a handless and faceless man is suspended in the air against six horizontal rows of barbed wire. Written in red, the word *UNDOCUMENTED* crosses the crucified body. Drops of red ink from the head down to the feet represent blood. Although Montoya does not consider himself a Catholic, the religious reference to the crucified Jesus is unavoidable. Another source for the artist, and for many others, is the imagery of the Jewish Holocaust. The ubiquitous barbed wire at Auschwitz and other concentration camps during the Nazi terror adds another layer of meaning. Used in relation to the border, barbed wire suggests a contemporary, ongoing holocaust. Most important, however, barbed wire in this and other pieces by Montoya functions as a direct reference to the border as a place.

The work of these two artists reflects the concerns and aesthetic propositions of the 1960s. Other artists, however, have gone through a transformational process toward less traditional approaches. The selection of artists in this essay not only represents the diversity of media and aesthetic strategies in their work but also reflects their individual genealogies. Strategies and media range from traditional forms, such as printmaking techniques, painting, and sculpture, to on-site installations, diverse approaches to public art, and visual projections of photographic material.

The contemporary physical, social, and cultural landscape of the border is a powerful, problematic space and place. The untitled photograph by the Mexican photographer Lourdes Grobet from the 1980s series *Tijuana, la casa de toda la gente*[11] and the monotype by artist Luis Montenegro from 1993, *Llegué del Otro Lado* (see Figure 9.2), are examples of these problematic landscapes. Each in a different medium, the artists use barbed wire as a protagonist-referent of place. Grobet's almost idyllic landscape, with truncated paths created by the feet of the migrants, can only be identified as the border because of the fence, which divides the scene. In Montenegro's piece, the fence occupies almost the entire space, as if engulfing the small image of a man trying to climb it. Red blood is splattered at the bottom of the fence, which rises to an endless sky.

In recent years, artists from other parts of Mexico have turned their attention to the border. (Most Mexican artists, especially those from Mexico City, have traditionally ignored it.) Such is the case of Silvia Gruner's installation at the border fence of *el bordo*, a new name for a special section of the boundary in Tijuana. In this piece, constructed for the project *inSITE94*, the artist literally incorporates the fence into the art.[12] Entitled *In the Middle of the Road/En la Mitad del Camino*, the fence in the background supports rustic wooden chairs in which sit three-dimensional figurines of the Mesoamerican goddess Tlazoltéotl in the act of childbirth. The goddess directs her gaze, multiplied by her repeated representations, toward the present-day undocumented workers who walk casually on *el bordo*, waiting for night to protect them from another gaze, that of *la migra* (the INS). After the Iraq War of the

Figure 9.1. Malaquías Montoya, *Undocumented,* 1981. Serigraph. Collection of Gilberto Cárdenas. By permission of the artist.

Figure 9.2. Luis Montenegro, *Llegué del Otro Lado,* 1993. Monotype. Private Collection. By permission of the artist.

1990s, this part of the fence was built with leftover metal landing strips used during the Gulf War. The use of these materials seems in an ironic way to symbolize the increased militarization of the border that has taken place in the past fifteen years.[13]

The fence that draws the division of the land is for Chicana/o and border artists a world of referents. Gregory K. Dreicer (1997: 8) in his introduction to *Between Fences,* an exhibition on the history of the fence in the United States, states: "We live between fences. We may hardly notice them, but they are dominant figures in our lives. Our past is defined by the cutting point of the barbed wire. . . . Fences are essential to the way we think about the land, the way we behave on the land, and the way we expect our land to look." Lucila Villaseñor Grijalva's *From the Other Side* and Ester Hernández's *Border Flower* (see Figure 9.3)—both works from 1994 and both monoserigraphs—feature the fence/barbed wire as the main image. Villaseñor's piece shows hands crossed like those of people detained by *la migra*. These hands are holding the fence in a futile sign of surrender. In contrast, Hernández's piece makes the wire fertile, with flowers growing out of the barbs.

Figure 9.3. Ester Hernández, *Border Flower,* 1994. Monoserigraph. Private Collection. By permission of the artist.

The border's barbed-wire fence not only dominates the lives of its people on both sides, but it also cuts, hurts, and dismembers. The fence and the divided land have served as receptacles for remembering fragmented realities and geographies for Chicana/o and border artists. A 1987 serigraph by Chicana artist Patssi Valdéz, *LA/TJ*, presents a fragmented reality and, at the same time, the effort to remember it (see Figure 9.4). This work, if read from the bottom up, starts with the depiction of a man wearing a *sombrero*, as agricultural laborers often do in many regions of Mexico. He is facing the barbed-wire fence. Both the gaze of the viewer and that of the subject are directed to follow, layer by layer, a journey that crosses the path of Interstate Highway 5, interconnected bridges dense with traffic, and landmarks of the city of Los Angeles such as the City Hall. The last image is the self-portrait of the artist, fragmented in two. On the vertical sides of this layered landscape, the letters LA and TJ form a puzzle. Its solution can be found only in the remembering of the layers.

Border art must be approached within a broad framework, situating it cross-culturally while, at the same time, foregrounding the specificity of its variegated geopolitical manifestations. As a place, the border between Mexico and the United States is seen as a landscape—a physical landscape as well as one of social, cultural, and artistic practices—where territorializing and deterritorializing forces play an intricate game. By using landmark buildings on both sides of the border simultaneously, Polish artist Krzystof Wodiczko conveys this sense of place in *The Border Projection* (1988). Wodiczko was invited by El Centro Cultural Tijuana, on the Mexican side, and by La Jolla Museum of Art, on the U.S. side, to work on a site-specific project. And while Poland and the border region are geographically very distant from each other in terms of border experiences, the histories of these two places have many parallels. Why Wodiczko? Why at the border? This project by this artist exemplifies the transnational notion of the border and its globalization as a space and place. He selected the museum complex of Balboa Park in San Diego, on the U.S. side, and the Omni Theater of El Centro Cultural Tijuana, on the Mexican side, for his photographic projections. This selection emphasizes the (de)territorialization processes that Mexican migrants experience. By projecting the images of hands weathered by hard work on the land, in poses that indicate police detention and arrest or the chains of slavery, the artist emphasizes

Figure 9.4. Patssi Valdéz, *LA/TJ,* 1987. Serigraph. Collection of Gilberto Cárdenas. By permission of the artist.

the services and the riches provided by undocumented Mexican workers. He also conveys the process of criminalization of their labor in the
United States. At the same time, the artist refers to displacement by
forcing the viewer to actually cross the border to see the work, thus
making him follow the migratory route of the undocumented worker.
However, the viewer will probably have documents (on the Mexican
side) to enable him to cross to the United States, and the viewers on
the U.S. side will have no problem crossing over to Mexico.

The border is also a locus of desire. Lucy Lippard contends that "a
map is not the terrain" and that "mapping change is one challenge and
mapping desire for change is another, which has long appealed to the
visual artists" (1997: 79). When Lippard refers to senses of place, she is
talking about senses in the plural. The idea of "senses of place" is pertinent to the border, because it "emphasizes the contradictions, dilemmas, shifting grounds and displacements that characterize our current
social approach to place" rather than the traditional term of "sense of
place," which confers the notion of "roots" (Lippard 1999: 25). Veneֲ-
zuelan-born artist Irene Pérez, who has lived in the United States for
more than eighteen years, addresses "senses of place" in her 1996 installation *Transplant*. She constructs this piece by filling an old suitcase
with soil, and it serves as a planter for a tree that emerges precariously
from the suitcase. Without touching the ground, the roots hang into
the air, as if flying. The artist sees the life of her grandmother, to whom
the piece is dedicated, as very similar to hers; her grandmother's life
was that of a migrant, since she always moved from one place to another, carrying her roots wherever she went. In this respect, roots become nomadic by being exposed to the diverse elements encountered
on the journey.

The Real and the Symbolic: Globalizing Border Spaces

For Mexicans (from the border or with border experience) and Chi-
cana/os, *la línea* is an area-receptacle of the collective memory of the
communities. The border is also the map of the divided heart, the permanent reminder, *el recordatorio*,[14] of the border as "an open wound."[15]
It is the place where xenophobia converges, where real political discrimination against the Latino minorities in the United States takes

shape. Propositions 209 and 187 in California or the Hopwood decision in Texas in the 1990s are only the most prominent examples. For the dispossessed inhabitants of this land, the migrants, *la frontera* is a war zone—sometimes cold, sometimes hot.

With the border paradigm, critical theory finds new explanations that help to account for global cultural phenomena. The border forces us to think of the margin, the end of one country and the beginning of another, each with a center of power, and one more powerful than the other. The border, and the multiple articulations that take place there, dislocate a vision from the center (centers of power) by reclaiming other visions from the limits (or outside the limits) as valid. The displacement of phallocentric Western cultures to the periphery or to the margins—and marginal cultures to the center—as well as the concept of cultural negotiation have contributed to new paradigms with regard to minorities in First World countries, their contributions in all spheres of life and culture, and their agency in non-Western cultures. The concept of the border in these new developments plays a central role, since the border is the place where the local, the global, and different cultures meet. The explosion of Chicana/o visual arts has given way to the creation of a new border iconography of *la línea*, of *el otro lado*, which by and large derives from seeing the border in the way that Gloria Anzaldúa (1987: 3) has described it: "This is my home, this thin edge of barbed wire."

The artistic explosion that started during the 1960s has gone through an intriguing process that combines tradition with innovation and also translates, fragments, brings together, and negotiates the border. It also speaks about, and from, a cultural space and, thus, about the power of a space and place that is deeply marked by "this thin edge of barbed wire." This language "sees" from the margin, from the limits to the centers, and questions and displaces those dividing lines. Paradoxically, the visual productions of this language, which displaces the centers to the margins, and the Mexican and Chicana/o border artists who produce it, largely remain outside the mainstream art establishment.

Yet, borders have become an essential factor of globalization, having been appropriated by multinational capitalism as a powerful marketing tool. The concept of the "border," developed in a located space and place between Mexico and the United States with its history and undeniable reality, is transformed into the "raw material" for globalization.

The border has become an artistic locus of multiple and global contradictions, displacements, desires, and migrations. For Ukrainian artist Ilya Kabakov, for instance, the border between East and West Germany becomes *Two Walls of Fear* (1990). In his work *Development Plan to Build Albania* (1992), American artist Peter Fend creates symbolic maps that redraw boundaries within a gallery space. Candy Noland from the United States builds a border in the confines of an office in *Office Filter* (1990).

Borders are mapped and constructed in the imaginary and in the real. The symbolic space of the border is found in both open fields and closed spaces. It would seem that the border has become a state of mind within the symbolic realm. But the boundary between Mexico and the United States remains as real as the fence, the river, and the desert. Artists such as Laura Cano and Carmela Castrejón with *Border to Border* (1991), José Antonio Aguirre with *Diálogo Fronterizo* (1992), Irene Pérez with *Dos Mundos* (1992), Patssi Valdéz with *LA/TJ* (1987), and Susan Yamagata with *A Silent Shame* (1994), together with the Border Arts Workshop for the 1990 Venice Bienniale, among others, create their images from the border, at the border, and within the border, in the spaces of the real and the symbolic. An installation by Marcos Ramírez, el Erre, *Toy-an-Horse* (1997) aptly addresses this point (see Figure 9.5). The giant two-headed horse sculpture, built with thin wooden strips and measuring ten meters in height, nine meters in length at its base, and four meters in width, was installed on top of the official demarcation line that divides Mexico and the United States at the port of entry (or departure) between Tijuana and San Diego. While one of the heads of the horse looks north to the United States, the other one looks south to Mexico. In the words of the artist, "the position of the sculpture questions the relationship of the two countries." Built from the border, at the border, and within the border, *Toy-an-Horse* can only convey the intention of the artist by its spatial location on that thin edge of barbed wire.

Conclusion

The visual arts produced by *fronteriza/o* artists on both sides of the border address the multiple negotiations of place and space, such as

Figure 9.5. Marcos Ramírez, El Erre, *Toy-an-Horse*, 1997. Site-specific installation. In *inSITE97, Tiempo Privado en Espacio Público/Private Time in Public Space*, San Diego/Tijuana, 1998. By permission of the artist.

conflict, places and people left behind, and the migrant experience. These creative articulations of the U.S.-Mexico border depict the asymmetries, contradictions, and negotiations that occur by virtue of this geopolitical boundary. Rupert García and Malaquías Montoya incorporate images of barbed wire to portray the division of the landscape, the criminalization of the border, and the conflicting interactions that occur there. But these artistic conceptualizations represent much more than a line that divides two nation-states. The imagery of barbed wire depicts that moment of crossing from Mexico to the United States for all Mexicanos, documented and undocumented, as well as the transformation from Mexican citizen to migrant—and, for some, from full participants in Mexican society into criminals, as the act of crossing turns them into "illegal aliens." The border transforms all Mexicanos into ethnic minorities as they enter the U.S. social landscape. This landscape is further complicated by the juxtaposition of the migrant's border experience with that of the Mexican citizen's border experience, as illustrated by Wodiczko. In his *Border Projection,* the migrant is symbolically tied to the border landscape and territorialized by labor while a simultaneous process symbolically (de)territorializes the worker by degrading or criminalizing the very same labor.

The border as place and space takes on personal significance for those confronted with the act of crossing from south to north, as both a symbolic and real marker that has profound effects on personal and familial realities. For many Mexicanos living in Mexican non-border states, the moment when they make their decision to migrate to *el norte* from states as far away from the border as Veracruz or Oaxaca marks the beginning of a process of cultural negotiations in which they bring the border into their lives. The real and the symbolic place and space of the border is the fundamental factor of the transnational experience. It becomes the new guest who inhabits and determines their lives. This guest is the line drawn in the landscape, and it is real, with real consequences.

Ultimately, Border art functions as a social criticism of the binational political boundary. Visual articulations of a transnational sense of "place and space," of "cultural and national identities," of the power of "place and remembered changing geographies," along with the globalizing of border space are powerful conceptualizations brought to life in such a way that Mexico and the United States are forced to acknowledge the existence of these realities. The symbolic becomes real, and, through the artists' representations, both nations are held accountable for the realities of the border experience.

Notes

1. For more information on the expansionist movement of the United States in the Southwest in different historical periods, see Merk (1963) and Sepúlveda (1983). For conflicts in Texas during and after the Mexican War, see Brinkley (1925). For a discussion about war, conflict, and disputes during the annexation process of the Mexican north, which is today the U.S. Southwest, see Balbotín (1883). For a contemporary look at the Treaty of Guadalupe Hidalgo and its consequences, see Gómez-Quiñones (1994). For the Texas case, see Montejano (1987).

2. For a contemporary approach to the concept of opportunity, see McKinney and Sharpless (1992).

3. The border as a key image in novels can be seen throughout this century. One of the earliest examples of the border as character is found in the work of Daniel Venegas (1984). In the last decade, Anglo writers such as Tom Miller (1981) and the compendium of stereotypes in the work of T. Coraghessan Boyle (1995) employ the border as protagonist. In the works of authors such as Boyle, the border as a geographical character exacerbates misconceptions. Chicano authors such as Víctor Villaseñor (1991) explore the historical role which the border has played in the lives of the writer's family and for the Mexican people on both sides of *la línea*. Norma Cantú's *Canícula, Snapshots of a Girlhood en la Frontera* (1995) presents a gendered character of the border. Rubén Ortíz (1993) sees the border as the fluid, porous space in which a new culture is emerging. And finally, Pat Mora (1993) discusses the border as a gendered psychological and cultural space.

4. Some of the earliest works of the twentieth century that focused on the border and dealt with issues of migration include the studies by McWilliams (1948, 1969). Groundbreaking works from the Mexican side are offered by Gamio (1931, 1969).

5. See Castillo (1986); Dillman (1969); Herzog (1990); Martínez (1986); Meining (1971); Ross (1978); and Tamayo and Fernández (1983).

6. A groundbreaking discussion on the gendered border can be found in Anzaldúa (1987). An old/new concept that has received serious discussion is *Nepantla*. As defined by Mora (1993), Anzaldúa (1987), and Cantú (1995), *Nepantla* is the Náhuatl name for the border—a land in the middle, a land in-between.

7. In the case of Baja California, the legend of the peninsula as an island populated only by women is still a story told to children. It is believed that the legend started with reports by the Spaniards, who were influenced by the work of García Ordóñez de Montalvo (1857). Another source comes from Mesoamerican mythology, where Cihuatlán was believed to be the place in the west where women who had died while giving birth went to accompany the sun in its travels. Cihuatlán means the place of the women, *lugar de mujeres*. See León Portilla (1989: 35–40). Another story told even today is that of Sir Francis Drake, the pirate, who is thought to have hidden his treasure along the remote beaches of Lower California. In Chihuahua the complex of Casas Grandes has inspired several *cuentos* (stories) in the region, related by parents to their children. The legend of giants who populated some of the land, particularly Baja California, adds another dimension to the mysterious origins of the region and of the peoples of *el norte, la frontera*.

8. This myth dates from the time of Prohibition in the United States. When the Volstead Act (1919) prohibited the production, distribution, and consumption of alcohol, Mexican border towns such as Ciudad Juárez and Tijuana became centers of entertainment for the Anglo population. There they were able to drink and gamble with no fear of the law, so the legends of the "black history of Tijuana" and the fame of "Juaritos" arose. Tijuana, for example, became notorious thanks to places such as Casino Aguascaliente, where Rita Cansino (later known as Rita Hayworth) danced and sang, and for its associations with prostitution, gambling, Mafia types such as Al Capone, and alcohol that seemed to flow in rivers. See Piñera (1985) and Bustamante (1986).

9. See García Riera (1986) and Iglesias (1991).

10. This is exemplified by the movie *Dances with Wolves*, in which Kevin Costner, the hero, plays the part of a white man who joins the "Indians."

11. The series was part of a research project coordinated by Néstor García Canclini (1989).

12. For a detailed description of this project, see *inSITE94*.

13. For an excellent study of the militarization process at the border, see Dunn (1996).

14. The word *recordatorio* in Spanish also means the notice of death. Other meanings for *recordatorio* refer to warnings and lessons. This word seems more accurate in this context than merely "reminder" in English.

15. Anzaldúa (1987: 3) states: "The U.S.-Mexican border *es una herida abierta* [an open wound] where the Third World grates against the First and bleeds. And before a scab forms it hemorrhages again, the lifeblood of two worlds merging to form a third country—a border culture."

References

Anzaldúa, Gloria. 1987. *Borderlands/La Frontera: The New Mestiza*. San Francisco: Spinsters/Aunt Lute Books.

Balbotín, Manuel. 1883. *La Invasión Americana de 1846 a 1848: Apuntes del subteniente de artillería Manuel Balbotín*. México: Gonzálo A. Esteva.

Boyle, T. Coraghessan. 1995. *The Tortilla Curtain*. New York: Viking.

Brinkley, William C. 1925. *The Expansionist Movement in Texas, 1836–1850*. Berkeley: University of California Press.

Bustamante, Jorge A. 1986. *Historia de la Colonia Libertad*. Tijuana, México: El Colegio de la Frontera Norte.

Cantú, Norma. 1995. *Canícula, Snapshots of a Girlhood en la Frontera*. Albuquerque: University of New Mexico Press.

Castillo, Víctor. 1986. "Desarrollo Regional y Frontera Norte: Conformación Regional, 1960–1980." In *Ecología y Frontera*, ed. J. Alvarez and V. M. Castillo, 71–87. México: Universidad Autónoma de Baja California, Escuela de Economía.

Dances with Wolves. 1990. Directed by Kevin Costner. MGM/United Artists.

Dillman, Daniel. 1969. "Border Town Symbiosis along the Lower Rio Grande as Exemplified by the Twin Cities: Brownsville (Texas) and Matamoros (Tamaulipas)." *Revista Geográfica* 71: 93–113.

Dreicer, Gregory K., ed. 1997. *Between Fences*. New York: National Building Museum, Princeton Architectural Press.

Dunn, Timothy J. 1996. *The Militarization of the U.S.-Mexico Border, 1978–1992: Low-Intensity Conflict Doctrine Comes Home*. Austin: University of Texas Press.

Gamio, Manuel. 1931. *The Influence of Migration in Mexican Life*. Typewritten copy.

———. 1969. *El Inmigrante Mexicano: La historia de su vida (Notas preliminares de Gilberto Layo sobre la inmigración de Mexicanos a los Estados Unidos de 1900–1967)*. 1st ed. México: UNAM.

García Canclini, Néstor. 1989. *Tijuana, la casa de toda la gente*. México: INAH-ENAH/Programa Cultural de las Fronteras, UAM-Iztapalapa/CONACULTA.

García Riera, Emilio. 1986. *Historia del cine mexicano* (Foro 2000). México: SEP.

Gómez-Quiñones, Juan. 1994. *Roots of Chicano Politics, 1600–1940*. Albuquerque: University of New Mexico Press.

Herzog, Lawrence A. 1990. *Where North Meets South: Cities, Space, and Politics on the U.S.-Mexico Border*. Austin: CMAS Books, University of Texas.

Iglesias, Norma. 1991. *Entre Yerba, Polvo y Plomo: Lo fronterizo visto por el cine mexicano.* Vol. 1. Tijuana: El Colegio de la Frontera Norte.

inSITE94. 1995. *A Binational Exhibition of Installation and Site-Specific Art.* San Diego: Installation Gallery.

inSITE97. 1998. *Tiempo privado en espacio público/Private Time in Public Space.* San Diego/Tijuana.

La Frontera/The Border: Art about the Mexico/United States Border Experience. 1993. San Diego: Centro Cultural de la Raza, Museum of Contemporary Art.

León Portilla, Miguel. 1989. *Cartografía y crónicas de la antigua California.* México: Universidad Nacional Autónoma de México, Fundación de Investigaciones Sociales, A.C., Lám. XLV.

Lippard, Lucy R. 1997. *The Lure of the Local: Senses of Place in a Multicentered Society.* New York: The New Press.

———. 1999. "No Places Like Home." *Art in America,* February: 25, 79.

Maciel, David R. 1990. "Mexico in Aztlán and Aztlán in Mexico: The Dialectics of Chicano-Mexicano Art." In *CARA, Chicano Art: Resistance and Affirmation,* 109–20. Los Angeles: Wight Art Gallery, University of California.

Martínez, Oscar, ed. 1986. *Across Boundaries: Transborder Interaction in Comparative Perspective.* El Paso, TX: Western Press.

McKinney, Joseph A., and Rebecca M. Sharpless, eds. 1992. *Implications of a North American Free Trade Region: Multidisciplinary Perspectives.* Ottawa: Carleton University Press.

McWilliams, Carey. 1948. *North from Mexico: The Spanish-Speaking People of the United States,* 1st ed. Philadelphia: J. B. Lippincott Co.

———. 1969. *Factories in the Field: the Story of Migratory Forms of Labor in California.* Hamden, CT: Archon Books. First published c. 1939.

Meining, Donald W. 1971. *Southwest: Three Peoples in Geographical Change.* New York: Oxford University Press.

Merk, Frederick. 1963. *Manifest Destiny and Mission in American History.* New York: Alfred A. Knopf.

Miller, Tom. 1981. *On the Border: Portraits of America's Southwestern Frontier.* Tucson: University of Arizona Press.

Montejano, David. 1987. *Anglos and Mexicans in the Making of Texas, 1836–1986.* Austin: University of Texas Press.

Mora, Pat. 1993. *Nepantla: Essays from the Land in the Middle.* Albuquerque: University of New Mexico Press.

Ordóñez de Montalvo, García. 1857. *Las Sergas del virtuoso caballero Esplandián, hijo de Amadís de Gaula (Sevilla, 1510).* Madrid: Biblioteca de Autores Españoles.

Ortíz, Rubén. 1993. *The Other Side: Notes from the New LA, Mexico City, and Beyond.* New York: Vintage Books.

Piñera, David, ed. 1985. *Historia de Tijuana*. México: UABC.

Ross, Stanley R., ed. 1978. *Views across the Border: The United States and Mexico*. Albuquerque: University of New Mexico Press.

Sepúlveda, César. 1983. *La Frontera Norte de México: Historia, conflictos, 1762–1983*. México: Porrúa.

Tamayo, Jesús, and José Luis Fernández. 1983. *Zonas fronterizas (México-Estados Unidos)*. México: CIDE.

Venegas, Daniel. 1984. *Las aventuras de Don Chipote, o cuando los pericos mamen*. Serie Frontera. México D.F.: SEP Culturas.

Villaseñor, Víctor. 1991. *Rain of Gold*. Houston: Arte Público Press.

Artists and Their Works

Aguirre, José Antonio. 1992. *Diálogo fronterizo*. Monotype. Private Collection.

Cano, Laura, and Carmela Castrejón. 1991. *Border to Border*. Installation. Border Art Workshop/Taller de Arte Fronterizo, BAW/TAF.

Fend, Peter. 1992. *Development Plan to Build Albania*. Tanja Grunert Gallery, Cologne.

García, Rupert. *¡Cesen Deportación!* 1975. Serigraph. In *CARA: Chicano Art, Resistance and Affirmation*, ed. Richard Griswold del Castillo, Teresa McKenna, and Yvonne Yarbro-Bejarano, 35. Los Angeles: Wight Gallery, University of California, 1991.

Grobet, Lourdes. *Untitled* (undated), black and white photograph. In Néstor García Canclini, Patricia Safa, photographs by Lourdes Grobet, *Tijuana, la casa de toda la gente*, 1st ed., INAH-ENAH; Programa Cultural de las Fronteras; UAM Iztaplapa, México, 1989.

Gruner, Silvia. 1994. *In the Middle of the Road/En la Mitad del Camino*. Installation. In *inSITE94: A Binational Exhibition of Installation and Site-Specific Art*, ed. Sally Yard. San Diego: Installation Gallery, 1995.

Hernández, Ester. 1994. *Border Flower*. Monoserigraph. Private Collection.

Kabakov, Ilya. 1990. *Two Walls of Fear*. Installation. In *Finite Nature of Freedom*, organized by the DAAD Gallery, Berlin, commemorating the fall of the Berlin Wall.

Montenegro, Luis. 1993. *Llegué del Otro Lado*. Monotype. Private Collection.

Montoya, Malaquías. 1981. *Undocumented*. Serigraph. Collection of Gilberto Cárdenas.

Noland, Candy. 1990. *Office Filter*. Touka Museum of Contemporary Art, Japan.

Pérez, Irene. 1992. *Dos Mundos*. Monotype. In *Imágenes de la Frontera: Monotipia/Monoprint Images of the Border*. Austin: Festival Internacional de la Raza, Galería Sin Fronteras, 1992.

———. 1996. *Transplant*. Multimedia installation. Artist's Collection. In *De Mujer a Mujer*. Austin: Austin Museum of Art, 1996.

Ramírez, Marcos, el Erre. 1997. *Toy-an-Horse*. Site-specific installation. In *inSITE97, Tiempo Privado en Espacio Público/Private Time in Public Space*, San Diego/Tijuana, 1998.

Valdéz, Patssi. *LA/TJ*. 1987. Serigraph. Collection of Gilberto Cárdenas.

Villaseñor Grijalva, Lucila. 1994. *From the Other Side*. Monoserigraph. Private Collection.

Wodiczko, Krzystof. 1988. *The Border Projection*. Photographic projection. El Centro Cultural Tijuana and La Jolla Museum of Art.

Yamagata, Susan. 1994. *A Silent Shame*. Multimedia installation. In *inSITE94*. San Diego.

CHAPTER TEN

Latina Entrepreneurship in the Borderlands

Family Well-Being and Poverty Reduction Policies

Bárbara J. Robles

Ethnic enterprises and minority small businesses grew at an unprecedented rate in the last decade of the twentieth century. Women-owned businesses have taken the lead in this growth spurt during the period 1987–1999 by 103% (U.S. Small Business Administration 1999). Latina-owned businesses have accounted for a large share of this increase. Between 1987 and 1996, these businesses grew by 206% and their sales rose by 534% (Center for Women's Business Research [CWBR] 1997b and 2000). During this same period, job creation by Latina-owned businesses grew by 487%. Between 1997 and 2002, Latina-owned businesses grew by 39%, and there were an estimated 470,344 such businesses in the United States. (CWBR 2001). These privately held, majority-owned Latina enterprises accounted for $29.4 billion in receipts and employed 198,000 workers (CWBR 2001). These indicators demonstrate the growth in Latina entrepreneurial activities in the United States and have finally captured the attention of community development researchers.

The data on Latina self-employment and entrepreneurship contradict the general stereotype of retiring, submissive, and silent women who take on a supporting and nurturing role in the Latino family with a similarly invisible and marginal service-oriented role in mainstream society and the economy (Abalos 1993). Moreover, the decade of the 1990s brought into focus the continuing demographic shifts within the Latino population in the United States as well as a new understanding of the intricacies of the role that Latinas play within the changing dynamics of the family. For example, between 1990 and 2000, Latino families in the United States almost doubled from 4.8 million to 7.4 million (U.S. Census Bureau 1990 and 2000). During the same time, Latino families residing in the four border states increased from 2 million to 4.1 million, a 105.7% increase (U.S. Census Bureau, State Facts 1990 and 2000).[1] Moreover, the change in the number of households headed by Latinas with children under the age of eighteen also increased nationwide and in the borderlands. From 1990 to 2000, Latina-headed households with children rose from 1 million to 1.57 million nationwide, an increase of 57%. For the border states, Latina-headed households with children for the same period grew from 337,718 to 531,718, an increase of 57.2% (U.S. Census Bureau 1990 and 2000).

These demographic changes have had a visible impact within Latino communities and, consequently, on mainstream society's awareness of Latinos/as in the United States. For example, not only are Latinas entering into the entrepreneurial market in record numbers, but they also are outpacing their male counterparts in political office. Since 1984, the number of Latinas elected to office nationwide has increased by 400%, nearly four times the rate at which Latinos are elected (Romney 1998). In 2001 the National Association of Latino Elected Officials (NALEO) reported that women comprise 38% of all Latino officeholders (Treviño 2001).

The U.S.-Mexico border presents an interesting scenario for Latino entrepreneurs. To understand the growth in Latino self-employment and entrepreneurial activity along the border, it is important to explore the dynamic factors behind the Latina "good news" story and to describe the socioeconomic forces driving these significant data. Placing this investigation within the cultural context of the Mexico-U.S. transnational community allows for an exploration of the factors that have led to the growth in entrepreneurial activity of Latinas in the borderlands. What emerges from this research is the recognition that community-based organizations (CBOs) and community-development financial institutions (CDFIs) coalesce with cultural factors to create social networks and tangible support systems for Latina entrepreneurs that translate into support networks for Latino families. Correspondingly, by supporting Latina self-employment and entrepreneurial activities, which supplement low-wage family income and contribute to family financial stability, policy prescriptions aimed at reducing the incidence of poverty along the U.S.-Mexico border can make a significant impact in Latino communities.

Latina Entrepreneurial Activity: Theory and Practice

The theoretical discourse on supply-and-demand-side factors of small business formation[2] and entrepreneurial activity tends to focus on performance measures and outcomes (Thornton 1999). These studies seek to understand the market dynamic of small business and entrepreneurial risk as contributing factors in the overall health and continued growth of the U.S. economy. What is neglected in these studies is the crucial interrelated sociocultural and gender dimensions of entrepreneurial behavior. There exists a growing strand of literature that intersects sociology, anthropology, and economics on ethnic entrepreneurial activities, which contributes to an historical and immigrant-oriented market assessment of ethnic small businesses but does not address in a comprehensive manner the gender dimension of the small business owner (Portes 1995).

Other studies (Rosa et al. 1996) focus solely on the gender dimension as a means to compare female and male business-owner performance characteristics and market concentration. Gender thus becomes the solitary empirical and observable factor influencing outcomes. These gender-oriented studies provide little or no direct assessment of the race-ethnic-cum-socioeconomic factors that play a significant role in the unique characteristics of women-of-color business owners. Nor do they address the labor market obstacles faced by female racial and ethnic job seekers that propel them into self-employment. Subsequently, little is known about women-of-color business owners, the economic sectors in which they operate, the implications for familial arrangements, and the wealth effects generated by female-owned businesses that impact the communities in which they are located.

Light and Gold in *Ethnic Economies* (2000) devote an entire chapter to gender roles and family participation in ethnic economies. They assert that there exists a multilevel sequence of "effects" influencing how ethnic economies evolve and transform entrepreneurial agents and the sociocultural environment in which they operate. These "effects" are described as "macro factors" that influence the demographic profiles of individuals and families and thus signal the extent of the resources, needs, and employment opportunities of ethnic families. Consequently, family characteristics influence economic status regardless of culture, educational level, or access to ethnic or class resources. Light and Gold also point out typical demographic characteristics such as sex ratios, median age, outmarriage, fertility, household size, marriage, and divorce rates as factors in establishing social habits and patterns. These, in turn, influence access to social capital that is related to educational outcomes and job-seeking capacity. Saunders and Nee (1987) find that Asian and Latino groups tend to have more married-couple families with higher rates of self-employment than ethnic groups with fewer married-family households. Many ethnic enterprises reverse gender roles and rely on family relationships to survive and succeed. Thus, a family's contributions to ethnic economic activity serve a communal purpose, allowing all of its members to add to the well-being of the kin unit. Women and children's labor contributions to ethnic family businesses are not viewed by family members as "exploitative" but rather as necessary inputs to the success of the household.

Light and Gold (2000) identify "middle range factors" relating how ethnic economic status is conditioned and affected by ethnic families' interaction with mainstream society through social and economic activities. These activities cover entrepreneurship, job seeking, resource access, and communal cultural capital, inheritance, and cultural change. For Light and Gold, the following are all perceived as circumstances that give further impetus to ethnic economies: the maintenance of shared family resources, women's entrepreneurial endeavors and female-centered transmission of cultural and economic resources, transnational ties with country of origin to increase social capital and the economic resource base, and growing pressures to assimilate by social forces at work in the host country.

Finally, Light and Gold explore "micro dimensions," which divide the family as a unit into individual ethnic agents or members within families and communities. The focus here is on the "microcosm" of families, which can often lead to "conflict." Families do not always portray "communal" characteristics. For example, disagreements over resource allocation and unequal concentrations of power imply a dynamic that leads to changing loyalties, rearrangements, and exclusion from familial economic and social capital resources, often impelling members of ethnic families to seek opportunities outside their circle. Gender relations undergo, often within one generation, a shift in women's position within the ethnic family. Indeed, Light and Gold cite several studies on migration and ethnic economic activity describing contradictory conditions that exist for gender roles in the host society. For example, ethnic women in the host country often ensure the continuity of country-of-origin cultural patterns via child rearing and are empowered with control over household resources due to longevity. Moreover, in the host country, women are central to establishing home-based economic activity and strengthening social and resource networking within ethnic communities. Since these host-country roles often differ from the more home-based roles of women formed in the country of origin, they can contribute to internal family conflict over male-female domains. The transitional and ongoing changing gender roles are further negotiated, balancing family survival needs with new exposure to differing cultural norms for women-based economic activities.

Clearly, the theoretical discourse on gender and ethnicity in entrepreneurial activities is not a linear continuum of relationships among and between ethnic families, communities, and the larger economy. Rather, theory requires a multidimensional perspective of the multiple features of ethnic and immigrant gender roles as dictated by culture-of-origin norms that are being rearranged and modified in the host country over time.[3] Family dynamics and sociodemographic features are undergoing transformation as women increasingly contribute toward entrepreneurial efforts. What is relevant here is that research, both qualitative and quantitative, continues to provide evidence and to

extend our understanding of the complexities of ethnic women entrepreneurs, their multiple roles in their communities, and their impact
on civil society. One salient reality emerges from the description of, and
research on, ethnic and minority small and microbusinesses: the establishment of ethnic entrepreneurial activity is positively correlated with
rising wealth accumulation for communities of color. This is especially
true for Latina entrepreneurs and Latino families in the borderlands.

Latina Entrepreneurship in the Borderlands

Between 1997 and 2002, Latino-owned businesses saw a decrease
in employees of 15.7%. However, the number of Latina-owned businesses increased by 39%, and sales grew by 8% (CWBR 2001). Increases in non-employer businesses along the U.S.-Mexico border have
contributed to the overall rise in Hispanic-owned businesses (see Figure 10.1).[4] The highest share of Latina business growth has occurred in
the four border states of New Mexico (20%), Texas (18%), California
(17%), and Arizona (13%) (CWBR 2001).

ACCION USA, a microlending organization, estimates that there are
over 13.1 million microentrepreneurs in the United States (Edgcomb
and Armington 2003). The overall self-employment rate for women
between 1983 and 1997 was 48% (U.S. Small Business Administration
1999), while the Latina self-employment rate between 1975 and 1990
doubled (Devine 1994: 23). The growth in self-employment between
1988 and 1998 for the Hispanic population was 30%, outpacing the
3.9% reported for the entire U.S. population (U.S. Small Business Administration 1998: 8). Currently, the rate of growth of Latina-owned
businesses outpaces Latino business owners and exceeds the rates of
new business growth for all other women and women of color (CWBR
1997b). In the border states of Texas, New Mexico, Arizona, and California, Latina-owned businesses saw a rapid rise in both the number of
new establishments (266,872) in 2002 and, in the same year, an increase in receipts totaling $16.8 billion, more than one-half of the total
$29.4 billion for all Latina-owned businesses in the United States
(CWBR 2001). (See Table 10.1.)

Even as the rate of change in generating new jobs has declined for
Latina business owners,[5] the rate of change for the self-employed along
the U.S.-Mexico border has risen significantly. Texas leads the border

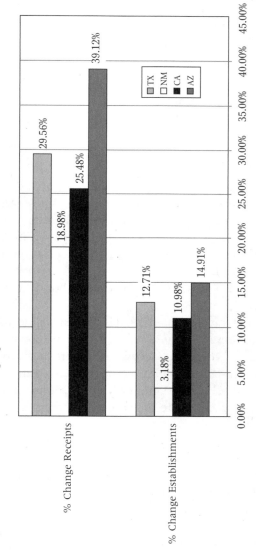

Figure 10.1. Borderlands Self-Employment, 1997–2001

Source: Non-Employer Statistics, Economic Census, 1997 and 2001, Bureau of the Census.

Table 10.1.   Growth in Latina-Owned Businesses, Border States, 1997–2002

State	% Change in Number of Firms, 1997–2002	% Change in Sales, 1997–2002	% Change in Employment, 1997–2002
Arizona	58.3	10.6	13.0
California	24.3	-7.9	-13.8
New Mexico	12.3	12.7	-18.5
Texas	38.0	150.3	-7.8

Source: Center for Women's Business Research, 2001.

states with substantial increases in self-employment in the McAllen and Laredo metro areas. Related to these increases are the unemployment rates along the border that are higher than those posted for the nation. For example, the annual average unemployment rate reported for McAllen between 1997 and 2001 was 15.4%, and in Brownsville it was 10.6% (U.S. Department of Labor, Bureau of Labor Statistics, 2003). (See Figure 10.2.)

The economic sectors in which Latina-owned businesses are located vary by state and region. Moreover, these businesses have shown the greatest gains in industries where they previously were not represented, such as construction and communications (CWBR 2001). The majority of Latina firms and self-employment are in the service sector. (See Figure 10.3.) This is especially so in the border region.

The Center for Women's Business Research (CWBR) conducted a survey of 404 Latina respondents who were randomly drawn from several listings of Latina business owners, and reported some intriguing demographic and cultural factors influencing these Latina entrepreneurs (CWBR 2000). The most compelling features of Latina-owned businesses were the emphasis on bilingualism and biculturalism and the fact that Latinas believed that their culture was an asset in owning and running a business. Latinas rely on personal, familial, and fictive kin resources (44%) to start up their enterprises, and 55% did not borrow capital or financial resources at all (CWBR 2000). The Latina

Figure 10.2. Metro Borderlands Self-Employment, 1997–2001

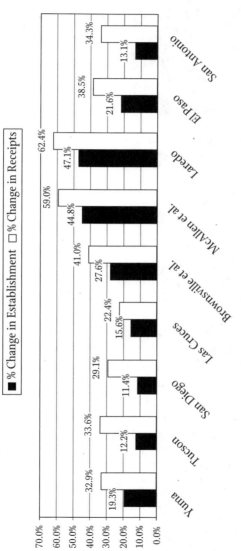

■ % Change in Establishment □ % Change in Receipts

Source: Non-Employer Statistics, Economic Census, 1997 and 2001, Bureau of the Census.

Figure 10.3.   Latina Businesses by Economic Sector, 2002

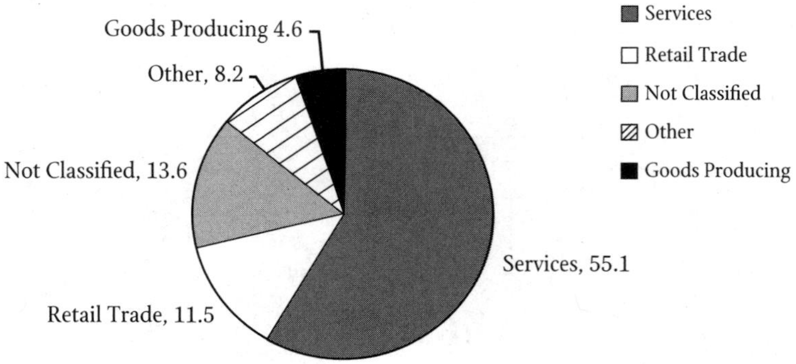

Goods Producing 4.6

Other, 8.2

Not Classified, 13.6

Retail Trade, 11.5

Services, 55.1

- ■ Services
- □ Retail Trade
- ▨ Not Classified
- ▨ Other
- ■ Goods Producing

Goods Producing = Agriculture, Construction, Manufacturing, Mining
Other = Financial/Insurance/Real Estate, Trasnportation/Communication/Public
Utilities, Wholesale Trade

Source: Hispanic Women-Owned Businesses in the U.S., 2002: A Fact sheet, http://
www.nfwbo.org.

survey responses indicate a more firmly entrenched reliance on family resources, with 75% of Latina entrepreneurs indicating that their business was family-run compared to Anglo (71%), Native American (66%), Asian (64%), and black (55%) female owner respondents (CWBR 2000 and 1998). Family-run businesses are defined as those with family members who are involved in the daily operations of running the enterprise. Some 68% of Latina family-run businesses reported moderate to large spouse involvement, and 32% reported that children play a large role as well.

Latina business owners, by and large, are older, married with more children, and less educated than their female business peers. Evidence from other studies indicates that married women business owners are generally older and have access to more family resources than do single, never-married female entrepreneurs, who also tend to be younger and reach higher levels of education (U.S. Small Business Administration 1998; Aldrich and Waldinger 1990).

Latinas distinguish themselves from their cohort of women business owners in their emphasis on how family contributions and support encourage their entrepreneurial drive. Responding to the survey question regarding "Motivations for Business Ownership" (CWBR 1998), 62% of Latina business owners affirmed, "To improve things for yourself and your family." African American businesswomen exceeded this figure with a 65% response rate for the same question, with Asians (52%), Anglos (58%), and Native Americans (60%) trailing. In a series of questions designed to shed light on "What Women Business Owners Like Best about Business Ownership," Latina women responded overwhelmingly (61%) to the category listed as "Being own boss/Being in control," with only Native American women exceeding this response rate (72%) compared to Asians (53%), African Americans (46%), and Anglos (50%).

Equally telling is the Latina response to the query, "Support Systems Used by Women Business Owners," to which 13% chose the entry, "Father," compared to Anglos (4%), Asians (5%), African Americans (7%), and Native Americans (8%). Of similar interest was the entry "Spouse/Significant Other," which had a 10% Latina response rate compared to Anglos (4%), Asians (4%), Native Americans (8%), and African Americans (9%). The question, "Business Information Sources for Women Business Owners," had several entries under "Family": Latinas signaled how much they relied on family as an information resource with a 35% response rate compared to Anglos (20%), African Americans (26%), Asians (22%), and Native Americans (20%).

Evidence from ethnographic surveys conducted in San Antonio, Texas, among Latina microbusiness owners confirms the national survey responses (Cavazos 2002). The Latina microbusiness owners relied on the previous experience of male relatives, spouses, and extended family kin as resources that were essential to starting up or continuing and expanding their enterprises (Cavazos 2002).

Latina entrepreneurs, both young and older, believe that the changing family and gender roles that have been evolving in U.S. Latino communities have opened new doors that previously were shut and bolted. Bettina Duran, an owner of a small business in Azusa, California, believes that Latina entrepreneurial drive arises from the fear "of making the same mistakes that our mothers did. We don't want to be dependent. We don't want to be stuck. We don't want to be complacent or apathetic" (Romney 1998). Ann Maria Arias, editor and publisher of *Latina Style* magazine, which offers seminars for Latina entrepreneurs, says, "Before, Hispanic women had always put ourselves at the bottom of the totem pole in terms of our family. Now, we want to take care of ourselves and, by taking care of ourselves, we're taking care of our families" (Romney 1998).

Latina self-employment, microenterprises, and small businesses focus on low capitalization (little to no start-up costs) and display a high degree of sweat equity (personal labor efforts and own savings). Moreover, the use of bicultural and bilingual assets in start-ups and operations often go unnoticed, such as language switching, which is a substantial part of daily life along the southwest border. The types of services that Latino microentrepreneurs engage in include cultural food preparation in their homes for particular customers or for sale at vendor stalls and sites. These activities tend to increase during cultural holidays and festivals. Small entrepreneurial vendor stands that sell *raspas* (ice cones), handmade candies, and traditional Mexican foods fall under the "service sector" category. Other examples of Latina entrepreneurial activities, which are often placed within the service (if sewing for hire) or retail categories, involve sales of handmade crafts, religious items, and traditional wedding, *quinceañera*,[6] or First Communion finery. These small cottage industries are under researched, but every Latino community harbors female microenterprises and informal entrepreneurial activities that serve to supplement family income.

Bilingualism and biculturalism, although surprising to many observers unfamiliar with the borderlands, are an integral part of entrepreneurial activities. For example, biculturalism is present during the making and selling of such items as *las arras, el lazo,* and *los cojines* for Mexican American weddings or *nopalitos* and *capirotada* foods during Lent. Moreover, cultural practices continue to require items that many Latina women make and sell in their own communities. These expressive crafts, items, and activities include Spanish and bilingual greeting cards; candles with specific messages and images of *santos; yerberistas* (herbalists); women hired for *limpiezas espirituales de casas* (spiritual house-cleanings and energy centering, similar to Feng Shui and nearly as old); and *sobadoras* (neither chiropractors nor masseuses, they are trained to combine massage with nerve-system/energy alignments through kneading). Many services that require bilingualism and translation or interpretation also proliferate: bicultural and bilingual insurance agents, Spanish- and English-language video rental storefronts in *colonias* (unincorporated townships), small community *tienditas* with an array of Latino and U.S. foodstuffs and household sundries, and talented Latina entrepreneurs teaching informal classes in *ballet folklórico* to community youth.

One can own a storefront selling Mexican and Latin American curios, crafts, and art and have an expanding tourist-oriented customer base without being bicultural or relying on linguistic fluency. However, one can also own a storefront selling the same items as well as local Mexican American artwork and crafts, thereby engaging the community by employing one's own bicultural and bilingual community roots as an entrepreneurial asset, and be doubly successful, since a tourist customer base has been cultivated along with a local customer base. Latino microenterprise owners indicate that their own biculturalism is an asset when it comes to customer service and satisfaction (Robles 2002).

Intergenerational Transmission of Entrepreneurial Attitudes

David Abalos (1993) describes the escalating changes in Latino family dynamics due to the demise of the Latina matriarch associated with the waves of immigration during the first half of the twentieth century and, for the majority of borderlands Latino families, the period connected to the Mexican Revolution. He points to the nexus of interactions between the host society, cultural norms of the Latino family transferred to the new home country, exposure to economic opportunities for all members of the Latino family via public education, and the generational transformation of gender roles. The role of women in the Latino family was traditionally viewed as that of mediator and mitigator of societal racism aimed against male heads of household. By maintaining cultural norms and transmitting cultural values retained from the country of origin to the next generation, Latinas played a stabilizing role in the family. In essence, they have been the "keepers of the flame" in a traditional hearth/home role by providing sanctuary to family members discouraged by the hostility and obstacles of the host country's labor markets and institutions.

Extended Latino families capitalize on the blending of two cultures along with the dynamism that this encourages. Specifically, this allows for extended market opportunities via language and country-of-origin dualism along with transnational business networks. Research has shown that the best predictor for a successful venture is having had a family member who owned a business (Raijman 2001; Grameen Bank n.d.). Entrepreneurs in the extended family or fictive kin who pass on entrepreneurial know-how to children and to other family members create survival skills that are often required in areas with low job creation and repressed wages. Many of the entrepreneurial activities engaged in by women in Latino communities are culturally dictated and seasonal.[7] These female and often home-based activities play a significant role in passing on entrepreneurial skills (which encourage social and cultural capital) to younger family members; also, these activities keep supplemental entrepreneurial earnings within the community.

Latino Families in the Borderlands

The historical ties with Mexico that are evident in borderlands language, culture, and daily economic activity create a unique transnational environment for Latino families residing along the border.[8] This also contributes to the diversity of family arrangements along the border, in metro areas, and in rural ethnic enclaves such as *colonias*. For borderlands Latino families, economic mobility depends upon extended family resources and on learned economic survival strategies that, in turn, depend upon class and community resources. These social and cultural family and community resources can be difficult to quantify but are observable in effectiveness. For example, young children are often left in the care of grandparents, aunts and uncles, cousins, or *comadres* or *compadres* (fictive kin) during short and medium spells of seasonal employment or entrepreneurial buying trips. These types of family arrangements help to defray the costs of employment seeking for wage earners and of inventory stocking or establishing resource networks for microbusinesses. Additionally, Latino families pool transportation resources, reducing the costs of entrepreneurial activities and job maintenance. Children often serve as translators and language mediators for older family members with limited English fluency. Bilingual family members become resources for extended family and fictive kin when navigating employment opportunities or microbusiness activities; in essence, the children's bilingualism becomes a cultural asset for all of the family members.

Economic mobility is also related to educational opportunities. Low educational attainment rates are especially pressing along the U.S.-Texas border with Starr County, which has the lowest educational attainment rate of the twenty-five-year-old and over population (34.7%

Table 10.2.   Socioeconomic Indicators for Border States, 2000

Indicators	Texas	New Mexico	Arizona	California
Percent Latino	84.4	50.6	34.1	28.9
% HH w/child <18 yrs	53.9	40	34.4	37.8
% Families w/child<18 yrs	57.5	51.4	46.2	51.1
Avg. Family Size	3.52	3.19	3.27	3.53
% Homeowner	68.0	70.1	65.6	55.6
Median Value Home	$47,819	$70,257	$95,650	$163,600
% Grandparents in HH w/Grandchildren	15.0	7.5	6.1	6.9
% Grandparents Responsible for Grandchild	5.5	4.1	2.7	2.2
Median Family Income	$27,984	$32,835	$37,292	$44,332
Per Capita Income	$11,682	$13,800	$15,963	$18,083
HH Median Earnings	$25,110	$28,172	$32,689	$39,469
Median Earnings Male, FT, YR Workers	$23,816	$28,697	$29,513	$34,864
Med. Earnings Female, FT, YR Workers	$17,357	$19,429	$22,649	$27,165
% Families w/Income 0-$15,000	24.5	19.1	12.4	9.3
% Families w/Income 0-$25,000	43.5	36.0	26.5	20.0
% Families w/Income 0-$35,000	58.7	51.7	41.4	31.7
% HH w/Earnings w/Public Aid	20.1	14.2	9.4	10.3
% Families w/child<18 below Poverty	38.4	29.0	20.5	15.4
% Individuals below Poverty	30.4	22.2	15.5	12.5
% Non-High School Grad	43.2	27.9	20.0	18.5
% High School Grad or Higher	56.8	72.1	80.0	81.5
% College or Higher	18.3	23.2	30.2	36.2

Source: Census County Data, 2000, Bureau of the Census.

have a high-school degree). Correspondingly, over 50% of the population report a below-poverty-level status. (See Table 10.2.) Studies indicate that low educational attainment rates are also correlated with low earnings and low median household and family income data (Thomas-Brietfeld 2003; Sorenson et al. 1995; "Education Pays" 2002). The pattern is especially stark for Latino families in Texas as compared to the rest of the border states (see Figure 10.4). Families with incomes between zero and $15,000 are substantial in Texas (24.5%) and New Mexico (19.1%). Increasing the income range from zero to $25,000 raises the proportion of families falling into this income category in Texas (43.5%), New Mexico (36%), Arizona (26.5%), and California (20%). Over 50% of families have incomes between zero and $35,000 in Texas (58.7%) and New Mexico (51.7%), while Arizona reports that 41.4% fall into this income category, and 31.7% earn between zero and $35,000 along the border in California (U.S. Census Bureau, County Census Data 2000). (See Table 10.2.)

Additionally, the rate of poverty is higher in Texas but also pressing in New Mexico and Arizona (see Figure 10.5). Since the passage of the Welfare Reform Act of 1996 (PROWA), receipt of public cash-assistance income in all of the Border states has declined significantly during the 1989–1999 period: Texas, -71.1%; New Mexico, -50.4%; Arizona, -85.6%; and California, -60.9%. Equally disturbing are the changes in median household income for the border states during the same time: Texas, 13.8%; New Mexico, 9.1%; California, 2.2%; and Arizona, 13.4%.[9] The increases in median household income do not substantially offset the declines in public assistance income in the borderlands.

These stressful economic conditions generally encourage informal economic activity and, observably, this occurs with a high degree of frequency along the U.S.-Mexico border. The key to harnessing informal economic transactions is to create a network of supportive microbusiness services housed in culturally competent community-based organizations that transition the informal business activities into microenterprises (Robles 2003). In order to do so, community-based organizations must cultivate trust, talent, and skills. In an era of non-reversible devolution, microbusinesses substitute for the increasing scarcity of public assistance dollars, supplement family income with small microbusiness loans, and create additional earnings opportunities for struggling families (Clark and Kays 1999). Moreover, Latina

Figure 10.4. Borderlands High-School Completion Rates for U.S. Population 25 Yrs and Over, 2000

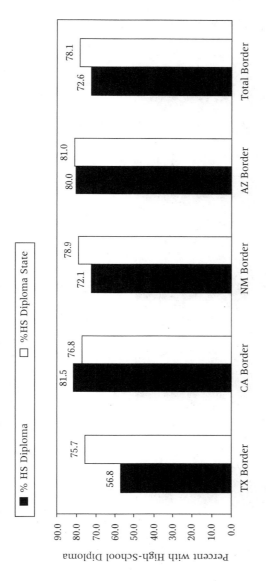

Source: County Census Data, 2000, Bureau of the Census.

Figure 10.5. Borderlands Poverty Rates, 2000

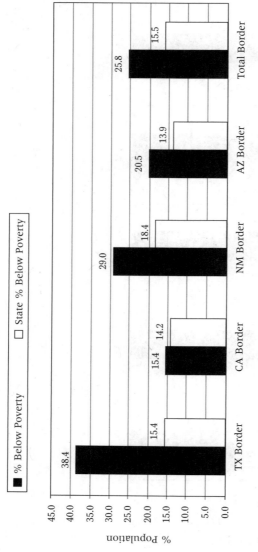

Source: County Census Data, 2000, Bureau of the Census.

self-employment and microenterprises located within ethnic rural enclaves and ethnic metro areas contribute to the retention of income generated within the confines of Latino communities. For example, in San Antonio, Texas, Perla Cavazos (2002), using ACCION Texas data, reports that microbusinesses increased mean monthly revenues by 76.9% (after two microloans). For microentrepreneurs with one microloan history, average monthly revenues were $3,810, and for clients with two microloan histories, mean monthly revenues were $6,741.[10] The majority of microbusinesses are in the service sector (55%) and in the production/industry sector (28%). The median monthly household income was $2,452 for the sample of microbusinesses (n = 630).

Supportive Policies for Family, Cultural Responsiveness, and Community-Based Organizations

Latina entrepreneurial activities rely on family, culture, and community resources to start up their enterprises and increase the income-generating opportunities that economic survival requires. Nonprofit organizations providing support services, governmental agencies administering programs, and local, state, and federal policies aimed at increasing the economic well-being of Latino families and borderlands communities fail to meet "outcomes" and "results-oriented" measures when they do not account for the bicultural and transnational economic environment that characterizes the borderlands' metro and rural communities. Foundation evaluations have documented that attempting to institute and replicate programs and services that have succeeded in urban and rural communities elsewhere in the United States do not result in the same successful and sustainable outcomes in the borderlands (Robles 2003). Assessments indicate that cultural responsiveness is the missing element in programs imported into Latino communities.

For example, Individual Development Account (IDA) programs enroll three categories of the working poor as stratified by income: extremely poor, middle poor, and high poor. The IDA programs match participant savings deposits by a ratio of 1-to-1 or 3-to-1. This means that for every dollar saved by the program participant, the program funder deposits a matching dollar or three-dollar amount. Some IDA program evaluators have found that the extremely poor save at a higher rate than do the middle and high poor participants (Clancy et al. 2002). However, attempting to implement IDA programs along the border even by culturally responsive community-based organizations does not result in success. These IDA programs restrict eligibility through asset tests and limit withdrawals of funds saved for certain family investment events such as home purchases, microbusiness start-ups, or school tuitions. Many border families refuse to participate because of these strict withdrawal rules and indicate that they are better off saving in a community *tanda*.[11]

The individualism inherent in the slow accumulation of a small amount of saved funds over time and deposited in some vague and "unconnected-with-community" bank or financial institution is not as attractive a prospect for accumulating savings as is a "communal/collective" initiative. *Tanda* members vicariously "engage" in each *tanda* participant's spending or investment decision. It is a matter of more than engaging in savings behaviors; it is a celebration of the "event" for which the money was saved. One borderlands CBO executive director who participates in many *tandas* recounted the satisfaction of seeing one of her *tanda paisanos* receiving the monthly "pot." The following week, the same man drove a new car when he deposited his weekly *tanda* contribution and commented that he no longer had to worry about constant breakdowns and getting to work on time. There is a strengthening of community building and solidarity in such collective economic activity. These informal community savings and mutual aid behaviors parallel the formation in the United States of credit unions.[12]

Cultural Capital and Latino Families

One important aspect of Latina microbusinesses and entrepreneurial activities that directly impacts the well-being of Latino families that does not appear in data collected by microfinance organizations or by local, state, and federal agencies engaged in supporting microenterprise activities is the use of cultural capital. Cultural capital is defined as an intangible asset that occurs within ethnic enclaves where rewarding cultural norms and behaviors can be crucial to the success of an enterprise (Edin 2001). Language switching between Spanish and English is part of borderlands culture and occurs daily in a variety of transactions, often without the speakers being cognizant of the degree of switching they engage in. Another distinct cultural asset is affiliation and sponsorship through fictive kin relations, in particular, the connections formed by *comadres* and *compadres* along with the religious-based fictive kin relationships of *madrina* (godmother) and *padrino* (godfather). Thornton Dill *(1994) explains that the system of *compadrazgo*[13] links members of communities across class and wealth resources, links an individual with a distinct occupational status, and creates opportunities to access extended social networks through political ties and patronage. For Latina entrepreneurs, this implies extending their networks and accessing resources that otherwise would be inaccessible (see Figure 10.6).

Cultural Responsiveness and Community-Based Organizations

Community-based organizations (CBOs) such as community development corporations (CDCs), community development financial institutions (CDFIs),[14] and community development housing organizations (CDHOs) serve a variety of economic and sustainable development functions and are the source of much-needed revitalization capital, service networks, and resources for struggling Latino enclaves. These organizations provide child care, health care, immigration services, affordable housing, housing rehab, support services for the elderly, food banks, entrepreneurial and microbusiness technical assistance, tax preparation and filing services, and a host of youth programs that alleviate constrained school budgets. However, the degree of "success" that many of these organizations experience in Latino borderlands communities is predicated on the degree of cultural competence present in the services that they provide to families and small and microbusinesses. Without understanding the manner in which many informal economic activities driven by cultural factors occur in Latino communities and become part of daily life, many nonculturally competent CBOs are not successful in delivering relevant or effective social services (Edgcomb and Armington 2003). In fact, many top-down nonprofit organizations and university satellite programs fail to fully

Figure 10.6. Latina Native-Born and Immigrant Entrepreneurs Involving Family in Enterprise by Generation, 2000

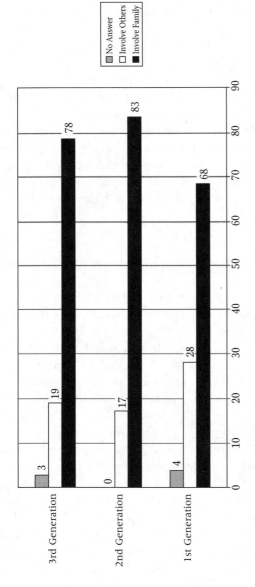

Source: Center for Women's Business Research, "The Spirit of Enterprise: Latina Entrepreneurs in the U.S.," September 2000.

collaborate with key Latino community leaders and organizations that could easily provide a foundation upon which CBOs could build a permanent presence and establish trust.

An additional factor that arises in this context is the intersection of border culture and class. This unique configuration of culture and class often escapes or bewilders nonprofit service providers who believe that language fluency is sufficient to initiate entry into low-income and struggling Latino communities. There is no substitute for time spent cultivating networks and creating trust within the community. Moreover, it is insufficient to provide "mediating" employment to community members without also committing to upward mobility within the nonprofit. To do otherwise is simply to recreate the top-down decision making for allocating precious CBO resources toward particular programs without fully collaborating with community members as to their appropriateness or effectiveness. Clearly, for CBOs to successfully provide services in Latino communities, they must be willing to engage with them as full partners in program design, implementation, and outreach.

The nonpartisan political support given to microfinance lending organizations in the United States is a clear indicator that microenterprise services and programs meant to encourage self-sufficiency and transition individuals from welfare to work are part of asset-based policies that have gained national attention. Many communities of color have responded to welfare reform by simply engaging in economic survival strategies that help to make ends meet. Microenterprises have grown exponentially precisely because, in relevant ways, they have been ignored by mainstream institutions. In particular, researchers in this area do not acknowledge the "transnational technology transfer" component of microenterprise and microlending programs from developing countries in Latin America to the United States. The microfinance/microenterprise phenomenon in the United States is in essence the importation (especially in the case of ACCION microlending programs) of Latin American models to alleviate poverty in Latino communities north of the border.

The formal financial sector does not find it profitable to loan money in small amounts or to customers deemed "uncreditworthy." Community-based organizations such as CDFIs have taken over as community financial service providers. A CDFI is similar to a community development corporation (CDC) but focuses on providing the community members with capital and other financial products and services that mainstream banking institutions do not offer to low-income people.[15] But just as they seek to assist individuals and families to become self-sufficient through microenterprises, CDFIs must remain solvent and operating in order to continue serving struggling communities. The certified CDFIs that operate along the U.S.-Mexico border are small in number but large in impact. From the U.S. Treasury's certification list of 643 CDFIs in the United States, I estimate that nineteen operate in the borderlands (U.S. Department of the Treasury 2003). Of these, three significant microlenders are ACCION Texas (the largest in the United States), ACCION New Mexico, and ACCION San Diego, all affiliates of ACCION USA, which is in turn an affiliate of ACCION International.[16] For many of the CDFIs, the self-solvency (self-sufficiency) of their operations and organization is paramount, coupled with the need to expand services (grow to scale) in order to meet the growing demand for their expertise and culturally responsive assistance and support.

Even as nontraditional sources of capital become available in the form of rotating credit associations, for-profit and not-for-profit micro-lending agencies, and business trade credit, the traditional banks, capital markets, and other financial institutions cannot escape the demographic shifts occurring in the United States and, in particular, in regional markets. The financial services industry is only recently beginning to recognize the growing economic implications of the increasing presence of regional and transnational ethnic entrepreneurial customers. This is an issue of great significance in the borderlands. The traditional finance sector is one of the most crucial sectors of the economy for regulating economic growth, and yet it appears to lag behind in terms of "inclusive incorporation" of differing needs of participants.

Comprehensive Community Wealth Accumulation Policies

Past public policies that resulted in discouraging or mitigating wealth accumulation in communities of color play a direct and powerful role in ethnic entrepreneurial activities located both inside and outside ethnic enclaves and communities. The issues of wealth stagnation and wealth reversals during episodes of economic growth and prosperity are particularly salient to discussions of ethnic/racial entrepreneurial activities and the health of ethnic economies and enclaves.

Researchers, entrepreneurs, and public policy experts will need to craft new policies on issues addressing the increasing gaps in wealth among the various populations in the United States and their consequences for civil society. We have sufficient innovative community initiatives that, if supported by local, state, and federal policies, could rapidly decrease the economic stress currently being felt in the borderlands. An example of such policies are comprehensive wealth-building programs that tie the refundable Earned Income Tax Credit to affordable homeownership and to other asset accumulation, such as Children's Education Savings Accounts that are not included in asset tests for other incomes programs. A very troubling part of current policies meant to increase self-sufficiency for individuals and families is the mismatch between asset-development programs and incomes-based programs. For example, programs encouraging families to contribute to Children's Education Saving Accounts are considered to be strong asset-based policies but conflict with incomes-based programs (such as food stamps or supplemental security income) that consider the children's accounts as "family assets" and thus can disqualify families from cash-assistance programs.

Additionally, poorly designed tax credits such as the dependent-child and elderly-care nonrefundable credits are only useful to families with sufficiently high incomes and a correspondingly high tax liability. To make these policies truly effective in creating opportunities for self-sufficiency for the working poor, we must redesign these particular tax credits into refundable tax credits. The prevalence of families receiving this mixed message—on the one hand, policies encouraging self-sufficiency and frugal economic behaviors that build up savings, and on the other hand, incomes-based policies that require asset limits in order to qualify—creates confusion and mistrust. The transitioning period for families moving from welfare assistance into self-sufficiency can become a nightmare. Correspondingly, the lack of cultural knowledge by policy and program administrators and service providers sends additional messages of noninclusiveness toward Latino working poor communities. In the areas of program implementation and service provision, government institutions can be indifferent to the needs and cultural behaviors of transnational working-poor communities in the borderlands. One very real community response is to retreat, remain isolated, and disengage from civic participation. How welcoming our government and democratic institutions are can be measured by the degree of commitment to serving our less wealthy communities.

Conclusion

This chapter set out to explore the intersection of Latina entrepreneurial activity supplementing, or "patching," family income with community-based organizations that display a cultural understanding of the communities in which they operate and how this intersection contributes to family well-being. We have seen that Latina entrepreneurship is intimately intertwined with cultural roles and enhances family resources within the context of the unique transnational economic environment of the U.S.-Mexico border. Because entrepreneurial activities create self-employment and microbusinesses create employment opportunities for family, fictive kin, and other community members, they become a crucial component in reducing the incidence of poverty in the borderlands and in retaining earnings within the community. Self-employment and microenterprises have grown while public assistance has declined. Devolution does not appear to be a temporary measure. We must acknowledge that public assistance dollars cannot substitute for the absence of living wages, access to educational opportunities through quality schooling and enrichment programs for youth, and, most significant, affordable health care. One conclusion that cannot be made simply because I have documented economic resiliency and survival strategies among working-poor and low-income families is that microenterprise is the "silver bullet" that will universally reduce poverty in the borderlands. There is a vast difference between "income patching" and sustainable financial stability and economic well-being. What is important to note about this increasing entrepreneurial phenomenon is the significance of Latino working-poor and low-income families' healthy economic behaviors despite the policy neglect and lack of government investment dollars in the region.

I have also examined the crucial role that culturally competent community-based organizations play in struggling Latino communities.

The CBOs and CDFIs that maintain a permanent presence along the border and that employ cultural responsiveness in delivering services increase the probability of successful program outcomes and sustainable results in a number of wealth-building activities. Of course, this does not imply that community-based organizations can completely replace the role of public-sector agencies. However, the CBOs often act as facilitators between struggling communities and government entities and this type of partnership brings a degree of network and social capital into the dialogue regarding which programs and which policies are relevant for Latino working-poor families.

Confronting transnational families and Latina microbusiness owners residing in the borderlands are issues that can also result in social equity and permanent change. For challenges facing transnational families such as accessing education, home ownership and asset building are also the same avenues that present opportunities for Latina entrepreneurial activity. In regard to community development and family economic stability, cultural behaviors can be viewed as deterrents, which is generally the case in public education or in home-mortgage markets, or as assets, which is the case with Latino entrepreneurs employing bilingualism and biculturalism to successfully operate their enterprises.

Appendix

Twenty-nine Borderlands Counties

Texas:	Brewster
(*16 counties*)	Cameron (Brownsville-Harlingen-San Benito metro)
	Culberson
	Dimmit
	El Paso (El Paso metro)
	Hidalgo (McAllen-Edinburg-Mission metro)
	Hudspeth
	Jeff Davis
	Kinney
	Maverick
	Presidio
	Starr
	Terrell
	Val Verde
	Webb (Laredo metro)
	Zapata

New Mexico:	Eddy
(*7 counties*)	Doña Ana (Las Cruces metro)
	Lea
	Luna
	Grant
	Hidalgo
	Otero

Arizona:	Cochise
(*4 counties*)	Pima (Tucson metro)
	Santa Cruz
	Yuma (Yuma metro)

California:	Imperial
(*2 counties*)	San Diego (San Diego metro)

Notes

1. The four border states are Texas, New Mexico, Arizona, and California. See appendix for list of counties.

2. Small firms are defined as having fewer than five hundred employees (U.S. Small Business Administration 1999), whereas microenterprises are defined as having one to five employees with less than $35,000 needed in start-up capital (Association for Enterprise Opportunity 2006).

3. Some ethnic communities arrive in the host-country with home-country cultural norms strongly supportive of female economic activities outside the household. These cultural norms are reinforced in the United States. However, many ethnic communities struggle with women-based enterprises outside the home and negotiating such gender-role modifications. This is heightened by exposure to U.S. markets with high female labor participation outside the home, which often provokes additional stressors on immigrant family integration into the host country.

4. Non-employer businesses are essentially the self-employed, that is, businesses that do not employ workers. Microbusinesses or microenterprises are defined as businesses with one to five workers, including the owner.

5. New job declines can be related to a variety of factors during the 1997–2001 period. The decline in border manufacturing during this time has spillover effects on small business suppliers and could have contributed to the decline. Contributing to the decline in employment are the close ties to Mexico's economy, which suffered a financial markets adjustment in 1995 that resulted in a slowdown in economic activity along the border, particularly in the retail sector.

6. A *quinceañera* (*quince* is Spanish for 15, *año* is Spanish for year) is an Hispanic family and community rite of passage for young women turning fifteen. A religious ceremony along with a *fiesta* celebrate the transition from girlhood to young womanhood with all its attendant responsibilities and status (On Air Column 2002).

7. The most recognizable entrepreneurial activity among Latinas in their communities is the making of such cultural food as tamales, *buñuelos*, pastries, and so on, for holidays and high holy days.

8. A narrow definition of the borderlands is used in this section and includes twenty-nine counties (in four states) contiguous to the Mexico border. All data listed in Table 10.2 include only those counties located in the corresponding state contiguous to Mexico. All figures appearing in this section use the same county definition. See Appendix.

9. All percent-change calculations are in 2002 real dollars (U.S. Census Bureau, County Census Data 2000).

10. Calculations are in 2002 current dollars.

11. A *tanda* is a rotating credit-saving association formed by trusted members of a community. Each member is scheduled to receive the aggregate monthly "pot" (accumulated collective funds) at a specified date, and each member contributes a fixed amount, say, twenty dollars, on a weekly basis. One person holds the entire amount during the monthly accumulation. *Tandas* can have anywhere from five to twenty-five-plus participants. The "pots" can be substantial, and *tanda* participants are quite adept at scheduling their turn to coincide with an important family expense (a reunion in Mexico, a wedding, a baptism, the start of a school term). For an in-depth description of Chicano and Mexican participation in *tandas*, see Vélez-Ibañez (1983).

12. Historically, working conditions created by the Industrial Revolution gave rise to cooperative credit associations and mutual aid societies for low-wage workers. Ultimately, these community associations grew into our present-day credit unions (Moody and Fite 1971).

13. *Compadrazgo* is a Spanish term used for capturing the supportive nature of "godfathering" in Latino communities. The female version is *co-madrazgo*.

14. Community development financial institutions can be organized to target a variety of needs such as a community development bank, credit union, venture capital fund or, for my purposes in this chapter, a microenterprise loan fund, also known as microfinance or microlending organizations.

15. The Community Reinvestment Act (CRA) of 1977 stipulates that mainstream banking institutions must serve all their potential customers by geographical operations. However, these institutions have a long history of closing branch banks in low-income neighborhoods, thus denying ethnic and racial small businesses their start-up capital, and not actively pursuing low-income customers. However, the $38 billion-remittance market by Latino temporary and transnational workers is arousing more interest in the traditional financial services industry.

16. In 1961, ACCION International was launched in Venezuela by an American law student. He and his friends started grassroots community development programs that addressed the most pressing needs of the urban poor. These "ACCIONistas" created programs that were exported from Venezuela to Brazil, Peru, and Colombia. By 1970 the programs had moved toward economic opportunity and self-help and had begun working with entrepreneurs in the informal economy by offering them "microloans."

References

Abalos, David T. 1993. *The Latino Family and the Politics of Transformation*. Praeger Series in Transformational Politics and Political Science. Westport, CT: Praeger.

Aldrich, Howard E., and Roger Waldinger. 1990. "Ethnicity and Entrepreneurship." *Annual Review of Sociology* 16: 111–35.

Association for Enterprise Opportunity. 2006. "What Is a Microenterprise?" *About Microenterprise*. Available at http://www.microenterpriseworks.org/about/whatis.htm.

Barret, Giles, Trevor P. Jones, and David McEvoy. 1996. "Ethnic Minority Business: Theoretical Discourse in Britain and North America." *Urban Studies* 33(4–5): 783–906.

Bates, Timothy. 1990. "Self-Employment Trends among Mexican-Americans." Center for Economic Studies, Bureau of the Census, Working Paper CES 90–9.

Cavazos, Perla. 2002. "Measuring Asset Development among San Antonio Microentrepreneurs: An ACCION Texas Impact Study." Master's Professional Report, LBJ School of Public Affairs, University of Texas at Austin.

Center for Women's Business Research (CWBR). 1997a. "Latina Entrepreneurs: An Economic Force in the U.S." Press Release. Available at http://www.womensbusinessresearch.org/presreleases/9-26-2000/9-26-2000.html.

———. 1997b. "Minority Women-Owned Firms Thriving." Press Release. Available at http://www.womensbusinessresearch.org/presreleases/6-25-1997/6-25-1997.html.

———. 1998. "Women Business Owners of Color: Challenges and Accomplishments." Survey.

———. 2000. "The Spirit of Enterprise: Latina Entrepreneurs in the United States." Survey.

———. 2001. "Hispanic-Owned Businesses in the United States, 2002: A Fact Sheet." Available at http://www.womensbusinessresearch.org/minority/hispanic.pdf.

Clancy, Margaret, Mark Schreiner, and Michael Sherraden. 2002. "Saving Performance in the American Dream Demonstration—A National Demonstration of Individual Development Accounts." Final Report. Center for Social Development, Washington University, St. Louis, October.

Clark, Peggy, and Amy Kays. 1999. *Microenterprise and the Poor: Findings from the Self-Employment Learning Project Five-Year Survey of Microenterprise*. Washington, DC: Aspen Institute.

Darity, William, Jr., Darrick Hamilton, and Jason Dietrich. 2002. "Passing on Blackness: Latinos, Race, and Earnings in the USA." *Applied Economics Letters* 9: 847–53.

Devine, Theresa J. 1994. "Characteristics of Self-Employed Women in the United States." *Monthly Labor Review* 117(3): 20–34.

Dill, B. Thornton. 1994. "Fictive Kin, Paper Sons and *Compadrazgo:* Women of Color and the Struggle for Family Survival." In *Women of Color in U.S. Society,* ed. Maxine Baca Zinn and B. Thornton Dill, 149–70. Philadelphia: Temple University Press.

Edgcomb, Elaine, and Maria M. Armington. 2003. *The Informal Economy: Latino Enterprises at the Margin*. Washington, DC: FIELD, Aspen Institute.

Edin, Kathryn. 2001. "More Than Money: The Role of Assets in the Survival Strategies and Material Well-Being of the Poor." In *Assets for the Poor: The Benefits of Spreading Asset Ownership,* ed. T. Shapiro and E. Wolff, 206–51. New York: Russell Sage Foundation.

"Education Pays." 2002. *Occupational Outlook Quarterly* 46(1): 52. Available at http://www.bls. gov/opub/ooq/2002/spring/oochart.htm.

Fairlie, Robert W., and Bruce D. Meyer. 1996. "Ethnic and Racial Self-Employment Differences and Possible Explanations." *Journal of Human Resources* 31(4): 756–93.

Flota, Chrystell, and Marie Mora. 2001. "The Earnings of Self-Employed Mexican-Americans along the U.S.-Mexico Border." *Annals of Regional Science* 35: 483–99.

Grameen Bank, USA. n.d. "Self-Employment in the United States." Available at http://www.gfusa.org/gbrp/sel.html.

Gregory, Peggy. 2003. "The History of Latino Community Involvement: A Literature Review." Working Paper. University of California, Davis.

Hurtado, Aida. 1999. "Cross-border Existence: One Woman's Migration Story." In *Women's Untold Stories: Breaking Silence, Talking Back, Voicing Complexity,* ed. Mary Romero and Abigail J. Stewart, 83–104. New York: Routledge.

Kennickell, Arthur B., Martha Starr-McCluer, and Brian J. Surette. 2000. "Recent Changes in U.S. Family Finances: Results from the 1998 Survey of Consumer Finances." Division of Research and Statistics, Board of Governors, *Federal Reserve Bulletin* 86(1): 1–29.

Light, Ivan H., and Steven J. Gold. 2000. *Ethnic Economies*. San Diego, CA: Academic Press.

Moody, Carroll, and Gilbert Fite. 1971. *The Credit Union Movement: Origins and Development, 1850–1970*. Lincoln: University of Nebraska Press.

Olson, Patricia, Virginia Solis Zuiker, and Catherine Phillips Montalto. 2000. "Self-Employed Hispanics and Hispanic Wage Earners: Differences in Earnings." *Hispanic Journal of Behavioral Sciences* 22(1): 114–30.

On Air Column in *Voices,* vol. 28, Fall–Winter 2002. Available at http://www. nyfolklore.org/pubs/voic28-3-4/onair.html.

Portes, Alejandro, ed. 1995. *The Economic Sociology of Immigration: Essays on Networks, Ethnicity, and Entrepreneurship.* New York: Russell Sage Foundation.

Raijman, Rebeca. 2001. "Determinants of Entrepreneurial Intentions: Mexican Immigrants in Chicago." *Journal of Socio-Economics* 30: 393–411.

Robles, Bárbara. 2002. "Latino Microenterprise and the U.S.-Mexico Border Economy." *Estey Centre Journal of International Law and Trade Policy* 3(2): 307–27.

———. 2003. "Low-Income Families and Asset Building on the U.S.-Mexico Border." Session Report (February 2003), Annie E. Casey-LBJ School of Public Affairs, Consultative Session, November 15–16, Austin, Texas.

Rochin, Refugio I., Rogelio Saenz, Steve Hampton, and Bea Calo. 1998. *"Colonias and Chicano/a Entrepreneurs in Rural California."* Julian Samora Research Institute, Research Report no. 16.

Romney, Lee. 1998. "Latinas Get Down To Business." *Los Angeles Times,* November 13.

Rosa, Peter, Sara Carter, and Daphne Hamilton. 1996. "Gender as a Determinant of Small Business Performance: Insights from a British Study." *Small Business Economics* 8: 463–78.

Saunders, Jimmy M., and Victor Nee. 1987. "The Limits of Ethnic Solidarity in the Ethnic Enclave Economy." *American Sociological Review* 52: 745–67.

Sorensen, Stephen, Dominic J. Brewer, Stephen J. Carroll, and Eugene Bryton. 1995. "Increasing Hispanic Participation in Higher Education: A Desirable Public Investment." *Rand Internet Policy Brief, IP-152.* Available at http://www.rand.org.

Thomas-Brietfeld, Sean. 2003. "The Latino Workforce." National Council of La Raza, Statistical Brief, no. 3. Available at http://www.nclr.org/policy/briefs/SB%203%20Latino%20 workers-FNL.pdf.

Thornton, Patricia H. 1999. "The Sociology of Entrepreneurship." *Annual Review of Sociology* 24: 19–46.

Treviño, Marisa. 2001. "Latinas Increasingly Running for, Winning Office." *Women's e-News.* Available at http:// www.womensenews.org (last accessed January 24, 2004).

U.S. Census Bureau. 1990 and 2000. http://www.census.gov.

———. 1990 and 2000. State Facts. http://www.census.gov.

———. 2000. County Census Data. http://www.census.gov.

U.S. Department of Commerce. 1992. "Survey of Minority-Owned Business Enterprises." Washington, DC: U.S. Census Bureau, Department of Commerce.

———. Economics and Statistics Administration, Bureau of the Census, 1997. Non-Employer Statistics, Economic Census (EC97X-CS4, January 2001).

————. Economics and Statistics Administration, Bureau of the Census, 2001. Non-Employer Statistics, Economic Census (NS/01, September 2001).

U.S. Department of Labor, Bureau of Labor Statistics News Release. 2003. "Metropolitan Area Employment and Unemployment: November 2003." Washington, DC.

U.S. Department of the Treasury. 2003. "Certified Community Development Financial Institutions." CDFI Fund.

U.S. Small Business Administration, Office of the Advocacy. 1998. "Women in Business." Washington, DC.

————. 1999. "Minorities in Business." Washington, DC.

Vélez-Ibañez, Carlos G. 1983. *Bonds of Mutual Trust: The Cultural Systems of Rotating Credit Associations among Urban Mexicans and Chicanos*. New Brunswick, NJ: Rutgers University Press.

CHAPTER ELEVEN

Public Policy Changes on the U.S.-Mexico Border

Irasema Coronado

We annually celebrate the Fourth of July with a paean to immigration, the force that tamed this vast continent and built this great Republic. This is not simply history; immigration continues to refresh and nourish America; we would be better off with more of it. Indeed, during the immigration debate of 1984 we suggested an ultimate goal to guide passing policies—a constitutional amendment: "There shall be open borders."
> —Robert L. Bartley, *Wall Street Journal,* July 2, 2001

Long-term, established residents of the border region have learned to negotiate border policies and use them to their benefit. Nonetheless, geographic boundaries and the resultant barriers of unilateral policies directly and indirectly affect the lives of residents along the U.S.-Mexico boundary. There, policies and the politics they generate are part of the extraordinary experiences that border residents face in the challenges of daily life. Proffered in this collection of chapters are a series of snapshots of resilient and resourceful transborder families who have found a way to improve their lives under the shadow of globalization. As this body of work illustrates, public policy on the border is not bilateral; and, in some cases, I argue that public policies should be binational. For example, if both the United States and Mexico enact environmental policies related to air quality, common sense would dictate that these policies should be consistent at the U.S.-Mexico border. Likewise, it is important that other policies that are to be enforced in the region be congruent, on both sides; if not, there is a risk that policy making will be an exercise in futility.

This chapter unfolds with a history of public policies, including a brief overview of the Bracero Program and the Border Industrialization Program (BIP), and their impact, with a discussion of how globalization has led to the current state of affairs on the border. Next, the chapter addresses the shortcomings of public policies that often lack a bilateral perspective, and how such unilateral policies fail to address the needs of residents on the border. The chapter reveals how women negotiate the border and respective government policies in a creative manner to meet the needs of their families. Most public policies at the border are not binational, and this body of research points to this lack. As the border region continues to reach farther into the United States, beyond the contiguous borderline to places such as Albuquerque, New Mexico, San Antonio, Texas, and Los Angeles, California, transnational families are affected in important ways. Finally, I speak to the needs of the borderland families and children in the realms of economic, immigration, labor, and homeland security policies; and, with this perspective, I present a series of relevant and critical binational public policy recommendations.

What Happened? *Qué pasó? Braceros* to *Maquiladoras*

In response to the U.S. labor shortage during World War II, Washington and Mexico City negotiated the Bracero (laborer) Program, a temporary plan that offered Mexican workers entry into the United States. With American men away fighting the war, women replaced them in the factories, which left no one to pick the crops in the fields. At the end of the war, theoretically, the men would come home, and the women—tens of thousands of "Rosie the Riveters"—would take up their previous roles as homemakers. In this scenario, the *braceros* would return to Mexico. Like all public policies, the Bracero Program had positive and negative externalities. For one, many established relationships between workers and employers continued after the program ended. Thousands of *braceros* simply crossed back into the United States as undocumented workers and reappeared at the same ranches and farms where they had worked previously. Growers benefited from having the flow of reliable, cheap labor while the *braceros* earned U.S. dollars. The official Bracero program in theory provided the Mexican workers with certain benefits, such as health care coverage, lodging at the place of employment, and some protections against exploitation. U.S. agencies stipulated wages and working conditions and, in principle, supervised operations in the field. In practice, however, supervision was often quite lax, allowing departures from the mandated standards that sometimes fell to below-contract wages, miserable working conditions, and virtual peonage (Reubens 1986).

The Mexican government established a savings account for the *braceros* to serve as a future pension. A part of all earnings (10%) would be collected by the employers, deposited in American banks, and transferred to the Banco de México, S.A., which would then deposit the funds in the Banco Nacional de Crédito Agrícola and the Banco del Ahorro Nacional. According to a study commissioned by the Servicio de Investigación y Análisis, División de Política Social de la Cámara de Diputados, over $168,254,140 (Mexican pesos) were deposited in 1945 alone (Sandoval de Escurdia et al. 2003). Many of these deposits were never seen by former *braceros*, who sued the Mexican government for the lost funds. In response to this suit, the Secretaría de Gobernación initiated a program to, first, register all former *braceros* who had paid into this savings plan, and second, to pay them compensation of approximately $38,000 *pesos*, or $3,800 dollars (Chaparro 2005). Several former *braceros* have requested an extension to register, because many of them are attempting to find the original documents that verify their participation in the Bracero Program, a prerequisite to receiving compensation.

As the Bracero Program was ending, the international division of labor was exacerbated. In 1965 the Mexican government unleashed a new economic development strategy, the Border Industrialization Plan

(BIP) that married American corporations' need to maximize profits with the cheap labor that Mexico offered. The BIP provided incentives for companies looking to relocate to the northern Mexican border cities that became prime locations because of their proximity to the U.S. market. Hence, many corporations found their way to Nuevo Laredo, Reynosa, and Matamoros, in Tamaulipas; Ciudad Juárez, in Chihuahua; Nogales, in Sonora; and other border cities.

Many American companies began to move their labor-intensive operations south of the border to increase profits and take advantage of the cheap, abundant work force. Beneficial tariff laws and favorable taxation policies drew corporations and manufacturers and specialized workers to the border plants. *Maquiladoras* were exempted under the 1973 Foreign Investment Law in Mexico, which required a minimum of 51% Mexican ownership of all businesses (Clark, Sawyer, and Sprinkle 1990). These forces (incentives) fueled the rise of the *maquiladora* industry on Mexico's northern border (Nash and Fernández-Kelly 1983). American corporate officers applied capitalist principles to the *maquiladoras,* such as the division of labor, self-interest, and the function of markets, and concluded that an additional way to save money was to pay their workers less.

The international division of labor and the BIP had unintended consequences for border residents. Exponential growth in population drawn to jobs at the border and the inability of local governments to provide basic infrastructure led to demands on public agencies and institutions and to serious, complex environmental problems. People lacked access to safe drinking water, and to wastewater and sewer services. Public transportation was limited and forced the proliferation of crowded, poorly constructed residential areas near the plants. Because newly arrived immigrants to Mexico's northern border did not have the resources to rent apartments or buy homes, many resorted to becoming squatters (Coronado 1998; Cravey 1998). These unplanned housing settlements, known as *colonias populares,* emerged in many cities on both sides of the border. Indeed, the ongoing presence of *colonias* reflects the reality of the poorest living conditions of all Americans. *Colonias* are found along the California, Arizona, New Mexico, and Texas border with Mexico. In Texas alone, for example, there are over 2,294 *colonias,* with over 400,000 residents along the border with Mexico (*Colonia* Faqs n.d.)

The large number of workers seeking opportunities in the northern Mexican states had consequences for both sides of the border. A study of Texas border cities found that changes in the level of *maquiladora* employment had a great impact on employment rates in the communities of El Paso, Laredo, McAllen, and Brownsville (Patrick 1990). A 10% increase in *maquiladora* jobs resulted in a 2–3% increase in employment in El Paso and McAllen, and a 3–4% increase in Laredo and Brownsville (Holden 1984). These cities also experienced a real estate boom because American corporate officers and managers transferring to Mexican border cities lived on the U.S. side (Staudt and Coronado 2002). These economic, global, and demographic forces exposed a border that extended beyond national lines, transmuting a construct of societal and economic inequities (Fatemi 1990; Kopinak 1996).

With the passage and implementation of the North American Free Trade Agreement (NAFTA), the economic integration of Mexico, the United States, and Canada deepened. More U.S.-based corporations continued to move into Mexico, along with banking and other services. Well-connected Mexicans bought their nation's second-largest commercial bank from the government for $3.3 billion and sold it to Citigroup for $12.5 billion (Faux 2005). In 2005, the Maytag Company moved parts of its operations from Illinois to Reynosa, Tamaulipas, leaving 1,600 Americans unemployed (Moberg 2005). In March 2006 one of the largest refrigerator plants in the United States—Greenville, Michigan's Electrolux AB—ceased production there and moved to Ciudad Juárez, with approximately 2,700 American workers losing their jobs. Moreover, the Associated Press reported that GE refrigerators are now being made at the company's new plant in Ciudad Juárez (Gilot 2006).

A combination of factors in the transition from *braceros* to *maquiladoras* has changed the economic circumstances and employment opportunities for new immigrants and longtime border residents, ultimately leading to increased poverty and marginalization of some families living along the U.S. borderline. The relocation of American companies to Mexico's northern border does, as mentioned earlier, create employment, although, some observers would argue, not enough for U.S. border cities. Texan cities such as Laredo, El Paso, and Eagle Pass benefit from their port-of-entry locations. Moreover, transportation, warehousing, packaging, and other businesses in these U.S. border cities directly benefit from the location of *maquiladoras* in Mexico.

Mexico's northern border states have benefited as well from globalization in that they have the highest per capita income in Mexico. The location of American-owned *maquiladoras* has led to increased employment in Mexico, albeit at low wages. *Maquiladoras* continue to be the top foreign exchange generator for Mexico, at $18.4 billion in 2003, followed by oil at $15 billion, and then remittances (Coronado 2004).

Globalization and the Immigrant Experience

As globalization has unfolded, the border region has become a focal point for the movement of goods and services, people, and capital across political boundaries. All of these transactions impact border communities. The movement of goods exerts pressure on infrastructure and contributes to air, water, and soil pollution and other environmental problems, such as the transboundary movement of hazardous materials and illegal dumping. People moving from one side of the border to the other witness congestion in the lines on the international bridges as well as at the pedestrian points of entry. It is ironic that the American-born children of Mexican immigrants are now finding job opportunities in Mexico and not in the United States. Between 5,000 and 8,000 people who live in El Paso cross daily into Ciudad Juárez to work, mostly in the *maquiladora* industry (Rivera 1998; Staudt and Coronado 2002).

The immigrants who came into the United States from circa 1900 to the 1960s were socialized into American life and culture in part because of the availability of jobs that paid well in comparison to Mexican wages and that also provided benefits such as health care and life insurance. Full-time work and decent wages enabled new immigrants to live well. However, by the 1970s, they faced a bleaker future, largely because they had started out at a greater disadvantage (Borjas and Scrivener 2005). While Borjas and Scrivener argue that assimilation is the key to success in the United States, I contend that fewer economic opportunities that could lead to financial assimilation exist. In the 1970s in El Paso, the garment capital of the world, people earned between $9.00 and $12.00 per hour working at Levi's, Farah's, or other clothing factories. A manufacturing job socialized immigrants into the workforce and shaped their assimilation into U.S. society. Obtaining credit was an integral part of their success if they were to achieve the American dream. Two important variables—a certain income threshold and verifiable long-term employment—yielded access to credit and thus to major purchases such as a car or a house, possibilities that did not exist for them in Mexico (Coronado 2003).

When viewing the border region as a whole, it is important to acknowledge how internal immigration to Mexico's border cities presents challenges to border communities. Mexicans who migrate to the borderline also must learn to adapt to a new way of life. There are tensions between the new migrants and the established residents of Mexican border cities. Similar tensions appear in the United States as longtime border residents argue that the children of newcomers are burdening the schools and are demanding more government services (Staudt and Coronado 2002). On the U.S. side, as companies moved their labor-intensive operations south, American workers lost their jobs, health insurance, retirement pensions, and hope. For example, the El Paso garment industry suffered major losses and relocations in the 1990s in the post-NAFTA era. As factories and firms left the border region (some overnight), "the costs and consequences of these problems were often passed on to workers" (Ortiz-Gonzalez 2004: 82). Loss of jobs, in some cases, translated into loss of homes and cars and into bad credit. As a result, immigrants became the scapegoats of the greater force of globalization driven by corporate profits (Calavita 1996).

The 1970s saw the emergence of the energy crisis and an economic downturn in the United States, and economic recession proved to be an important factor facilitating a rise of immigration restrictionist sentiment (Nevins 2002). The number of migrants from Mexico grew significantly in the mid-1980s in the context of a serious downturn in that nation's economy (Nevins 2002).

I would argue with those who say that Americans started to lose their jobs with the advent of NAFTA. I contend that this job loss began in the 1950s and 1960s with the international division of labor. As multinational corporations continue to exploit cheap labor, workers on both sides of the border lose out. Both suffer unemployment, downgrades in benefits, increased hours, and lower wages. The spiral of lower wages on the U.S. side results in workers' inability to pay bills, buy homes, or pay college expenses, all of the elements that ultimately contribute to successful participation in American society (Staudt and Coronado 2002).

Unilateral Border Policies

Negotiating unilateral government policies is part of everyday life for U.S. and Mexican border residents whose lives daily intersect this political boundary. Mexicans wanting to legally enter the United States are acutely aware of the documentation required by the U.S. government that will allow them to do so. Border residents know what must be done in order to comply with these policies. For example, to obtain a U.S. travel visa, Mexican residents must demonstrate that they have money in a Mexican bank. To comply, the person borrows money to open an account and then obtains the necessary documents to satisfy the official consular requirements. Or, as Mexican residents shop in American stores, they are acutely aware of Mexican policies that determine what one can bring back into Mexico without paying a penalty tax. To survive at the border, one must master the art of circumventing these unilateral policies.

Access to health care is a serious and prevalent issue that results in significant cross-border utilization of services from both sides (Brandon et al. 1997). The poor and medically uninsured border residents of Mexican origin who reside in the United States tend to rely on less expensive Mexican physicians and medicines. Likewise, there are cases when Mexicans cross to the north to avail themselves of specialized medical services not available in Mexico. As a result, and despite the increasing restrictions on the importation of medicine into the United States from Mexico, border residents find creative ways to meet their health care needs (see Márquez, chapter 6 in this volume). Some families residing in the United States resort out of necessity to smuggling medicine purchased in Mexico into the United States. Participant observation research and my own personal experiences indicate that Mexican pharmacies provide a physician-signed prescription for proof to U.S. Customs officials that the medication was legitimately ordered. Dental work is less expensive on the Mexican side, and some Mexican dentists offer free transportation for their American patients to their offices. These same dentists advertise in the Yellow Pages and give a toll-free number U.S. phone number. Restrictive policies clearly complicate life for border residents and raise unnecessary obstacles for families whose lives are dependent on the cross-flow and movement of border life.

Policy Impact on Border Families and Children

Recent Homeland Security policies have created additional burdens for those families who are dependent on cross-border activities. For some, they face longer wait times at the international bridges and undergo greater scrutiny upon entering the United States. In the case of the Mexican maids or child-care providers who work in the households of Americans, Homeland Security restrictions force many to stay overnight in the United States rather than return home to their own families. They fear being "caught" working illegally. Additionally, when U.S. Border Control becomes stricter, there is an increase in documentation fraud that translates into higher smugglers' fees. The issue becomes deadly serious when tighter border security can even lead to loss of life as migrants risk crossing through desolate areas (Andreas 1998; Wood 2001). For border families, greater enforcement coupled with long waiting times to cross alienates families who are spread across the divide (Staudt and Coronado 2002). Ultimately, low-income border residents are faced with serious choices such as not crossing into Mexico to visit a doctor or buy cheaper prescription drugs or food, all of which negatively impact the quality of their subsistence. Another critical factor comes in the heavy reliance by Mexicans on the remittances sent back from their loved ones who are working in the United States. For many, this money serves as the family's sole source of income. New policies are needed to deal with bank cards and sending fees. The high costs of sending remittances tie up investment capital, thus reducing the impact on human resources (education, new schools, teachers) and community resources (parks, hospitals, construction of modern schools, investments in businesses). Banks have implemented new procedures for taxing remittances, which would place a double tax burden on immigrants in the United States who often have tax money withheld from their paychecks and do not receive refunds (De la Garza and Lowell 2002).

Another critical impact on immigrants has come in the form of increased policy restrictions aimed directly at immigrant communities.

Border states have implemented aggressive policy changes to reduce the amount and type of social benefits available to immigrants. As seen in 1994, the state of California passed Proposition 187, controversial legislation that restricted public benefits to all immigrants including health care and access to primary and secondary education (González-Baker et al. 1998). In an ideal world, one solution for protecting immigrants' rights could be through bilateral policies between the United States and Mexico. Unfortunately, the historical pattern of such bilateral policies has been that they are difficult to negotiate and even more difficult to implement (Staudt and Coronado 2002). For example, the implementation of the 1983 La Paz Agreement, created to protect the environment along the U.S.-Mexico border, faced serious problems in that the accord failed to "adequately address the how to, the when, and the concomitant funding streams needed to address border problems" (Staudt and Coronado 2002: 78).

Finally, there is the unique issue of education. Historically, Mexican parents have taken extra measures so that their children can attend American schools. Their primary goal is to provide the best education possible for their children, regardless of on what side of the border the better opportunities lie. Parents recognize that success in today's world requires their children to be well educated and to have an excellent command of the English language. At the same time, there are many situations where families from the U.S. side cross their children to Mexican schools so that they can master the Spanish language. While families on both sides make sacrifices to ensure that their children can negotiate border life, Mexican and American school districts experience overcrowding and are inadequately funded.

Border crossers and their families are adaptive and are turning certain new policies into opportunities that positively impact their lives. For example, border institutions of higher learning in the United States allow Mexicans to pay in-state tuition. In addition to tactically using the educational systems on both sides, some border residents have found it more economically feasible to purchase homes in Mexico with U.S. credit as U.S. housing costs have increased exponentially. Returning Americans have formed communities where they outnumber Mexican citizens. Moreover, Mexican residents are seizing the opportunity to secure loans from the various U.S. banks that are now lending money for people to purchase homes in Mexico (Holden 1984).

The Transboundary Life

A whole new dimension of business activity has emerged that links Mexican immigrants in the United States with their home country—bus and air travel, telephone cards and calling plans, television programs, and the Internet—that ultimately nourishes the transboundary life-style. In the past, immigrants tended to cut the ties back to their homeland; now, however, newer and more abundant options in technology, affordable transportation, and the proliferation of a viable market have facilitated connections between Mexican immigrants and their country of origin. Family unity remains central to this expansion of services.

American television stations carry ads for telephone companies touting transborder calling cards. The same commercial strategies are sold to immigrants and allow them to talk with their families in Mexico as well as farther into Latin America. For example, calling cards, sold in Mexico for between $3.00 and $10.00, are advertised directly to immigrants in the United States as well as to family members left behind. A recent advertisement encouraged children, "Now you can call your father in the U.S."; and store fronts flaunt signage, "Calling cards sold here" (Staudt and Coronado 2002).

Similarly, international television networks keep people in closer touch with their country of origin. Today, immigrants in the United States can watch newscasts from Mexico as well as their beloved soccer matches, entertainment shows, and, of course, the very popular *telenovelas,* or soap operas. Throughout major U.S. cities and the entire border region, immigrants keep informed about the latest Mexican political, social, and economic events covered by the conglomerate Spanish-language networks of Televisa, Telemundo, and Univisión. Equally important, Mexicans watch American channels, movies, and newscasts. Satellite television, cable, direct TV, and Internet cafés link people in both directions and offer a cultural symbiosis that is, at the same time, instructive, informing, and enlightening. Transborder families who learn to negotiate both sides of the border have economic and social advantages, and the appropriate use of technology has led to a better quality of life for them.

Public Policy Recommendations

In general, both the United States and Mexico should work together to minimize income inequality, assure basic needs, and provide quality education and affordable medical care for residents on both sides of the border. Collaboration in these areas only enhances the quality of life for people and communities. Success requires respect for the organizational and operating processes of educational systems, health systems, professional preparations, higher education, the criminal justice systems, and the governmental institutions, structures, and functions in both the United States and Mexico. There are many precedents where the United States and Mexico have worked together. For example, in regard to the environment, the two countries signed the 1983 La Paz Agreement over commerce issues, and the more recent NAFTA went into effect in 1994. Over time, the United States and Mexico have signed over two hundred agreements on a wide range of significant issues. In the spirit of that cooperation, I offer policy recommendations in six areas.

Crossing the Border

For every holiday season such as Christmas, Easter, and the Day of the Dead, long lines await *paisanos* at crossing points as they return to visit family in Mexico. Similarly, Easter Week and summer vacation bring many Mexicans to the United States. Governments on both sides should initiate transborder reforms that facilitate the crossing process. If movement of people at the bridges were expedited, U.S. and Mexican businesses would benefit through the increased purchases of goods and services by visitors. This increase would lead to additional sales taxes and a positive cash flow to local governments.

- Better technology on both sides would facilitate quicker crossings as well as faster detection of criminals such as sexual predators and drug dealers.
- An expedited clearance program for frequent crossers could be implemented similar to the existing FAST bilateral initiative,[1] which expedites the clearance of commercial shipments.

- A public transportation system for easily crossing the border—that is, designated bus lines that run directly to the bridges, or trolleys that easily take people across—would facilitate traffic.
- The Mexican government could allow *paisanos* to enter their vehicles without having to pay the import tax and also permit them to take gifts into Mexico without paying duties.

Health Care

Both governments need to take into account that transborder families capitalize and maximize health resources in both countries. Economy-minded border residents are aware of what health-care services are available to them on either side of the border. Families who live in the region deserve a health-care system that builds upon the cross-border utilization of services.

- Make portable health insurance available to border residents that would pay for health services wherever they were delivered.
- Implement a cross-border database for pharmaceutical dispensation of prescriptions.
- Train doctors and other health professionals on cultural differences and offer them sensitivity training.
- Create and disseminate borderwide preventative medical programs that are bilingual and bicultural.
- Make health-care brochures and other literature accessible while taking into account illiteracy and the need to disseminate information in different ways, such as radio, television, the Internet, and public notices.
- Implement campaigns in which medical care providers, practitioners, pharmacists, and *promotoras de salud* inform border residents about the dangers of over-the-counter medicines.
- Initiate immunization campaigns for children throughout the borderlands.

Binational, Bicultural, and Bilingual Education

Educators and policy makers should value and respect bilingualism and cultural diversity. A need exists to educate people of Mexican origin in the United States about Mexico, as well as about immigration processes while in Mexico. There is also a need to educate Mexicans about Mexican Americans, Chicanos, and American culture. In today's world, learning both Spanish and English has become a marketable skill for residents of both countries.

- In the U.S. educational system, efforts to accommodate different teaching and learning styles must be implemented, especially with children who speak a language other than English.
- More schools need to take into account the transnational life-style produced by globalization and develop adaptive strategies to understand and harness the "funds of knowledge" of children (and families). Bilingualism, the experiences of those who regularly return to their country of origin (or their parents'), and cultural traditions should be incorporated into American classrooms as resources that Mexican children bring to the schools.
- A significantly high homeownership rate exists for Latino families residing in the borderlands, but it does not translate into appreciating housing values. Local de facto segregation cannot deliver the healthy school budgets that lead to quality education. In order to raise educational attainment rates among youth in the borderlands, school financing must be divorced from local property values.
- El Paso and neighboring Ciudad Juárez could become models for a binational and bilingual educational system by capitalizing on each other's strengths.
- Ciudad Juárez's medical school could provide instruction in English in order to meet El Paso's elusive goal of opening a medical school.
- Cross-border student exchanges at all grade levels would give children from both countries the opportunity to learn each other's language and culture.
- In El Paso today, many nurses trained in Mexico work as nurses' aides, or Mexican teachers work as teachers' aides, because their degrees are not recognized in the United States. The implementation of a binational accord to recognize such credentials would reduce underemployment of degreed professionals and the basic misuse of human capital.

Binational Employment

An established historical pattern exists of northern Mexican families relying economically on a member who earns his or her living in the United States. For example, at the border, many Mexican women work in the United States as maids, babysitters, or caretakers for elderly Americans. Families in the United States benefit from this arrangement because they are able to afford these cheaper services, and families in Mexico benefit because a member is earning U.S. dollars.

- Establish a decent living-wage policy for both sides of the border.
- Offer the ability to move freely and legally between Mexico and the United States for the purposes of work.
- Establish a program that provides retirement and health insurance benefits and college funds for the children of *braceros* and other temporary workers.
- Allow corporations to profit by producing goods more cheaply across the border but ensure that they bear some responsibility to those workers who increase the corporations' profits through their cheaper labor costs.

Decent Housing as a Human Right

The availability of adequate and affordable housing is essential for transforming mere shelter into quality homes. Ensuring that border residents have access to housing at affordable prices is essential to the future of border communities and the well-being and prosperity of transnational households. Moreover, potential homebuyers must be given assistance and information about mortgages and financing options, loan amounts, and house prices. Given adequate opportunities to purchase or build homes, they contribute to the economic vitality of their border communities and can have a significant impact on housing markets.

- Establish more self-help building projects that capitalize on the available resources of a community. For example, in the state of

Guanajuato, Mexico, and in Presidio, Texas, adobe housing is being promoted as both affordable and in harmony with the environment.

- Provide workshops and technical assistance to people who are building their own homes so that they can adhere to sound building codes.
- Offer creative financing to promote home ownership for low-income families.

New Economic Realities

The borderlands exhibit classical wage repression in a variety of industries located in the area. Increased diversification of industrial and economic enterprises with appropriate use of the region's natural resources will take coordinated effort between public and private entities on both sides. Such changes must consider the economic needs of the border worker.

- Establish binational policies requiring *maquiladoras* to offer temporary workers' benefits.
- Increase the amounts of low-interest loans that are specific to qualified women who want to establish their own small businesses.
- Create a series of Border Small Business Centers that link Mexican and U.S. universities to binational business opportunities.
- Increase local, state, and federal employment retraining programs.
- Since Latinos in the United States have the lowest Earned Income Tax Credit (EITC) participation rates compared to other ethnic groups, every effort should be made to promote the EITC and make it more readily available to struggling working American residents.
- Establish awareness campaigns and offer more free bilingual tax-filing services.
- Implement antipoverty programs on both sides of the border in order to enhance the quality of life of residents in the region.
- Establish binational financial literacy programs that include an understanding of the global economy, basic consumer information, and personal finances.
- Establish policies to reduce the predatory lending that targets low-income and working-poor border families.

- Establish policies to support banking opportunities for working-poor communities.
- Promote the partnering of community-based organizations with credit unions to lower the cost of financial services for working-poor families.
- Build on the borderlands *cundina,* a self-help concept where small groups of individuals create partnership savings plans. Participation in this type of savings plan becomes a recognized form of credit.

In order to bring these recommendations to fruition, it is important for policymakers on both sides of the border to work jointly and collaborate in developing policies that address the needs of transnational families. Border residents deserve and benefit from policies that strengthen families and communities and create mechanisms of cooperation.

Note

1. In 2004 the U.S. government instituted FAST, a bilateral initiative that seeks to ensure security and safety while enhancing the economic prosperity of both countries. FAST is an expedited clearance program for known low-risk shipments. Under FAST, Mexico and the United States have agreed to harmonize their processes for clearance of commercial shipments. http://www.kewill.com/tradepoint/articles/FASTPoint/Commissioner%20Bonner%20dedicates%20FAST%20lane%20in%20Laredo,%20Texas.htm.

References

Andreas, Peter. 1998. "The Escalation of U.S. Immigration Control in the Post-NAFTA Era." *Political Science Quarterly* 113(4): 591–615.

Borjas, George J., and Robert W. Scrivener. 2005. "Globalization and Immigration." In *Globalization: What's New?,* ed. Michael M. Weinstein, 77–95. New York: Columbia University Press.

Brandon, Jeffrey E., Frank Crespin, Celinda Levy, and Daniel M. Reyna. 1997. "Border Health Issues." In *Border Health: Challenges for the United States and Mexico,* ed. John G. Bruhn and Jeffrey E. Brandon, 37–72. New York: Garland.

Calavita, Kitty. 1996. "The New Politics of Immigration: 'Balanced-Budget Conservatism' and the Symbolism of Proposition 187." *Social Problems* 43(3): 284–305.

Chaparro, Ramón. 2005. "Pedirán prórroga para registrar a más ex-braceros." In *El Diario de Juárez.* http://www.diario.com.mx/servicios/hemeroteca/nota.asp?notaid=99c4b002b1ca12124bbbf9270f2eeb5d (accessed March 4, 2005).

Clark, Don P., W. Charles Sawyer, and Richard L. Sprinkle. 1990. "Determinants of Industry Participation in Offshore Plants: The Case of *Maquiladoras* in Mexico." In *The Maquiladora Industry: Economic Solution or Problem?* ed. Khosrow Fatemi, 91–102. New York: Praeger.

Colonia Faqs. n.d. http://www.sos.state.tx.us/border/colonias/faqs.shtml.

Coronado, Irasema. 1998. "Who Governs in a Binational Context? The Role of Transnational Political Elites." Ph.D. diss., University of Arizona.

———. 2003. "*La Vida en las Colonias de la Frontera/*Life in *Colonias* on the Border." *Latino Studies Journal* 4: 193–97.

Coronado, Roberto. 2004. "Workers' Remittances to Mexico." *Business Frontier* 1. http://dallasfed.org/research/busfront/bus0401.html.

Cravey, Altha. 1998. *Men and Work in Mexico's Maquiladoras.* Lanham, MD: Rowman and Littlefield.

De La Garza, Rodolfo O., and Briant Lindsay Lowell. 2002. *Sending Money Home.* Lanham, MD: Rowman and Littlefield.

Fatemi, Khosrow, ed. 1990. *The Maquiladora Industry: Economic Solution or Problem?* New York: Praeger.

Faux, Jeff. 2005. "NAFTA at 10: Where Do We Go from Here?" In *Globalization: The Transformation of Social Worlds,* ed. D. Stanley Eitzen and Maxine Baca-Zinn, 74–77. Belmont, CA: Thomson Wadsworth.

Gilot, Louie. 2006. "End of an Era." *El Paso Times,* March 5, 2006, E1.

González-Baker, Susan, Frank D. Bean, Augustin Escobar Latapi, and Sidney Weintraub. 1998. "U.S. Immigration Policies and Trends: The Growing Importance of Migration from Mexico." In *Crossings: Mexican Immigration in Interdisciplinary Perspectives,* ed. Marcelo M. Suárez-Orozco, 79–112. Cambridge, MA: Harvard University Press.

Holden, Richard J. 1984. "*Maquiladoras* along the Texas/Mexico Border: An Econometric Evaluation of Employment and Retail Sales Effects on Four Texas Border SMSAs." Texas Department of Community Affairs, Regional Economic Development Division, February 1984. http://usinfo.state.gov/wh/Archive/ 2005/Nov/01-410479.html.

Kopinak, Kathryn. 1996. *Desert Capitalism: Maquiladoras in North America's Western Industrial Corridor.* Tucson: University of Arizona Press.

Menjívar, Cecilia, and Nestor Rodriguez. 2005. "State Terror in the U.S.-Latin American Interstate Regime." In *When States Kill: Latin America, the U.S., and Technologies of Terror,* ed. Cecilia Menjivar and Nestor Rodriguez, 3–27. Austin: University of Texas Press.

Moberg, David. 2005. "Maytag Moves to Mexico." In *Globalization: The Transformation of Social Worlds,* ed. D. Stanley Eitzen and Maxine Baca-Zinn, 92–97. Belmont, CA: Thomson Wadsworth.

Nash, June, and Maria Patricia Fernández-Kelly. 1983. *Women, Men and the International Division of Labor.* Albany: State University of New York Press.

Nevins, Joseph. 2002. *Operation GateKeeper: The Rise of the "Illegal Alien" and the Making of the U.S.-Mexico Boundary.* New York: Taylor and Francis.

Ortiz-Gonzalez, Victor M. 2004. *El Paso: Local Frontiers at a Global Crossroads.* Minneapolis: University of Minnesota Press.

Patrick, Michael J. 1990. "The Employment Impact of *Maquiladoras* along the U.S. Border." In *The Maquiladora Industry: Economic Solution or Problem?* ed. Khosrow Fatemi, 57–70. New York: Praeger.

Reubens, Edwin P. 1986. "Temporary Foreign Workers in the U.S: Myths, Facts, and Policies." *International Migration Review* 20(4): 1027–47.

Rivera, Carlos. 1998. "Mexican Auto Worker: I Would Like to Help the GM Workers Win." http://www.wsws.org/workers/1998/july1998/mex-j25. shtml, World Socialist Web Site (last accessed on July 25, 1998).

Sandoval de Escurdia, Juan Martín, Richard Muñoz, and Maria Paz. 2003. *Análisis sobre la situación general de la migración 2003.* Servicio de Investigación y Análisis, División de Política Social de la Cámara de Diputados LIX Legislatura. http://www.ciepac.org/otras%20temas/migrantes/anamigracio.pdf.

Staudt, Kathleen, and Irasema Coronado. 2002. *Fronteras No Más: Toward Social Justice at the U.S.-Mexico Border.* New York: Palgrave Macmillan.

Wood, Andrew Grant, ed. 2001. *On the Border: Society and Culture between the United States and Mexico.* Lanham, MD: SR Books.

Ana Marie Argilagos is senior consultant, Planning, Research, and Development Unit, Southwest Border/Indian Country, Annie E. Casey Foundation.

Amanda G. Bailey is affiliated with the Public Policy Institute of California.

Irasema Coronado is an associate professor in the Department of Political Science at the University of Texas, El Paso.

Marie-Laure Coubès is a researcher with El Colegio de la Frontera Norte Ensenada San Antonio del Mar.

Amelia Malagamba-Ansótegui is an assistant professor and Southwest Borderlands Scholar at Arizona State University's Herberger College of Fine Arts.

Raquel R. Márquez is an associate professor in the Department of Sociology at the University of Texas, San Antonio.

Yolanda C. Padilla is a professor in the School of Social Work at the University of Texas, Austin.

Catalina Palmer is an analyst with La Red por los Derechos de la Infancia de México.

Mary A. Petrón is an assistant professor in the Department of Curriculum and Instruction at Texas A&M International University.

Belinda I. Reyes is an assistant professor at Raza Studies in the College of Ethnic Studies at San Francisco State University.

Bárbara J. Robles is an associate professor in the School of Social Work at Arizona State University.

Harriett D. Romo is an associate professor in the Department of Sociology at the University of Texas, San Antonio, and director of the Mexico Center.

Patricia Sánchez is an assistant professor in the Bicultural-Bilingual Studies Division at the University of Texas, San Antonio.